PRAISE FOR *THE NEW RULES OF INVESTING*

"*The New Rules of Investing* presents a compelling argument that the investment environment has changed in consequential ways in the twenty-first century. In readable prose, it explains how investors can react to powerful new forces and shocks. These structural changes in process and in prospect are usefully captured in the 5 Ds: debt, deglobalization, decarbonization, digitalization, and demographics. A very useful framework for navigating in a rapidly changing world."

—**MICHAEL SPENCE**
Nobel laureate in Economic Sciences (2001)

"Most Wall Street figures aren't very good at explaining to lay people the complicated global macroeconomic issues materially affecting wealth creation in the twenty-first century. Mark Haefele is the exception to the rule. Using personal stories from clients and from his own life, coupled to a historian's keen eye for detail, Haefele brings to life everything from the tide-shifting role government intervention is playing in today's markets to the quirky way our personal money issues sabotage our financial results—and what you can do about it. This book is well worth the investment."

—**JEAN CHATZKY**
New York Times and *Wall Street Journal* bestselling author;
CEO, HerMoney.com

"*The New Rules of Investing* cuts through the daily noise and helps the modern investor think differently about markets, portfolios, and world events."

—**DAVID M. RUBENSTEIN**
Cofounder and cochairman of Carlyle

"At Joint Special Operations Command, we oversaw the translation of national threat assessments, strategy and policy into the actions that delivered non-linear national security outcomes. Mark explains, in practical terms, how a global investment operator converts strategies into diversified actions for consistent risk-adjusted returns."

—**REAR ADMIRAL HUGH WYMAN HOWARD III**, US Navy (Ret.)

Former commander, Naval Special Warfare Command

"I have seen Mark implement successful and robust investment strategies over the past decade in a challenging global environment. His approach is highly effective."

—**AXEL A. WEBER**

Former president of the Deutsche Bundesbank, former member of the European Central Bank Governing Council, and former chairman of UBS Group AG

The
NEW RULES
of
INVESTING

ESSENTIAL WEALTH STRATEGIES
FOR TURBULENT TIMES

MARK H. HAFELE
with RICHARD C. MORAIS

HarperCollins
Leadership

An Imprint of HarperCollins

Published by HarperCollins Leadership, an imprint of HarperCollins Focus LLC.

Any internet addresses, phone numbers, or company or product information printed in this book are offered as a resource and are not intended in any way to be or to imply an endorsement by HarperCollins Leadership, nor does HarperCollins Leadership vouch for the existence, content, or services of these sites, phone numbers, companies, or products beyond the life of this book.

The names and certain identifying details in this book have been changed to protect the privacy of individuals.

The information provided in this book is for general informational purposes only and does not constitute financial advice. Readers should seek professional guidance before making any financial decisions. The author and publisher are not responsible for any losses or damages resulting from actions taken based on the information in this book.

ISBN 978-1-4002-4964-0 (ePub)
ISBN 978-1-4002-4963-3 (HC)

Library of Congress Control Number: 2024948681

Printed in the United States of America
24 25 26 27 28 LBC 5 4 3 2 1

This book is dedicated to
Andreas
Hannah
Hilary
Lena
Jürg
Simon

CONTENTS

Disclaimer

FOREWORD

A Peek Under the UBS Hood

My colleagues and I at UBS are continuously striving to serve our clients in new and innovative ways, which is why I am pleased to share with you *The New Rules of Investing: Essential Wealth Strategies for Turbulent Times*, penned by our global wealth management chief investment officer, Mark Haefele.

The book is a must-read—and not just for investment professionals. You will discover how profoundly the world and markets have changed in the twenty-first century, in part due to the intervention of governments and central banks. You will gain fresh insights into investor psychology. And, of particular note, you will learn how 160 years of Swiss private-banking experience have coalesced to forge UBS's unique wealth-management system.

Indeed, as Mark's book underscores, the value we create at UBS flows directly from our global network of highly accomplished clients and from our trusted advisors who allow us to execute our approach to managing, protecting, and building wealth in all corners of the globe and for generations to come.

Mark not only explains the "science" and algorithms behind modern wealth management but also the "art" of what we do—the way we harness our clients' deepest issues and passions to help them navigate challenges and opportunities in a way that is personally *meaningful* to them. In the process of reading this book, you will not only receive a unique perspective into UBS's craft but also learn how our extraordinary clients are pointing us in a new direction and how we are likely to be investing in the years ahead.

SERGIO ERMOTTI
UBS CEO

INTRODUCTION

My name is Mark Haefele, and most likely you haven't heard of me.

I am the chief investment officer of global wealth management at UBS, the Swiss universal bank headquartered in Zurich. I was an American-born middle-class kid who somehow became a dark-suited Swiss banker advising some of the wealthiest individuals and families in the world. Despite my low visibility, I am told that I am an influencer, albeit one you will never see on TikTok kissing Chihuahuas or lip-syncing Taylor Swift hits.

My credibility, the draw of my global following, stems from the simple fact that from a nondescript office in Zurich, I oversee the investment process for one of the largest pools of private capital in the world.

That means, in concrete terms, my team and I manage and provide advice to $4 trillion of UBS's total $5.7 trillion in invested wealth,[1] and, of that pool of assets, we are actively managing client assets of $350 billion. Warren Buffett, arguably the world's most famous investor, oversees some $300 billion in portfolio assets at Berkshire Hathaway, which I hope puts what we do in perspective.[2]

Let me give you a taste of what I do. In October 2022, UBS took over the entire five-star hotel the Fontenay in Hamburg, Germany, so that forty highly accomplished billionaire clients, who had flown in from around the world for the event, could have a safe and private place to network with their peers. It was such an important occasion the whole congress was carefully orchestrated and hosted by the bank's exceptionally talented wealth management president, Iqbal Khan, who also happens to be my boss. Iqbal, an auditor by trade and by then one of the best-connected private bankers in the world, had choreographed every detail and handpicked every guest in the room. I was on set to interview a panel of global experts on the butterfly effect of geopolitical issues that were then dominating the headlines.

November was just days away, but it was, I recall, so warm that even the ducks on the Aussenalster Lake didn't know whether they should stay put or fly south. They were not the only ones who were befuddled. If I had to give you one takeaway from this gathering of intensely wealthy and influential people, a conversation repeated week after week when I met with them privately, it is that the world has somehow changed.

Some of the commentary was sobering. While I cannot reveal the identities of who was in attendance, a comment I heard from a former president of an EU country while I was moderating that morning's sessions made me sit up. This former president claimed that the war between Russia and Ukraine would last for years, and Russia wouldn't be allowed back into normal relations with the EU for at least twenty years *after* Putin had left the scene.

I instantly pivoted toward my audience and underscored the need to rethink the possible longer-term consequences of a lasting war in Europe.

Over the course of three days, while I was having one-on-one meetings with our clients, learning how I could help them achieve their goals, we heard from the industry and government leaders onstage. From well-connected sources in Asia and the United States, we learned that mainland China, outwardly supportive of Russia, was, at that point, being careful not to overtly cross America's red line by busting sanctions and providing Russia with material support, even while we all had a keen eye on mainland China's relations with Taiwan.

The chart showing the Russian markets' brutal plummet since the invasion was sobering, and a harbinger of what would probably happen to global markets if hostilities erupted in the South China Sea, disrupting the far more important Pacific Rim economies. That's what my team and I do: we look at the markets in a judgment-free way, putting aside all the political or moral ramifications of the hypothetical scenario we're entertaining, and instead ask ourselves, *Are our clients' portfolios robust enough to withstand whatever shock the world might throw at us?*

We were specifically asking ourselves: *What portfolio hedges do we have in place to blunt the fallout of such a catastrophic Pacific-basin war and disruption?*

But there was also information exchanged leaning toward the upside. The silver lining of the Russia-Ukraine war was that Europe was rapidly weaning itself off Russian oil and gas and furiously building up its green-energy infrastructure. Just days after our event, as if to underscore this point, the French senate passed legislation requiring the nation's large parking garages to put solar panels on their roofs, with one stroke legislating into existence some eleven gigawatts of homegrown energy, equal to the output of ten nuclear power plants.[3]

From the brilliant scientists flown in from Boston, we heard that the process of creating cutting-edge immuno-oncology drugs theoretically capable of eradicating certain cancers was migrating, even at the initial stages of discovery, from the laboratory to the laptop. We heard futurists and a Nobel laureate in economics riff about the future of work, about productivity, and about how cities themselves need to be reinvented for the new way people want to work.

The concept of impact investing, as a means to become a steward of the planet, was another topic that frequently came up. Despite the dire headlines emanating from the United Nations and academic studies about missed emissions targets, we were told that investing 2 percent of global gross domestic product (GDP) annually in environment-friendly technology and infrastructure could prevent catastrophic climate change.

After a gala dinner at Hamburg's newly opened museum Montblanc Haus, the event closed on the final day with a cofounder of one of the iconic firms of the digital age striding across the stage and pressing home his message that none of our companies would survive if we were "unwilling to disrupt" ourselves. The successful companies of our times must have a culture and "tolerance for risk" that endlessly "tries a lot of bad ideas"[4]—to find that one true gem on which tomorrow's fortunes are built. So perhaps it was no surprise that the financial sophisticates in the room knew they had to adapt.

But how? they asked me.

That's the subject of this book: how we must all change our way of investing to meet the needs of our times.

The sheer volume of assets my team manages at UBS means we can afford to go to great lengths in our efforts to provide our clients the information needed to make better investment decisions. But moving large amounts of capital in the markets also means the investment pronouncements I oversee can sway the direction of capital markets. These are some of the reasons why the globe's most powerful financial institutions and the very wealthy—those forty billionaires gathered at the Fontenay, for example—want to know what my team and I are thinking about the markets and what our latest ideas are about where they should be investing—and how.

Well, this book is not just for them or restricted to Wall Street professionals.

This book is equally for *you*. It is meant to help you, the lay reader, become a better investor and, I hope, help you steadily accumulate wealth over the course of your life, in all its varied material and nonmaterial forms. You might miss a few of my more technical financial and economic explanations along the away, but that's okay, because they are not the core of what it means to become a better investor. If you stick with me through the unfolding chapters, you will, I promise, walk away with a deeper understanding of how markets really work, while also learning practical tips on how to create greater wealth during your lifetime.

In broad strokes this is what I will help you understand:

- How to follow the money to see how the world has profoundly changed
- How this change has made investing more complex

- How it requires you to change your approach to investing
- Why the risk-adjusted returns of self-directed clients underperform clients who work with advisors to invest in our asset-allocation solutions
- Why you should think about your wealth in three portfolio "buckets"
- Why possessing self-knowledge and incorporating your personal money issues into your investment process are important
- That the most inspiring investors today are transforming how we invest in the future through a technique called *impact investing*
- That, if you follow the money, as we will do, it is possible to imagine how investing will be different by the middle of the twenty-first century
- How cultivating humility is essential to becoming a successful investor

Now why, you might ask, would I share my knowledge with you?

The simplest answer is that at age fifty-three I am in that stage of life when I am concerned less with writing my résumé than I am with writing my tombstone. This is one way I hope to give back to the world.

But that's a grandiose response. The more mundane and important truth is I needed to write down and articulate my own thinking about investing over the next twenty-five years because it is going to be different from the past twenty-five years in many ways. I would go so far as to say that many of the time-tested rules of investing, when put in practice today by the average investor, are dangerous to their wealth.

A key to investing successfully for the future is understanding where the big pools of capital, both private *and* public, are flowing, and incorporating that understanding into your investment process. I can't stress that enough. Arguably the most profound change underfoot in capital markets these past few decades—a force so powerful it has upended how we invest—revolves around governments' increased role in the global economy.

Another key to becoming a successful investor is understanding who you are, where your skill level is at, and how wealth benefits can flow from an investor operating with a sense of humility. If you think you are going to be the next Warren Buffett, terrific; I think there is information in this book you will find useful. But the book is also an argument that you are probably not able to pick stocks as Warren Buffett did when he started Berkshire Hathaway. The world has changed too much. And that is okay. In fact, that's probably a good thing, as long as you adapt your investment plan accordingly.

What I mean is this: the 1970s called on a rotary phone and is demanding its investment theory back. Stock picking in the form of Buffett-style value investing—the skill of finding company shares that are a good value relative to their earnings potential, which is an investing technique still celebrated in hundreds of new books continuously rolling out—is not where most people should be spending their time as they learn about investing and managing their wealth.

I am not saying that reading the financial statements of hundreds of companies to locate a mispriced gem is impossible today, and I am not saying that bargain hunting isn't fun. But as a wealth-generating strategy, it ain't what it used to be. For most of us, trying to spot undervalued stocks when they are out of favor in the hope they will become sexy again is a recipe for failure in today's financial markets, largely due to all the macro and structural changes that have unfolded in recent years and are still underway. The supremely talented can still do it. But many of us professionals have come around to admitting we can no longer use these outdated techniques the same way.

Even David Einhorn, one of today's great Buffett-style value investors known for his stellar results at the hedge fund Greenlight Capital, has gone public about how he was forced to change his value-investing approach. He now views markets "as fundamentally broken" and attributes this breakdown in traditional investing to the fact that passive investing has so completely taken over the landscape. "The value industry has gotten completely annihilated," Einhorn recently admitted on Bloomberg Radio's *Masters in Business*.[5]

The first part of this book is about how the investing world has changed since I began as a value investor thirty years ago, and why you need to understand the big changes if you want to have any hope of developing a successful investment strategy in today's world. But there is more. I also learned in the past thirty years that being narrowly focused on developing a successful investment strategy is not the way for most people to effectively protect and grow their wealth. What I believe makes my view of investing unique is that it is informed by the knowledge I have gained in my role as private banker to the world's great and influential investors.

After a hedge-fund career, I am now the longest-serving private banker on the executive committee in the UBS Global Wealth Management division, and much to my own surprise, I have become one of those insiders in the secretive world of Swiss banking. That means I personally meet with hundreds of the world's wealthiest and most influential families to discuss how they protect and grow their wealth.

The world's billionaires (as well as hundreds of thousands of other investors) turn to UBS to protect and grow *generations* of their families' wealth. What they have collectively taught me about wealth far exceeds what I've taught them, and the techniques and attitudes that they deploy on their journey to increased wealth should help set this investment book apart in a crowded field.

In the end, all the investment theory in the world is useless, even dangerous, if real people don't have effective ways of applying those ideas to their real-world investment portfolios. UBS would in fact not be UBS if our advisors were not capable of holding an introductory meeting and demonstrating their value to prospective clients so that they can win new business and keep it. What are they doing in these meetings to show commonsense people the value of entrusting their wealth to UBS? We are going to show you the "hacks" we have developed over the past 160 years that are proven to work for real people, not just theoretical "rational actors" or the ultrarich.

But the knowledge flows the other way, too, and here's one essential lesson I have learned from my clients in my transition from hedge-fund manager to billionaire advisor: it is likely that you manage your *investments*, as I did when I started out in the industry almost thirty years ago. In contrast our successful clients manage their *wealth*. That's an important distinction. This worldview is not just about learning how these wealthy clients achieved a different mindset for how to use money as a tool to increase the quality of their lives. It is also about how this mindset leads many of our top clients to focus on a *different* way of investing. After showing you how they see the investing world today and teaching you how to follow in their footsteps, we're going to put all these wealth-management techniques together with some examples from real clients.

The issue at the heart of this distinction between wealth management and investing is the understanding that our clients are, well, people. They are out there living their lives; they are not the mythical "theoretical profit maximization machines" that so many economic and investment books are based on. All the textbooks in the world can't prepare you for what it is like to be a real person investing in the real world. That's why I am going to spend time addressing "soft" issues such as your personal hang-ups around money, so that your process ultimately expands enough to be about managing and building wealth in the broadest sense—and not just about anxiously tracking the day's hot stock or index fund.

Don't despair. It's confusing, I know, even for the wealthiest and most talented. But the new rules of investing I outline will address these micro issues and the new macro reality we live in and provide you with a solid, actionable framework for managing (or working with others to manage) your wealth in an ever-changing environment.

Before we plunge in, please know that the most important concepts to take away from this book, from an investor's standpoint, are learning how to allocate assets and then learning enough about your personal money issues to avoid sabotaging your results.

But the most important point to grasp about how the markets have changed in the past decades, and how we must change our investment strategies accordingly, is following the money, and today it's government intervention that's shaping markets.

Since that profound macro issue affects everything we do as investors, I begin this book by explaining this big shift before we get down to the essentials of portfolio construction and how to manage your wealth in a more fulsome way. That's why chapter 1 looks at how a changing world is forcing us to reorganize our investment thinking around what we call *the 5Ds of disruption*.

Chapters 2 and 3 look at how buying what the government is buying became the big new investment strategy during the 2007–2009 financial crisis and how to use this strategy in the future. Chapter 4 switches gears to argue that while you should understand that the investing world has changed, the fundamentals of asset allocation remain the core of successful investing.

Chapter 5 contains practical advice about knowing yourself, and why that is essential if you want to be a better-than-average investor. Becoming a great investor is never about beating others at the investment game but, as Warren Buffett and his mentor have often pointed out, all about mastering your emotional money-related issues.

In chapter 6 we will discuss how over 160 years of experience working with actual clients led us at UBS to combine both traditional and behavioral finance in the UBS Wealth Way* investment system. This real-world investing approach has helped thousands of people improve their returns and feel more secure about their investment plans.

In chapters 7 and 8, we turn to the emerging investment trend of the twenty-first century, which our clients are creating and leading. We're going to show you, via real-life client stories, how these innovators are mashing up the rules in this book by infusing their investment choices

---

* UBS Wealth Way is an approach incorporating Liquidity. Longevity. Legacy. strategies that UBS Financial Services Inc. and our financial advisors can use to assist clients in exploring and pursuing their wealth-management needs and goals over different time frames. This approach is not a promise or guarantee that wealth, or any financial results, can or will be achieved. All investments involve the risk of loss, including the risk of loss of the entire investment. Time frames may vary. Strategies are subject to individual client goals, objectives, and suitability.

with personal purpose and meaning at the same time they are investing in and around the great issues of our age. How impact investing, currently practiced by a tiny elite, is likely to develop in the future and within the mainstream is the subject of our final thoughts. The last chapter is a bonus rule, and it makes the case that humility is the most underrated of investor qualities and demonstrates how it can pay for itself when facing the fury of the markets—a lesson applicable to all the previous rules.

By the end of this book, you will have digested real-world client studies drawn from all over the world and enough investment theory to emulate the practices we have demonstrated to work. All of this should empower you to make a more informed decision about how you invest, how much to manage yourself, and what to look for in partners or advisors.

Finally, I hope to give you tools that help you learn—all so you can be happier with both the results and the process.

RULE 1

FOLLOW THE
BIG MONEY

In the past five years we have had a global wave of new infections, injections, invasions, inflations, interventions, and intelligences unknown in human history. We have seen interest rates[1] and oil prices[2] go negative and long-dormant inflation return.[3] US government debt has been downgraded again.[4] The Doomsday Clock, which symbolically measures the threat of nuclear war, is set close to midnight,[5] and world leaders disagree about whether climate change or artificial intelligence poses the greater existential threat to humanity. Meanwhile, as demographics shift toward urbanization, 99 percent of the world's population breathes unhealthy air,[6] and every baby is born from a placenta containing microplastics.[7]

Many clients tell me they are not just confused about how to invest in a changing world; they fear that existential threats to humanity are piling up as never before.

Yet for investors, has the world really changed all that much? As the old warhorses of Wall Street are inclined to say, "in times like these" it is important to remember there have always been times like these, or, as another saying goes, "The world doesn't end very often." In my view, if you follow the money, it is relatively easy to show that the investing world has changed dramatically, and this should lead investors to reorganize how they think about free markets; to wit: they are a lot less free.

Still, clients aren't the only ones who think the investing world has changed. Given the title of this book, *The New Rules of Investing*, you will not be surprised to learn that I also think the investment landscape has changed since I started a hedge fund nearly thirty years ago.

GOVERNMENT AND THE ECONOMY

Consider the US government's share of total economic output and how that share has grown over the years, particularly since the pandemic. Never before in history have governments around the world purposely shut down their economies and then shocked them back to life with massive stimuli; as the following chart shows, only in the World War II period has government spending matched the level of spending we have experienced in recent years.

The US government accounts for a growing share of the US economy
US government spending, in % of GDP

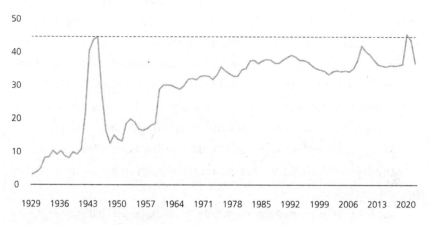

Source: IMF, UBS, as of July 2024

It isn't just that the US government's total share of our economy spiked in response to the COVID-19 crisis; it's what's happened since then. After

World War II the government's share of the US economy promptly dropped to the high teens, but since the COVID-19 pandemic the government's new baseline share of the economy has been between 35 percent and 40 percent. The government's share of the economy has been steadily growing for decades, regardless of which political party is in power.

If we want to follow the money, we must understand government spending. This spending is Big Money. The continuously growing US government accounts for over a third of the nation's economy and is increasingly crowding out the private sector.[8]

Whether you think this change is a good thing or a bad thing, you can't ignore it as an investor—even in the "free-market" economy of the United States.

PUT ASIDE YOUR JUDGMENTS

I have spent my entire professional career studying that space where governments and markets intersect, so I know well that this discussion about government intervention will trigger people. Some of you will be highly offended by any suggestion that you should track government subsidies for profit, and I get why the idea might upset you. But the point I repeatedly make to our UBS clients is that it's immaterial whether we personally think that top-down interference in free markets is a politically right or wrong move.

Like you, I have views on what a better society and world would look like, and I support these views in my private life. In my professional life, however, **clients seek my advice not to explain how the world *should* work but how the world *does* work**.

If you are a passion-driven person and concerned about the state of the world and your kids' and grandkids' future—if you believe it's vitally important to adhere to your moral code when dealing with the outside world—then my "cold" investment strategy will probably be hard to follow, whatever side of the political spectrum you fall on. Later we will show when it is appropriate to drop this observe-only discipline and how our clients are successfully incorporating their values into their investments to have a positive impact on the world.

But, for the moment, let's not argue about whether the world is getting more dangerous. Let's see instead what assets might benefit or lag because governments around the world have increased their defense spending 9 percent in 2023 to a new record high. Fact: defense spending is growing three times faster than the global economy.[9]

Similarly, we're not going to debate the existence, causes, or solutions of climate change. We're going to follow the money and point out that the International Energy Agency (IEA) calculated that over 50 percent more investment was made in so-called clean energy than fossil fuel extraction in 2023, with that trend increasing.[10] In Texas, often seen as ground zero for Big Oil, public and private investment in clean energy and transportation was up 37 percent in 2023, to $239 billion,[11] or roughly the entire GDP of Greece.[12] To put that into further perspective, it is worth noting that the Texas economy is larger than Russia's, whether we look at it before or after the Russia-Ukraine war—and it even makes its own famous vodka.[13]

My amoral approach to understanding how the economy works; my insistence that you dryly observe what is going on and drive your political or religious ideology out of your investment process; my recommendation that you follow the money and the data and divorce yourself from what that money flow is telling us about the state of the world—for many of you it will be too much to take. It will probably feel as though I am urging you to go against your code, pushing an investment approach that's in direct conflict with the way your parents brought you up to be and behave.

You won't be alone. There are times when, in office meetings, I am asked to give my investment view and I focus solely on the financial ramifications of a government policy, completely indifferent (as an investor) to the moral or social fallout of that policy, and my counterparts' expressions make it clear what they are thinking: *This dude is seriously strange.*

If you're thinking that, well, I get it, but let me point out there is a subtle but profound difference between an *amoral* investment approach and an *immoral* investment approach. I'd even argue that looking hard at the amoral reality of the markets, the way markets respond in real ways to shifting money flows, is itself a kind of virtue.

Don't judge. Just observe.

If it helps with this mental realignment I am urging you to undertake, consider the Serenity Prayer, which is often used in recovery programs and expresses a worldview found in various guises in many religions and spiritual movements across the globe.

> God, grant me the serenity
> to accept the things I cannot change,
> the courage to change the things I can,
> and the wisdom to know the difference.[14]

When you have your investment hat on, I'm advocating for a kind of nonspiritual, financial-market version of the worldview expressed in that prayer. Don't fight the reality of the markets and the state of the world; accept them for what they are, but do change what you have control over, which is how your investment strategy fits in with this new reality unfolding before us. Follow the difficult advice in this book with this higher purpose in mind—increasing and managing your wealth prudently, all while staying focused on the endgame of finally having the resources to pursue the moral causes that mean a lot to you personally.

That's what some of my most successful ultra-high-net-worth clients do, and in the process many of them achieve immense personal satisfaction and a deep sense of moral purpose from impact investing, which we'll get to later.

GOVERNMENT SHARE OF GDP IS JUST ONE ISSUE

Now back to my larger point about how investing has changed because government purchases have and are changing. The government's share of

GDP shown in the previous chart represents a nation's fiscal spending or fiscal policy, which is something we often hear about in the news. Fiscal policy is the use of government spending and taxation to influence the economy. We won't debate the details of that right now, so let's just call it "spending." But there is a whole other kind of government spending that is important to investing. That's *monetary policy*, the term that describes what central banks do to promote growth and employment.

Some of the most consequential buying or investing today is government buying that does not even show up in the government expenditure illustrated in the previous chart. I'm talking about the asset-purchase programs done by the US Federal Reserve and other central banks. These purchase programs are usually referred to as *quantitative easing* and are intended to spur economic growth. Whether they have achieved their mission is not my point. Rather, it's recognizing that more than $6 trillion of bonds, stocks, and mortgage-related purchases have had an impact on financial markets and investors.[15] The following chart spells out how the Federal Reserve has become a major buyer of financial assets since the beginning of the Global Financial Crisis. As we will see, investors need to take heed that this is also a major change in the way markets operate.

The Fed's balance sheet has expanded significantly since the 2008 financial crisis
Federal Reserve balance sheet, total assets, in USD tn

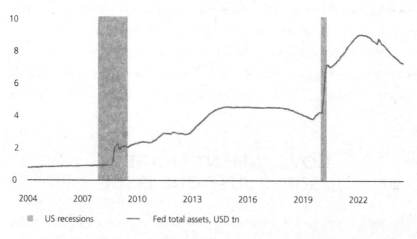

US recessions   —— Fed total assets, USD tn

Source: Federal Reserve Bank of St Louis, UBS, as of July 2024

6

Now, I started this chapter by saying that clients are increasingly overwhelmed by changes that pose existential threats to humanity, and I follow that up with charts about government expenditure and purchasing. Why?

That's because, to respond successfully to change, we need to reframe our fears about the latest headlines into investment risks and opportunities. That means acknowledging where change is taking place, understanding that change from an investment perspective, and converting that knowledge into action.

Furthermore, I will force us to think about problems not just as problems but also as opportunities. When clients come to us overwhelmed by perceived problems, we want to help them make sense of what they are seeing and feeling.

The way we try to make sense of the current world is to reframe concerns around what we call the **5Ds of disruption** that are changing the investing landscape to create new risks and opportunities. If we follow the Big Money, we see the Big Money is government spending, and governments have identified some even bigger problems to spend it on—the 5Ds.

The 5Ds are, in no particular order, **debt, deglobalization, demographics, digitalization**, and **decarbonization**. All these disruptive forces are related in one way or another to government spending, and all these trends are bigger than any one company, sector, asset class, market, country, or region. They are global forces cutting across the world economy, and I am starting with these 5Ds to show you how a changing world is forcing us to reframe much of our investing around bigger issues than what kinds of earnings we expect from companies in the S&P 500 next quarter or even next year.

DEBT: A PARADOX

There is an old joke that if you borrow $100 from a bank and can't pay it back, it is your problem, but if you borrow $1 million from the bank and can't pay it back, it is the bank's problem. Well, whose problem is $307 trillion?[16]

That's where total global debt stands today.

Debt has ruined many a person, company, and nation throughout history, and yet that has not stopped developed nations from adding to their national debt. In the United States the debt-to-GDP ratio went from 31 percent in 1980 to 133 percent during the 2020–2021 pandemic, before falling back to around 122 percent today.[17]

US debt, at $35 trillion,[18] has led Phillip Swagel, director of the nonpartisan Congressional Budget Office (CBO), to warn that the budget is on an "unprecedented" trajectory that risks a currency crisis.[19] Federal Reserve chairman Jerome Powell has publicly stated it is "now time, or past time, to get back to an adult conversation among elected officials about getting the federal government back on a sustainable fiscal path." US Treasury Secretary Janet Yellen, when appearing before Congress, has similarly argued that it is "critically important" that the federal government return to "fiscal responsibility."[20]

The US government is currently spending more on the gross interest payments servicing its debt than it is on its national defense.[21] The CBO predicts that the government's interest costs in 2030 will reach 3.3 percent of GDP, exceeding the previous post–World War II high of 3.2 percent, recorded in 1991.[22] The United States was recently the fourth- or fifth-most indebted developed nation in the world, depending on the time period, after Japan (236 percent of GDP), Greece (185 percent of GDP), and Italy (134 percent of GDP).[23]

These figures explain why more and more investors are worried about the long-term debt sustainability of industrialized nations.[24] To compensate for the risk that at some point in the future developed countries may struggle to finance their deficit spending, the markets could seek higher interest rates on government debt, just as people pay a higher interest rate on loans if they have a lower credit score than their neighbors. The knock-on effect of higher national debt levels is greater uncertainty for investors. Higher interest rates could put pressure on the growth of the economy and lower the tax revenues collected by the government.

What all this debt means for investors is not so straightforward. My chief investment office colleagues and I believe it is no longer clear whose problem the debts are. One danger is for investors to assume that the market will have the final say on this interest and debt in the future. Politics will play its role, not least because low interest rates can help governments avoid making tough decisions on taxes and spending. So bear this in mind: in a new world of high government debt, political decisions, not markets, will increasingly decide whether "safe" assets such as bonds become risky and stocks become relatively safe.

Policymakers' preferred path to relief would be debt reduction through robust economic growth, which could materialize out of the widespread use of artificial intelligence, abundant renewable energy, and revitalized local supply chains—three things that governments and private capital are investing in. If these investments don't yield higher growth and productivity, however, other means might also be needed.

Don't assume that governments will pay back all the debt at market rates. Governments don't have to play fair. They may force down rates; they may default; they may trigger inflation. Oil-rich Russia shocked the world when it defaulted on its ruble-denominated debt back in 1998,[25] then technically defaulted again in 2022, when, cut off from its foreign holdings because of the Russia-Ukraine war, it missed paying interest on its foreign-currency obligations.[26] More recently, in the world at large, interest rates on government debt have been suppressed by the debt-purchase programs of central banks, who are nominally independent but are ultimately accountable to the same governments issuing the debt.

Global debt levels are international problems that make our investment future more complicated than simply finding a fair value for securities in a free market. Going forward, no one knows how different nations—which is to say politicians, some of whom are populists—will choose to deal with spiking debt burdens.

But that's also our first clue as to how we should address the debt concern from an investor's perspective: **diversify your portfolio globally**

across different political economies. Even if one nation ends up in a default or scarred by high inflation, it may be that other political economies fare differently and better, based on different choices made.

The increasing role of governments in markets means that politics is playing a more important role in this arena, so fair-value calculation spreadsheets—the technique investors use to spot individual stocks or bonds that are undervalued—matter far less than they once did. In other words, there are unpredictable factors that could determine market outcomes. We are not yet at the point where studying politics has replaced understanding finance, but that might only be because both voter and government behavior remain so unpredictable, even for the political scientists.

Still, there are some things we can know about this new world. For example, a highly indebted world cannot afford widespread deflation. When there is deflation, wages and tax receipts are stagnant, making it harder to pay off existing debt. Conversely, inflation means that wages and tax receipts rise (even if there is no real economic growth), making it easier to repay old debts. We have already seen how scared policymakers are of deflation by the lengths they have gone to stop it.

When deflation threatened in the aftermath of the financial crisis, central banks introduced an unprecedented policy of *negative* interest rates. To encourage you to spend money or invest in risky things, to boost prices, they ensured you would have to *pay* just to keep your money in the bank. In 2019 a Danish bank was the first to pay people to take out a mortgage.[27]

As we saw during the pandemic, faced with the risk of deflation, governments in the United States and Europe chose policies that eventually led to an overshoot of inflation.[28]

Investors must be cognizant of the fact that broadly, in a more indebted world, the risk of higher inflation increases. Politicians and policymakers have a tradition of leaning toward a little bit of inflation to help ease them out of fiscal problems, because it's a drip-feed solution that compounds over time and doesn't hit the voting populace all at once. But for investors inflation makes traditionally safe assets such as cash and bonds riskier to hold over the longer term. Most bonds pay a fixed income, regardless of whether one dollar is enough to buy four shots of bourbon, as it once could, or a small bottle of water, as it does today in some places, if you're lucky. Meanwhile, cash on deposit often pays less than the rate of inflation, which means that the amount of goods it can purchase reduces over time.

In contrast, assets such as commodities or real estate tend to rise together with inflation, in part because these are essential items that people are always willing to pay for. Similarly, the stocks of companies with pricing power should be able to grow earnings in line with inflation as such businesses are able to raise prices during periods of inflation. There are also some bonds, such as inflation-linked bonds, whose payouts rise together with inflation.

CRYPTOCURRENCIES ARE NO PANACEA

The notion that the global financial order could one day suffer or collapse under the weight of its debt has understandably given rise to a survivalist impulse to do whatever it takes to escape the financial system we have, and perhaps create a new system in the process. That impulse, for good or bad, stands behind the rise of cryptocurrency, but I am highly doubtful that cryptocurrencies will save us.

Cryptocurrencies are perceived by officials to be both a threat to the existing financial system and a facilitator of money laundering,[29] which explains why, when Bitcoin fell 50 percent in short order,[30] government officials went out of their way to say, "We told you so." The US secretary of the treasury pointedly warned Americans against "extremely risky" cryptocurrencies lacking "appropriate supervision and regulation."[31]

It's not yet clear whether government will ultimately regulate cryptocurrencies into submission and make them part of the world financial order, or whether cryptocurrencies will remain an alternative financial asset that rivals and threatens the status quo. Bitcoin has recently staged a comeback since ETFs investing in crypto have been approved and launched. That suggests, after the last wave of crypto frauds were exposed, the new asset class is inching its way toward the regulated mainstream and middle-class respectability.[32] There is of course always a chance that politicians seeking votes will float the idea they might change the official cryptocurrency policy—in some political circles there is talk of the US government stockpiling Bitcoin reserve—but speculating that a country will undermine its own currency monopoly with a sizable effort seems to me like a risky bet.[33]

In fact, if cryptocurrencies remain on an alternative path, the sector may eventually face its day of reckoning. I come to this conclusion because of what history teaches us. While governments will tolerate market forces and market pricing to a point, they will not allow market pricing or rival assets to destroy the existing financial system. In the end, nothing is allowed to challenge sovereign rights and sovereign currency.

During the Great Depression, for example, gold became too attractive an asset compared to cash, stocks, and bonds. A terrified populace was converting dollars to gold and hoarding the yellow metal, further withdrawing liquidity from the markets. The US government responded by bringing down the hammer on what was then perceived to be a rival asset class threatening the entire financial system.

In March 1933, Washington passed the Emergency Banking Act, which gave the US secretary of the treasury the power to *force* institutions to surrender any gold coins and certificates they might be holding,[34] an act that was then amended and expanded by subsequent executive orders signed by President Roosevelt.[35] Because it was possible for the government to seize their gold stashes, many wealthy Americans spent decades afterward hiding their precious holdings in offshore bank vaults. It was only in 1974 that President Gerald Ford finally repealed President Roosevelt's executive orders and Congress again restored to US citizens their right to own gold.[36]

The United States was not the only nation to go hard against its citizens in this way. In 1959, Australia passed a law that allowed it to seize gold from private citizens. In 1966, the UK government banned its citizens from owning more than four gold or silver coins, a law that stayed on the books until 1979.[37]

This is not some quaint lesson from the past. It's an enduring principle. In times of trouble governments and the ruling politicians of the day will do extraordinary things to preserve the status quo and prevent the financial system from outright collapse. The lengths to which the US government went to save the financial system during the Global Financial Crisis (2007–2009), after making several blunders, will be dissected at length in chapter 3. But, to my mind, it was Mario Draghi, the former European Central Bank (ECB) president, who best summed up the pervasive worldview of government when it has its back against the wall.[38]

In the summer of 2012, as a sovereign debt crisis in Europe brought into question the euro's very survival, Draghi stood up and announced at a global investment conference in London, "The ECB is ready to do whatever it takes to preserve the euro. And believe me, it will be enough."[39]

We live in the age of "whatever it takes."

Whoever thinks that cryptocurrencies will be immune from government intervention and escape a fate similar to gold's, if this new age coin is perceived to rival and threaten the existing financial order, is deluding themselves. The crypto market globally stood at $1.7 trillion at the end of 2023,[40] liquid enough to appear interesting for investors, but it remains one-fourteenth the size of the US commercial real estate market, another exotic asset class that is more solid and generally not held enough in investors' portfolios.[41] But the larger point I want to make here is that cryptocurrencies as an asset class remain so small that governments could quash them without a major disruption to global markets.

Hence my concern for those drawn to crypto: rather than trying to understand the existing system and learning how to invest accordingly, an increasing number of investors are thinking they can escape the prevailing system through cryptocurrencies—and are at heightened risk of losing their life savings in the process.

Gold is often cited as a classic portfolio hedge against inflation, even though it's often forgotten that desperate politicians in desperate times have been known to seize their citizens' gold. Furthermore, gold doesn't pay dividends, as stocks do. That's why, while there may be periodic opportunities to buy gold at cheap prices, we don't include gold in our long-term strategic asset allocations; we see better long-term options to hedge against inflation elsewhere.

To compensate for these inflationary pressures building in economies, which then rattle markets, we are increasing our asset allocations to what we call *high-quality equities.* Desirable global brands with strong balance sheets and good cash flow, diversified across geographies, can get away with raising their prices when inflation increases. Granted, stocks are more volatile than bonds over the shorter term, but this new world of investing is causing us to rethink what it means to be a safe or risky asset.

DEGLOBALIZATION: THE PLAYERS PULL APART

It is the official national security strategy of the United States to resist what it sees as the intention of the People's Republic of China and its allies to realign the international order toward China's interests.[42] China, meanwhile, sees America's attempts to maintain its power and the status quo as a mistake and a weakness.

This conflict will play out in many ways. For example, when the United States banned the export of sophisticated AI chips to China in fall 2023, the Middle Kingdom retaliated by restricting its graphite exports to the United States after it had already limited access to its gallium and germanium exports, all key elements needed to produce electric vehicles.[43]

This wasn't a one-off event. A 2023 study by the European Bank for Reconstruction and Development found that 30 percent of all critical products were under some form of trade restriction, compared with 5 percent in 2015.[44] The result? Trade as a share of global GDP has likely peaked for the foreseeable future, as the United States, Europe, and China increasingly exchange sanctions, tariffs, and export controls. Such tensions risk splitting the world into incompatible financial, trade, and technological blocs.

What does it all mean to investors?

In the near term, geopolitical tensions could reinforce inflation. One key outcome of rising tensions between the United States and China has been significant investment in their respective surrounding nations. Mexico has, for example, overtaken China as the United States' largest trading partner.[45] Nations such as India and Vietnam are similarly benefiting as supply lines shift and realign in Asia.[46]

Yet the process of shifting supply chains away from where goods might be produced most cheaply and efficiently (e.g., China) and toward where the supplies might be more secure (e.g., Vietnam or Mexico) is likely to increase consumer prices. That inflation will systematically erode the value of "safe" assets, so hiding from geopolitical concerns in these assets, such as cash, won't help.

Furthermore, it's likely that geopolitical tensions will increase risks in specific markets. Investing in an electric-vehicle maker based on estimates of consumer demand may not be sufficient in a world in which key supply chain components might get cut off at a moment's notice. Diversification across sectors and across companies with diverse supply chains becomes a more critical issue for investors.

Finally, investors will increasingly have to consider how the politics of their jurisdictions may interact with the politics of the locations of their investments. Europeans or Americans with investments in Russian securities in 2022 were suddenly and essentially faced with a 100 percent loss on their holdings, not because the investments were worthless *in themselves*, but because they were worthless *to them*.

We must also train ourselves to see that there are not just risks but opportunities in deglobalization. A rise in global defense budgets has been accompanied by growth in spending, country by country, on energy security, cybersecurity, and water security, all of which boost revenues at companies providing the infrastructure and services in those areas.

And, from a portfolio perspective, it isn't necessarily a bad thing if the US and Chinese spheres of influence increasingly split into distinct financial, trade, and technological blocs. A heavily interconnected world is efficient but fragile. A downturn in any one region can drag down the whole system. So, counterintuitively, reducing connections can in some ways make world economic growth more robust, and it allows investors to increase their portfolio diversification by holding investments in a variety of political blocs.

DEMOGRAPHICS:
THE ELDERLY MULTIPLY

Maintaining a steady population requires a fertility rate of 2.1 births per woman.[47] This year Korea's fertility rate is projected to fall to 0.68, representing a near halving from an already low level of 1.24 as recently as 2015. China, almost a decade after scrapping its one-child policy,[48] now has a realized fertility rate of just 1.09, down from 1.81 in 2017.[49]

Populations will shrink as a result. China's population, currently at 1.4 billion, is in decline and is expected to drop below 1 billion by 2080 and shrink to 800 million by 2100.[50] Korea's population peaked a few years ago at 52 million and is projected to collapse a stunning 40 percent, to 31 million, by 2080.[51] That same trend is unfolding across the globe. The EU's population hit a high of 746 million in 2020 and is expected to fall to 624 million by 2080.[52] The outlier here, in the developed world, is the United States, where the current population of 336 million is expected to rise to 391 million by 2080 before flattening out.[53]

While shrinking, the populations are also aging. By 2050 the world will have an estimated 459 million persons aged eighty or older, almost triple the number in 2021, when the figure stood at around 155 million. That same year the global population of those 65 and older will stand at 1.6 billion.[54]

Economic growth is a function of growth in the labor force, capital investment, and productivity, so all else being equal, a smaller and increasingly retired population will mean lower potential economic growth. There's more: a higher proportion of retirees relative to workers could also increase debt loads, because the elderly will consume more government services at a time when there will be fewer workers paying income taxes to fund those services. Retirees consuming more services from ever-fewer workers could send prices soaring higher. Automation and AI could have a role to play, but we still appear to be a long way off from robotic nurses, hairdressers, and cleaning staff.

The ripples from this megatrend roll out. Increased workforce demand from the high-income societies coping with aging populations could lead to increased migration from lower-income countries, creating additional political tensions. The current estimates for international migration stand at 281 million people a year, up from just 153 million in 1990, which means that 1 out of every 28 people on earth today is a migrant.[55]

Yet for investors there is another side to this demographic change. The United States already spends over 18 percent of its GDP on health care,[56] and Medicare alone represented 14 percent of all US government expenditures in 2023.[57] Health care is a growing industry because of changing demographics.

Many developing nations are getting older and wealthier but per capita spend only half as much on health care as developed nations.[58] The demographic shift coupled with the rapid advances in medical treatments and increased public and private spending on health care appears to be one of the most durable trends of our age—and an opportunity for investors.

DIGITALIZATION: THE AI GAME CHANGER

The rise of artificial intelligence could very well presage an era of higher productivity. By our calculations AI could potentially unleash an incremental annual increase of between 0.3 percent and 2 percent in US productivity alone.[59]

But the picture here is not as clear as it is in, say, the demographics or debt arenas. If you asked me how ChatGPT has materially affected the way we produce goods these past two years, there are anecdotal stories I can point to, but it's hard to quantify the extent of its influence. What I can tell you is that AI technologies have had a significant impact on financial markets over that same period. By offering a simple, tangible demonstration of the potential power of modern artificial intelligence, ChatGPT has unleashed a wave of investment and galvanized many portfolios.

Investors in the Magnificent Seven of the S&P 500—the big-tech-driven companies such as Microsoft and Amazon—have become AI beneficiaries. The S&P 500 companies added $8.2 trillion to their market cap in 2023, but the Magnificent Seven alone accounted for $5.1 trillion of that increased market value.[60]

Of course, the big question is "What's next?" Investors today are spending a lot of time debating the extent to which AI will contribute to higher economic growth or inflation or unemployment. The answers to these questions seem still too uncertain at this stage to have much meaning for investors. Still, there are aspects of this new industry we can focus on.

AI FAVORS INCUMBENTS AND LEADERS

Developing AI solutions requires attracting talent, gathering data, buying computing power, and reaching consumers. These things require scale, which incumbents have. This means that established tech giants are likely to continue benefiting the most from AI advancements.

AI AND GEOPOLITICS INTERSECT

AI is becoming increasingly intertwined with geopolitics. Countries are entering an AI arms race to gain technological superiority, which can lead to geopolitical tensions. Recent restrictions on AI technology by the United States, and retaliatory measures by China, are examples of this trend.[61] The strategic importance of AI means that geopolitical developments will significantly affect the AI industry. Watch out for them.

AI IS MAKING HUGE DEMANDS ON THE ENERGY SECTOR

AI may start to test the limits of our energy capacity. Some corners of the US have already hit their limit of how many data centers they can host.[62] Virginia is one example. There are 245 existing data centers in Virginia, which collectively consume 3.6 gigawatts of power.[63] California is close to being in the same boat. There are 208 data centers in California, with 53 of those clustered around Santa Clara.[64] There is, of course, a political aspect as well. The need to ramp up data centers to service AI is immediate, but building new power-station capacity is a slow political process, often entangled with commitments to renewable energy.

We think at this stage investors should focus more on the tech companies that have the scale and resources to lead in AI development. While this point might seem contradictory to the notion of diversification, I think that "not missing the winners" is an argument in favor of diversification, not in opposition to it.

Second, since geopolitics will likely have an increasingly important role in shaping outcomes in the AI sector, investors should stay informed about geopolitical developments and consider diversifying their portfolios to mitigate related risks.

Finally, the energy demands of AI present both challenges and opportunities. Investors should consider companies involved in energy infrastructure and renewable energy, as they will play a crucial role in supporting AI growth. Additionally, tech companies with efficient energy management solutions will be valuable holdings for investors.

Here's the upshot: while the long-term growth potential of AI is substantial, the short-to-medium-term picture is still unclear, and focusing on these key aspects will help investors make informed decisions and navigate the evolving AI market landscape. As with other technology booms, an initial surge in demand can often be followed by a digestion period for consumers and businesses—and the markets. For long-term investors, such volatile periods could present attractive entry points into the sector.

DECARBONIZATION: BATTLING HOT AIR

As I said earlier, this book isn't going to debate climate change. Rather, it's going to follow the money and observe facts, then consider how investors should respond to those shifting forces. Here are some facts I think are relevant.

Governments around the world have made renewable-energy policy a priority, as they try to cut fossil fuel dependence and the resulting carbon emissions that scientists say are a major contributor to global warming. The EU has led the way with a binding goal that renewable energy account for at least 42.5 percent of European energy consumption by 2030,[65] but they are aiming for renewable energy to supply 45 percent[66] of that consumption. The rapidly rising power needs of our increasingly digital world are already so large they are leading to political questions as to who should get the power we produce.[67]

The following IEA chart neatly reveals how this growing investment flow toward alternative energy is unfolding. As recently as 2015 global fossil fuel investments were outstripping investments in alternative energy. What followed then were three years where the two sectors were virtually neck and neck, before alternative energy finally peeled away and soared off into the ozone. The IEA estimates that $2.8 trillion was invested in all forms of energy across the globe in 2023, but that alternative energy now accounts for $1.7 trillion, or 62 percent, of this total flow of money.[68]

Investment in clean energy has risen, while fossil fuel investment has fallen
Global energy investment in clean energy and in fossil fuel, total in USD bn

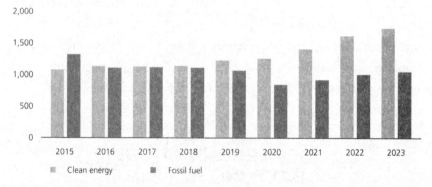

Source: IEA, UBS, as of July 2024

And now AI, as we've already noted, is leading to rapidly rising power needs in our increasingly digital world, which then leads to political questions at the intersection of these disruptive themes. Here, then, are some signposts to help investors find their way through the fog.

FOCUS ON RENEWABLE-ENERGY INVESTMENTS

Given the significant shift in investment toward alternative energy, there will still be a growing opportunity in renewable energy for a long while yet. Governments worldwide are prioritizing renewable-energy policies, and substantial capital is flowing into this space.

DIVERSIFY ACROSS ENERGY SECTORS

While renewable energy is on the rise, the transition from fossil fuel will take time. Diversifying investments across different energy sectors can help manage risk and capture opportunities in both traditional and alternative-energy markets. This includes investing in companies that are transitioning from fossil fuel to renewable-energy sources.

CONSIDER THE IMPACT OF AI ON ENERGY DEMAND

The rapid rise of AI and digital technologies is driving increased energy consumption and introducing unknowns. As we've mentioned, data centers in particular are significant energy consumers, and that could create an opportunity for companies that are developing energy-efficient technologies and solutions targeted toward them.

"But wait," you say. "What if a new administration gets elected and completely changes the previous administration's focus on renewable energy?" That's certainly possible, but the truth is that the changes in government policy in any one country would be just a drop in the global bucket.[69] The Big Money forces here are too big and powerful for any one nation to materially sway the direction this global money is headed.

In the longer term the smart folks in my office see the drive toward decarbonization as a net positive for global supply. Enabling a more abundant supply of energy at lower cost should contribute to higher potential growth, lower inflation, and more muscular supply chains.[70] For investors, solution providers as well as early adopters should stand to benefit the most from this massive migration to renewable energy.

Bottom Line

Even if you don't agree with every one of our 5Ds—debt, deglobalization, demographics, digitalization, and decarbonization—don't throw away this book yet. Reasonable people can debate precisely how to go about an exercise naming the top five investment themes of today and tomorrow. The larger point to grasp in this chapter is that the investment world has changed.

By following the Big Money—government spending—and the Big Problems governments around the world are increasingly focused on, today's investors can reframe an anxious discussion about existential risks into a practical discussion on investment risks and opportunities. The 5Ds are, as a result, often a great introduction to how our clients—and now you—can begin an investment journey that goes well beyond picking individual stocks and ultimately moves toward managing wealth in a way that addresses the larger forces at work in the global economy. But that's only the first step in the journey toward a comprehensive wealth-management strategy.

RULE 2

BUY WHAT GOVERNMENTS ARE BUYING

Investing in free markets is out.

Buying what the government is buying is in.

That's what you need to understand if you want to be an active investor in the twenty-first century. We can argue about how free the free market was before the financial crisis of 2007–2009, but the global trend toward government intervention in markets accelerated after the financial crisis and, as we saw during the COVID-19 years, shows no sign of abating.

To actively invest in markets today, it's a necessity to understand what governments are buying. If the US government is 35 percent to 40 percent of the nation's economy, it is arguably the single most important player in the markets, particularly when you consider that government incentives are then leveraged into even larger money flows by spurring related private-sector investments. This investment process starts by understanding how governments are shaping policy in reaction to the disruptive forces described in chapter 1, and to do that, we are going to—you guessed it—follow the money.

Let me show you what I mean. President Joe Biden signed the Inflation Reduction Act (IRA) in August 2022, providing billions of dollars in subsidies for an Energy Infrastructure Reinvestment Program, a policy meant to spur the nation's transition to a clean-energy grid.[1] The market responded. The US Infrastructure Development Index is up 46 percent as I write this, twenty-one months after the act was implemented.[2]

Similarly, the Biden administration's US CHIPS and Science Act of the same year provided $53 billion in incentives to bolster the nation's domestic semiconductor industry, policy that was in response to China's significant investments in its semiconductor technology.[3] Since the CHIPS and Science Act was signed into law, the iShares Semiconductor ETF (SOXX) has risen 77 percent.[4]

This new investment creed—**buy what the government is buying**—is relevant not just to the United States or a handful of other developed Western countries. It's become a global truth.

China is busy reshaping its domestic capital markets according to what is called a whole-nation theory of intervention, with various government entities, according to the press, guiding local investment banks via traffic-light signals on what companies can or cannot go public.[5] As reported in the *Financial Times*, initial public offerings (IPOs) for beverage makers and restaurants were getting a red light; those the Chinese government considers strategic industries of national importance—such as electric vehicles, battery makers, and solar panels—were getting a green light. Various institutions in China have reportedly been directed from the top down to support these strategically important IPOs, largely ensuring success. It is all part and parcel of China's grand plan to create an alternative to Western capitalism.[6]

The idea that beasts of burden will respond to incentives is so accepted in our culture, we often refer to using incentives to drive behavior simply as "the carrot and stick." Yet surprisingly few investors make the study of "carrots and sticks"—in particular those crucial government rewards and cudgels used to impose policies on vast swaths of people and markets—a central part of their investment process.

I would even argue that the beatings from the "sticks"—for resisting these government-incentivized directions of capital—are increasingly difficult to withstand, particularly for businesses determined to follow their own iconoclastic routes. Indeed, the cost of not marching in lockstep in the direction governments want industries to head is becoming so prohibitively expensive that fewer and fewer will dare risk defiance.

The US Justice Department recently sued eBay, potentially seeking $1.9 billion in fines, for merely distributing hundreds of thousands of emission-defeating devices that violated the Clean Air Act.[7] We're witnessing a growing movement to weaponize the new and existing environment-related laws on the books, and that is creating opportunities for larger and larger suits against perceived transgressors. In fact, we seem to have reached a tipping point where private entities are using punitive-damage suits to further enforce the government's drive toward the direction it wants society to go.

Does this sound like fantasy? In October 2023, Gramercy Funds Management, a US hedge fund, invested $550 million of its assets in a UK law firm, in the form of a secured loan, to finance massive environmental litigation claims against mining firms BHP and Vale, plus fourteen car manufacturers that were involved in so-called Dieselgate.[8] That's a scandal dating back to 2015, when car companies were found to be secretly using software to underreport car emissions.[9]

The European Court of Human Rights in Strasbourg, France, recently delivered its ruling in a case brought by more than two thousand Swiss women, the majority of whom are in their seventies, against Switzerland's government. They argued that heat waves fueled by climate change undermined their health and quality of life, which put them at risk of dying prematurely, and by not doing enough to prevent this from happening, the Swiss government violated their human rights. The Swiss women won their case.[10] This and other cases could open the door to civil liabilities.

Of course, it's not just the government's carrots and sticks we must follow. There are more obvious ways government interventions move markets.

Take Russia's invasion of Ukraine. When Vladimir Putin sent his soldiers over the Ukrainian border on February 24, 2022,[11] the flow of Russian energy to the West was disrupted, and EU natural gas prices per million metric Btu spiked 157 percent over the next several months.[12] This price jump was of course the direct result of Europe's very public energy choices over the previous decades, which made it vulnerable to such an energy-security chokepoint.

Not to be outdone, Western nations followed Russia's aggression with a government intervention that no investor can ignore.[13] Virtually overnight, governments declared Russia "un-investable," forcing Russian assets to become less than worthless[14] to those who faced criminal penalties for holding them.[15]

There's also more here than meets the eye. If you take a step back, you'll see that all these events—Biden's industrial policies, Xi's economic engineering, the fallout of the Russia-Ukraine war—are in some way related to a key trend, which is the way governments globally have shifted their investment priorities and controls toward what they think are the great competitive needs of the twenty-first century.

Western governments have, for example, radically changed the nature of their energy-industry incentives. They've largely withdrawn support from their coal industries, while increasing reliance on sources like natural gas and creating more incentives for the wind and solar industries. That's an important piece of intelligence for investors to know, and it flows directly from following the money. Big Money has Big Needs.

In fact, the rise in natural gas prices that was a by-product of the Russia-Ukraine war galvanized the EU's move toward renewable energy at a far faster pace. The EU Commission's REPowerEU Plan, passed just two months after the invasion of Ukraine, pumped EUR 300 billion in grants and subsidized loans into the continent's transition away from Russian energy and toward homegrown renewable energy.[16] Going forward, I am convinced we will see even more such government incentives supporting national energy security, which in turn will further shape the direction markets are headed.

Hedge-fund star Ray Dalio was for decades coy about his investment process, until a *New York Times* exposé and an underlying biography revealed that buying into government intervention was a significant way that Dalio made his wealth at Bridgewater Associates.[17] The Dalio reveal was a big deal when it came out[18] and produced a lot of controversy, but if the reports are right, the Wall Street billionaire was high-level schmoozing to get an edge on what governments were buying, all so his Bridgewater Associates could make money

But here's the thing: You don't have to be a government confidant to use this investment tool. You can buy what the government is buying from the comfort of your own living room, all with information that is publicly available on the internet. As we saw, the indexes for infrastructure builders and semiconductor manufacturers shot up after the Inflation Reduction Act and the CHIPS and Science Act were signed into law. The flow of funds from government spending usually follows after public announcements, and the big trends are simply too large to remain invisible.

And although this is not a foolproof set-it-and-forget-it strategy for the next fifty years, that doesn't mean returning to value investing—the process that starts with screening for low P/E stocks, which are company shares that are priced cheaply relative to the earnings the company is generating on a per-share basis—is the right answer. The world has changed too much.

Since 2015 growth stocks have massively outperformed value stocks, but for the aberrational year of 2022, when tech stocks got hit by a cyclical downdraft.[19] That value-stock rally was short lived. In 2023 large-growth stocks jumped 47.3 percent, according to Morningstar, outperforming large-value stocks by 36 percent, the second-biggest advantage for growth over value in the past twenty-five years.[20]

Of course, shadowing government purchases in the markets, as we recommend, doesn't eliminate the ability of some people to be great stock pickers, and it certainly is not a risk-free pursuit. If the government stops buying, the market flows can reverse, which means you need to sell before the government sells. Fortunately, that's going to be easier to deal with than you might think, since government policies often come to an end after they have become a victim of their own success.

Consider Germany's intervention in the solar-panel industry. Back in 2000 the German government unleashed its Renewable Energy Sources

Act, offering generous subsidies to encourage its citizens to buy solar panels for their homes and businesses, all while forcing utilities to pay a premium for energy supplied from such renewable sources.[21] This was a policy the political parties on both sides of the spectrum could all pretty much agree on, and for a while Germany became a leader in solar-energy production.

More than a decade after the Renewable Energy Sources Act was switched on, the German government reduced its solar-panel subsidies by 50 percent and then a further 30 percent, all in rapid succession.[22] Why? By 2012 the demand for solar panels in Germany was so great, and the industry growth so torrid, that the government felt it could no longer afford the policy and started aggressively cutting back its overly generous subsidies. Shares in solar-panel manufacturers promptly tumbled on the news, not just in Germany, but around the world.[23]

The point here is that the same abrupt ending could eventually happen with, say, President Biden's Inflation Reduction Act, which was passed by Congress and signed into the law of the land. The US government might eventually decide it can no longer afford the energy-credit subsidies and shut the party down, as happened in Germany with its solar-panel subsidies. But even if the subsidies become a victim of their own success, or a radical shift in government is able to undo a previous administration's particular legislation, that is usually a long way off in time and money. Between then and now, the government's subsidies will have years—potentially many years—to drive some industries and companies to grow faster than the growth rate of global or US GDP. Furthermore, as global investment in things like decarbonization ramps up, the specific policies of any one country become less consequential.

REWIRING THE WAY YOU THINK ABOUT INVESTMENTS

Thinking through the growing importance of government policy to investing, and the global power that the 5D disruptive forces have had in shaping our world, my colleagues and I at the UBS chief investment office found it was necessary to reshape our active investing strategies. In fact, we have started to put aside many of the traditional ways Wall Street has taught you and me to think about investments.

Wall Street organizes stock market knowledge by regions and sectors. Major stock indices, such as the S&P 500 and the MSCI Emerging Markets Index, are, for example, organized around regions like the United States, Europe, and emerging markets. The investment universe within a region is then subdivided into broad sectors like energy, materials, industrials, consumer discretionary, consumer staples, health care, and so on.

Each sector is then subdivided into industry groups. The energy sector is, for example, made up of both the oil and gas industry and the alternative-energy industry. The next grouping level down is sub-industries. The financial services sector contains both the banking industry and the insurance industry, for example, with the insurance industry further split into sub-industries such as automotive insurance, life insurance, and fire insurance.

Just because Wall Street wants you to think and organize your investments this way doesn't mean it will help you increase your wealth. Quite the opposite.

The top-down investment method we focus on at UBS instead researches and explores the macroeconomic, geopolitical, social, and technological trends that are being expressed in government policy. We discussed the 5Ds of change in the last chapter to showcase the need for applying a different investment strategy to today's world, but this chapter is more about *how* to change. As to the how, we are focusing more and more of our active investing efforts around **digital disruption**, **energy disruption**, and **health-care disruption**. We see these three trends as "trillion-dollar opportunities."

In an increasingly complex world, this focus helps prevent us from trying to boil the ocean with our expertise and research. Second, and more importantly, in making this shift to focus on active investing in digital, energy, and health-care disruption, we increasingly tie into the fears, passions, and excitements that surround how our ultra-high-net-worth clients want to invest.

Lucy* is the daughter of an East Coast business mogul who sold his business for $2 billion and then shortly afterward passed away, leaving her significant wealth. While growing up, Lucy got involved in local environmental issues, such as water scarcity, and that early exposure made her acutely aware that the world will run out of resources. When she became an adult, her sensitivity to environmental and climate change issues morphed into her investment and philanthropic passion. Today, Lucy is investing $70 million of annual liquidity in entities that try to solve the big environmental problems of our times. When we talk to Lucy about our focus on energy disruption, it not only connects us to her passion, it's also a way for us to apply our expertise in a meaningful way to what is important to her.

Yet from a practical standpoint, focusing on these themes is also valuable for active investors who are not professionals or ultra-highs. That's because the premise of this "Big Money = Big Problems" investing technique is to allocate your hard-earned capital to large, durable trends that don't change month to month or even year to year. You are entering these plays with a longer-term confidence and mindset. That mentally prepares you not to hit the sell button during the inevitable market fluctuations that force others to panic and dump assets when prices are temporarily low.

Furthermore, thinking this way doesn't require you to find a needle in the haystack of stocks, which is a huge plus. It also makes it a lot easier to reduce company-specific risks in your portfolio. By betting on broader themes, you are purposefully looking for a basket or ecosystem of investments that will benefit from these long-term trends, and the diversification of that basket of investments will help reduce the volatility if a particular stock or sector runs into problems for idiosyncratic reasons, like a bad CEO or a new competitor.

---

* Names and some personal details have been changed to protect identities.

Bottom Line

In chapter 4, I will make the argument that you are much better off allocating assets rather than trying to pick "hot" individual stocks. Yet even when investors I work with want to ignore that advice, they often see the logic of picking key themes from the 5Ds, as they believe it helps them narrow down the stocks they want to look at.

For my team of professionals, organizing our thinking around the macro issues governments are spending money on forces us to think outside of the industry silos, while also allowing us to laser-focus our expertise on fewer topics.

You should consider doing the same if you are going to be an active investor. Rewire and rethink your investment strategy in a world where free markets are out, and government intervention is in. That starts with unlearning how Wall Street has traditionally taught you to think about the world of investing: by regions, industry sectors, and companies. The successful investment strategy today is built on an understanding that the greatest opportunities of the future are lurking in those corners of the global economy where Big Money is trying to solve Big Problems.

RULE 3

UNDERSTAND HOW WE GOT TO WHERE WE ARE

If you look deeper into what happened during the Global Financial Crisis, you'll understand how the government intervention of that time wound up profoundly changing the markets we invest in today. It affects both our shorter-term trades and our longer-term strategic holdings. How we balance between the two is the subject of the next chapter on asset allocation. However, in this chapter, we want to focus on how the rulebook established during the Global Financial Crisis is very much still in play, creating massive money flows that like a large wave can either lift or sink your investment lifeboat.

The how and why of this phenomenon is what we need to unpack, and why I am again asking you drop any explicit and implicit value judgments you have about what governments and central banks did during that difficult time and are doing to this day—and instead coldly follow the money until you arrive at real insights into today's financial markets.

There's good reason for this ask. If you understand why we are where we are, if you grasp what policy and economic forces have been building over decades and are at play in today's financial markets, then it won't be as difficult to follow the buy-what-the-government-is-buying investment strategy that I recommend, even if you are philosophically opposed to this way of thinking. Understanding *why* you are investing a certain way will invariably make you a more confident and accomplished investor.

SEEDS OF UNDERSTANDING: HOW GOVERNMENTS AND MARKETS INTERSECT

The knowledge I gained about that nexus between markets and government intervention started my sophomore year at Princeton, when I took a course with the historian Sean Wilentz, who had a way of showing students the world doesn't always work the way people think it is working.[1] In that course, Wilentz assigned us *The Jungle*, Upton Sinclair's 1906 novel about Chicago's meat-packing industry, a muckraking work that exposed and brought viscerally home the filthy conditions of the city's unsanitary slaughterhouses.[2]

Instead of Sinclair's book leading to the end of the meat-packing business in Chicago, as I suspected would happen, it led to the *expansion* of the meat-packing business. That's because Sinclair's exposé led to the passage[3] of the Federal Meat Inspection Act of 1906.[4]

The meat-packers loved that their meat was thereafter stamped "USDA inspected," because that seal of approval made the US government complicit in their business and allowed for international expansion. Once they had the reassuring government-inspection stamp on quartered American steer carcasses, the meat wholesalers could successfully export their surpluses to the rest of the world.[5] In short, the market for American beef *expanded* after the government intervention, a positive example of how government intervention could in fact foster a new industry. I would be reminded of this lesson years later, when I started getting involved with impact investing.

But government intervention always has intended and unintended consequences, and it's the investor's job to parse out what real effect the policy will have on the ground, and then invest accordingly around that real rather than wished-for result. I caught an early glimpse of this distinction between intended and unintended consequences of government policy when I focused my independent studies at Princeton on the career of Walt Whitman Rostow, who went from MIT professor to President Kennedy's speechwriter to President Johnson's national security advisor.[6]

As I uncovered and eventually wrote up in my Harvard dissertation—"Walt Rostow, Modernization, and Vietnam: Stages of Theoretical Growth"—Rostow began his career as a brainy and charming history and economics PhD at Yale.[7] In 1940 he was tapped to join a team of fifty young economists creating the economics subdivision of the Research and Analysis branch of the Office of Strategic Services. That was the CIA's predecessor organization, and it was gathering and processing intelligence that would assist the Allies' war effort.

The Americans at the time were unhappy with the British bombing targets, biased as they were toward night raids and inducing civilian terror. The Americans wanted more strategic thought applied to bombing targets in Germany, which was why, in September 1942, young Rostow was figuratively parachuted into the newly created London-based unit called the Enemy Objectives Unit (EOU) to help compute what would be the best bombing objectives.

The EOU started by studying why Germany finally came to the negotiating table at the end of the First World War in 1918, and concluded the German government surrendered because it had run out of manpower and war material, not because the civilian population was terrorized and demoralized. That idea became the unit's guiding principle during WWII, and the EOU economists set out to trace the intricate connections between Nazi industries and the war effort then underway. The question they asked themselves: *What industries and which plants should be bombed to inflict the greatest disruption to Germany's military production?*

For a variety of reasons, the EOU settled on the nation's ball-bearing factories, providing key parts for heavy machinery. The EOU's strategic analysis of "destruction per unit cost" was in the end wrong, because they didn't know the Nazis had large ball-bearing reserves stashed around Europe, but that was not the important takeaway, as far as I was concerned.

Over the course of my investment career, I have often returned to Rostow's thought process during WWII and reapplied the EOU's way of thinking to the economic trends and market conditions I was facing at the time: *If you believe the global economy is heading in a certain direction, where should you target your precious and limited investment capital so you can most benefit from that overarching economic trend?*

There was one other crucial lesson I learned from Rostow: how intellectual "systems" dreamed up by economists can turn into government policy with real (and sometimes brutal) consequences for everyday folks. After WWII ended and the Cold War started, Rostow formulated his version of the idea that societies developed in economic stages, and that economic aid could help move emerging nations beyond the stage where they were vulnerable to a Communist takeover. Rostovian development theory became the backbone of American soft power under presidents Kennedy and Johnson, and contributed to the creation of both the US Army Green Berets and the Peace Corps.

While Rostow's economic theories told a story about how economic development would fight communism, once Rostow finally visited Vietnam he concluded the way to end Communist influence in developing nations was bombs.

Ultimately, lots and lots of bombs.

His ideas helped pave the way for the buildup of US military "advisors" in Vietnam and to the eventual carpet-bombing of large swaths of Southeast Asia when he became Johnson's national security advisor. Yet Rostow's economic theories remained useful to the Kennedy and Johnson administrations as they desperately struggled to come up with a policy on containing communism that both Republicans and Democrats could endorse.

Rostow created the story, backed by his economic calculations, that said, in effect, "Look, we are helping these people build a modern postwar economy in Vietnam that will eventually bring peace and prosperity and benefit to all of us. We just need to fight off the Communists for a few more years until capitalism can really take off." Through Rostow's views on economic growth and fighting communism, maybe some people were actually persuaded that there was a logic to the idea that "we had to destroy the village to save it." This was mad stuff. But the original research I conducted into Rostow was an insight into how the government policy that gets enacted tends not to be the smartest policy but the policy that allows the largest number of politicians to talk out of both sides of their mouth at the same time, while serving influential special interests.

After I went into finance, I started to see many examples of the way government policy had unintended economic consequences galore, distorting markets. Policy stood behind the accounting fraud we uncovered at Fannie Mae and Freddie Mac; behind the fast-growing global online-gambling industry of the early 2000s, disrupted finally when local government authorities intervened and smashed the industry's business model; behind the well-intentioned government efforts that unleashed the US's for-profit education industry and its attendant corruption. Once I realized the commonality in these events, I determined to make this understanding of government intervention even more important to how I invested in the future.

The watershed event in all of this—the catalyst that forever changed how we invest today and in the foreseeable future—was the Global Financial Crisis. Before the chaos of 2007–2009, many hedge-fund managers ignored big themes and macro investing. They proudly quoted the phenomenally successful Peter Lynch, who famously produced a 2,700 percent return at Fidelity's Magellan Fund when he ran it between 1977 and 1990, and repeatedly said in public, "If you spend thirteen minutes a year on economics, you've wasted ten minutes."[8]

After the financial crisis, the same hedge-fund managers sheepishly said to me, "Do macro or macro will do you." The logical follow-up question is this: What changed and what are the takeaway lessons still important for today's investors?

HOW WE GOT HERE

Many stock market investors have historically felt they could ignore macro investing and government intervention, because government kept a safe distance from playing a primary role in financial-sector bailouts. Throughout history, Wall Street has always been happy to profit from government policy and incentives, but when it came to financial panics, it was private capital, not public capital, that was expected to be the "lender of last resort" and save the day—with some exceptions briefly made during the Great Depression.

The Panic of 1907, also known as the Knickerbocker Crisis, is considered by economic historians to be the first worldwide financial meltdown, and it was similar to the Global Financial Crisis of 2007–2009 in that both panics started with New York–based financial institutions and markets before spreading to the rest of the world.[9] The 1907 panic, ignited by a failed attempt to corner the copper market,[10] ultimately led to US GDP falling 12 percent in 1908, a downturn that was second only to the Great Depression in severity.[11] But the bank run that led to the global market crisis in October 1907 only lasted a matter of weeks.[12]

That's because, the second week into the crisis, banker John Pierpont Morgan summoned the era's bank presidents and trust presidents to his library on Madison Avenue and locked the door.[13] He wouldn't let them out until they faced the severity of the market collapse and the risk of further contagion.[14] The New York stock market was at that moment falling nearly 50 percent from its peak.[15]

In the early hours, surrounded by the Gutenberg Bibles of his dimly lit library,[16] seventy-year-old J. P. Morgan and his peers hammered out a deal to create a trust company that would rescue Wall Street's key institutions on the brink of collapse.[17] The bankers put their own money on the line to end the panic, a mix of civic duty and profit-driven motives. Before the smoke cleared, Morgan had acquired strategic assets at fire-sale prices.[18]

That is pretty much how things worked for the next one hundred years. While the Panic of 1907 is often heralded as the event that sparked the creation of the US Federal Reserve System,[19] that did not mean that the US government immediately and fully embraced the role of lender of last resort.[20] That's because the government was still tiny. It didn't have the resources and wasn't a big enough part of the economy to do what the bankers could do. The US government's share of GDP was just 6.6 percent in 1907.[21] It stood at 34.2 percent in 2007 and reached an all-time high of 47 percent in 2020.[22]

Throughout the last century—except for some inconclusive intervention during the Great Depression—the US government kept J. P. Morgan's tradition alive during turbulent financial times by periodically leaning on a bevy of bankers to save the global financial system from total collapse. US policymakers did not have the appetite, or apparent authority or will, to save the world from a financial meltdown using public money. The government's instinctive response to a crisis was always, "Let's get J. P. Morgan in here and he'll put together a bunch of bankers to solve the problem."

In the latter part of the twentieth century, the J. P. Morgan role was usually filled by Warren Buffett,[23] and I would argue that too many investors who want to emulate the Sage of Omaha forget that a key factor of his outsized success was his ability to function as a "lender of last resort" when a crisis hit. It was Warren Buffett who provided, at good terms for himself, the bailout capital[24] needed by GE[25] and Goldman Sachs[26] when they were in precarious financial situations during the Global Financial Crisis, and then invested again in Bank of America during the 2011 debt-ceiling crisis.[27] His highly profitable playbook was only upended in the crisis of 2008, when government finally muscled in on his act and decided to out–Warren Buffett Warren Buffett.

I got an acute lesson in these workings in 1998, when I was in my late twenties, and my buddy Larry Kam and I created a long-short hedge fund called the Sonic Fund in our dorm rooms at Harvard. The hedge fund was structured so that we could either short stocks (bet that a company's shares would go down) or go long (bet they would go up) as we saw fit. The same year we launched our modest outfit, a much bigger hedge fund called Long Term Capital Management (LTCM) spectacularly collapsed.

LTCM almost brought down the entire global financial system before our eyes, and ultimately required a coordinated response from the authorities.[28]

LTCM was founded by John Meriwether, a former vice chairman and fabled bond trader at Salomon Brothers. His board included not one but *two* Nobel Prize–winning experts: Robert Merton and Myron Scholes,[29] known for creating the Black-Scholes-Merton model.[30] These guys were Wall Street legends and as smart as they come.

LTCM's business model was complex, but to boil it down, they would try to identify small differences in prices between similar bonds, differences which usually go away over a period of time. Initially, it worked, and Meriwether handsomely rewarded his investors between 1993 and 1998. But arbitraging tiny spread differentials in security prices requires huge amounts of leverage—borrowed money or debt—to make it anywhere near meaningful.[31]

So LTCM kept using more and more leverage.[32] At its peak in 1998, LTCM's $5 billion war chest reportedly controlled $130 billion in assets,[33] and the theoretical value of its positions exceeded $1.25 trillion.[34]

Then the outlier event happened.

In August 1998, Russia devalued the ruble and defaulted on its loans.[35]

There was an immediate need for quality and liquidity in the global bond market, and that made the prices for high-quality US Treasuries move in ways the academic models never predicted. The huge amount of leverage being used in LTCM's business model and its attempt to quickly sell everything to pay down that debt impacted bond prices around the world and set off a global panic.[36]

While the trigger, Russia's default, was a macro event far away, which then provoked all sorts of unexpected price adjustments in government bond prices closer to home, the heart of the problem was in fact what it usually is: people too smart, using too much leverage, building up too much concentrated risk.

But there was another important lesson below the surface of events.

While we were still firmly in the era of the investment gurus Warren Buffett and Peter Lynch—and their method of analyzing individual stocks for hidden values not yet recognized by markets—LTCM's collapse was nonetheless one of the early signs that in this new interlocking world of global markets, you could no longer ignore the macro, even if you only wanted to study individual stocks.

When LTCM was near collapsing,[37] and it had missed a small window to seize a rescue package offered by Warren Buffett,[38] the US government stepped in and made sure Wall Street saved itself. The consortium of banks the US Federal Reserve rounded together, ranging from Merrill Lynch to Goldman Sachs,[39] ultimately created a $3.6 billion fund that LTCM could draw on. That fund allowed LTCM to weather the massive waves it helped create, before finally limping into a safe harbor for an orderly liquidation.

No public money was ever used to save LTCM. It was all private capital.

The LTCM rescue was firmly part of that one-hundred-year period when the financial system was encouraged to heal itself. When a financial crisis hit, if you wanted to understand how the powers that be were going to navigate their way out of it and even profit from the turmoil, you had to understand what was going on in the banker's smoke-filled room, not what was going on in the government.

The Global Financial Crisis changed that.

I believe that government intervention not only led to the ultimate resolution of the Global Financial Crisis but also was inadvertently responsible for creating the crisis in the first place. It was only through systemic government intervention that the financial bubble of the mid-2000s could have ever gotten as big as it did. That's because a root cause of the crisis was the United States' housing-market distortions created by government-sponsored enterprises (GSEs).

GSEs are quasi-governmental agencies created to boost the flow of credit to specific corners of the US economy, such as to education or agriculture.[40] In this case, the principal actors were Fannie Mae and Freddie Mac, originally created by government for the noble purpose of expanding the housing market for more Americans.[41]

These GSEs essentially increased the liquidity and size of the nation's mortgage and housing market by raising money cheaply with a "sort of, almost, maybe, not really" government guarantee, then bulk buying and repackaging banks' home loans. By offloading the mortgages to the GSEs, the local banking institutions' balance sheets were freed up to recycle their money back into more and lower-priced mortgages for the public.[42] Good luck getting a thirty-year fixed mortgage anywhere else in the world, but the American middle class could almost take it for granted thanks to GSEs. That predictability made it possible for more families to use a big mortgage to buy into the American dream of homeownership.

Make no mistake: Fannie and Freddie remade America.

The GSEs decreased the cost of the American dream of mortgaging a single-family home in the suburbs, and that increased the mass migration out of the cities. They accelerated the reshaping of the American landscape into low-density neighborhoods that needed yet more cars to get around.

The system worked, and the US housing market expanded robustly for decades. But the implicit government guarantee that Fannie Mae and Freddie Mac enjoyed meant taxpayers ultimately shouldered much of the risk around ballooning mortgage debts. That's what we all lost sight of. As long as the GSEs kept adding low-cost mortgage debt into the system, they fueled increased housing demand and spiraling prices. Those "reliable" house-price increases showed up in the statistics for so long they created the illusion that house prices only went in one direction. The phenomenon went on for so long that the risk models started to spit out unreliable data that the housing market was getting safer and safer.

That's why you could hear Fed chairman Alan Greenspan arguing before Congress and the media it was highly unlikely that a national real estate bubble would ever occur or that housing prices could collapse like equities,[43] and why financial professionals were similarly making comments like "housing prices never fall." But the Freddie-and-Fannie-provided mortgage-debt "subsidy" continued for so long and became so big, it was a major factor in the housing bubble, and it was only because the real risk was hidden with the taxpayer and not talked about that the banks could build all their questionable housing and economic models. This allowed even more leverage on top of the Freddie and Fannie securities.[44]

Well, it doesn't take a mathematical genius to understand the danger here. We all know that the more people who can afford homes, the easier it is for prices to go up. As illustrated in the Hollywood movie *The Big Short*,[45] if an exotic dancer can speculatively own and finance five houses and a condo, something might be up, and it's entirely possible housing prices could collapse.

Yet what member of Congress is going to deny the average person the chance to use the system to get ahead, just like the wealthy and privileged do? Who wants to pop the balloon? So the horror that was building was allowed to continue until the world blew up.

The lesson: government intervention is a mighty sword that cuts many ways, and understanding where the blade is coming down, both the intended and unintended consequences of that policy, is a key job of the successful twenty-first-century investor. In this case the crisis brewing was a version of what we highlighted previously—well-intentioned US government policies provided a "carrot" subsidy for the housing market that was so successful it became the victim of its own success.

It's also why, as outlined in chapter 1, government debt is a disruptive force that is starting to impact our asset allocations.

Once we experienced the first tremors of the financial crisis in 2007, the US government then created an arguably bigger problem via a catastrophic set of mixed messages.[46] It did so by first stepping in to help save the distressed Bear Stearns on March 16, 2008. That's when JPMorganChase agreed to buy Bear Stearns for two dollars a share[47]—1 percent of the firm's value fourteen months earlier[48]—but did so with $29 billion provided through the back door by the Federal Reserve.[49] That government-financed rescue prompted a collective sigh of relief. After the S&P hit a 1256.98 low on Bear Stearns blowing up in March,[50] it climbed 15 percent to a 1440.24 high by mid-May.[51]

For the first time since the Great Depression, the Federal Reserve loaned public money to rescue a financial institution on the verge of collapse. The fall of Bear Stearns was undeniably a major new development and seemed like a turning point in the financial crisis. The government blinked and started intervening to save Wall Street from itself.

I am not going to tell you that Larry and I, running Sonic Capital Management, instantly recognized this as a historic rupture in the development of capitalism and profited from it. The best I can say is, we realized we weren't sure what was going on and became more cautious. It was a weird situation. Not only were valuations high, which made many investments unattractive, but also you couldn't get too bearish because the government had just shown it was willing to jump in to stop a sell-off. Often when governments start to panic, savvy investors start looking to buy.

Well, we soon discovered that the Bear Stearns intervention was a head fake. When the Federal Reserve decided it did not have the authority to save debt-laden Lehman Brothers in September 2008,[52] there suddenly was, the markets realized, no lender of last resort.

It wasn't Warren Buffett.

It wasn't the government.

One of the reasons this Bear Stearns–Lehman Brothers head fake was so devastating was because Ben Bernanke was Fed chairman—and everyone thought they knew where he stood.

Ben Bernanke had been an economics professor at MIT, Stanford, and Princeton.[53] The Great Depression was his scholarly expertise; one of his better-known books was a Princeton University Press collection called *Essays on the Great Depression*.[54] Bernanke was well aware[55] of the great economist Charles Kindleberger, who famously summed up the cause of the Great Depression as the fact that neither the Bank of England nor the Federal Reserve realized the global nature of the crisis and ever stepped in as lender of last resort.[56] This was not some fringe economic view about how to stop a depression. This is what I was taught at Harvard and by Charles Kindleberger himself, whom I used to visit at his retirement home while I was writing my dissertation.

Bernanke believed that the US Fed had helped turn the 1929 recession into a global calamity through two major mistakes: it had first allowed the money supply to contract during the crisis, rather than juicing the system with liquidity as the circumstances required,[57] and then it had passively let banks fail, rather than assisting them through their worst days, which further catastrophically damaged credit markets and destroyed the economy's ability to right itself.

So Bernanke grasped what might need to be done and understood that the Fed had many tools at its interventionist disposal, all of which could be used to shock the system back into recovery mode. Back in 2002, during a speech Bernanke gave at the National Economists Club in DC—in that case about what tools the government could use to fight deflation—the future Fed chairman presciently observed, "But the US government has a technology, called a printing press (or, today, its electronic equivalent), that allows it to produce as many dollars as it wishes at essentially no cost."[58]

That was why the market rallied after the Bear Stearns scoop-up.

With Bernanke in charge, the government would act as a lender of last resort. The worst firms, the unlucky firms, would go under, but that was business as usual. We had the guy in place who understood the role of the government as a fire-break for contagion. For that reason, so many investors believed that Bernanke would bail out the system if it faltered again—and maybe even start running the printing press.

Then the Lehman Brothers collapse happened, triggering the S&P's 57 percent collapse from its high in October 2007 to its low point in March 2009.[59]

It was such a scary period. The more you knew, the worse it seemed.

The US government had recognized that with Bear Stearns, the financial system needed a lender of last resort, and it had taken almost unprecedented action to step in and be that lender to try to save the financial system.

After Lehman, however, the muddled message was something like, "We know the financial system needs a lender of last resort. We convinced you of that with Bear Stearns. But we, as the US government, now don't think we have the power to save it."

That's how and why we ended up with Treasury Secretary Hank Paulson on his hands and knees begging Nancy Pelosi, the Speaker of the House, for help.[60] Paulson and Bernanke needed the full weight of the US government behind them.

On October 3 the US Congress passed the Emergency Economic Stabilization Act of 2008.[61] The profound shift in government policy had finally come about. That massive piece of legislation created the Troubled Asset Relief Program (TARP), a $700 billion fund that was tasked with pumping liquidity back into the financial system and stabilizing the banking institutions that were mass-dumping risky assets, further leading to price declines.[62] It was the last act of the seriously desperate. The banks' funding had dried up, and most were on the verge of collapse.[63]

Again, this is not a story about how I foresaw the financial crisis, made a fortune, and lived happily ever after. That is somebody else's book. Rather, years of experience and battle scars meant I had developed a sensitivity to risk. I had my investment system in place, which was a balanced portfolio of asset allocations. My stock allocation was down during this bear market, and normally I would rebalance it by buying more stocks, but forcing myself to rebalance in that free-falling market was too painful.

I was scared. Things seemed to be getting worse and worse.

This was a time when people started to confidently bet on the financial system's total collapse and destruction. I remember thinking it was like the movie *Jurassic Park* when the raptors start testing the fence for weak points.[64] Traders were similarly pushing on the banks to try to break them. I was not prepared to play this dangerous game, because if the government got its act together, those negative bets could easily get wiped out. And if the raptors broke through the fence and the system collapsed, I wasn't sure I could collect my winnings anyway. Worse still was the knowledge that smart investors I knew were starting to bury gold on their property and hoard food.

But fortune finally favored the prepared mind. Citigroup was riddled with subprime mortgage loans and sitting on $306 billion in troubled assets;[65] by November 2008 the colossal bank's shares had in short order fallen 60 percent to $3.77.[66] That's when Citi asked for government help.[67] On November 23 the US government announced it was guaranteeing Citigroup's loans and securities that were backed by residential real estate. Citi would absorb all portfolio losses up to $29 billion, after which the US government would assume 90 percent of the losses, first through TARP, then via the FDIC. These two government institutions would in exchange be issued $7 billion in preferred stock in Citigroup, and the shares would pay the US Treasury an 8 percent dividend.[68]

The US government, not its proxies J. P. Morgan and Warren Buffett, was finally and fully signed up to be the lender of last resort. The government was seriously back in the business of providing market support, after losing its nerve over Lehman.

Larry, that gifted reader of financial statements, found the nugget in the government's technically verbose rescue package, when yet more details emerged in late February 2009.[69] The US government was converting its Citi preferred stock for common stock at $3.25, a significant premium to the stock's share price at the time, but the market was disappointed by the announcement and proceeded to drive Citi's common stock down to $0.97 over subsequent days.[70]

Larry had to explain this to me twice because the enormity of it all left me speechless.

I said, "Wait a second. They're buying Citi's stock, and we can now buy this stock cheaper in the open market than what the government is going to pay us for our shares?" Larry nodded and slowly repeated that the government was in effect putting a floor to the bank's stock.

"But this is national news!" I said, stunned.

The government's intervention in Citi had far broader implications for the markets. It was, in many ways, the moment when Buffett-style value investing died. The imperative for investors to drop their micro-obsessions and think about how macro events were affecting markets was born.

The government was not investing in Citigroup because it had done a lot of research and determined that Citigroup stock was an undervalued gem ready to take off. The government was investing because they didn't want Citi going to zero and taking the economy with it.

That was not value investing. That was not stock picking in the traditional sense. It was about the government making a trade so big it could stop all risk assets from falling even further.

At the time, there were Nobel Prize–winning economists calling for the nationalization of US banks.[71] But US Treasury Secretary Timothy Geithner made a massive investment call and took us in a different direction. The US government was going to invest public capital into private companies and recapitalize the US banking system.

WE MAKE OUR MOVE

This, finally, was the major shift in macro policy that could be big enough to make a difference in equity markets. Larry and I decided to start buying shares again, and that night I explained it all to my wife.

"I'm going to rebalance our money back into stocks now," I said. "But you need to know, if this fails, we're not going to have a lot of money left. So should I do it?"

"Go for it," she said. "It makes sense, I've got a stable job, and if it doesn't work out, it wouldn't be the first time you started from scratch."

I started reallocating assets to equities.

Once the government intervention started to work and markets began to rebound, even savvy investors started to wonder if it was time to get off the government ride. But I started to realize that now that it had congressional authority to act, the government was going to lean into this intervention racket.

On Sunday, March 15, 2009, Fed chair Ben Bernanke went on the popular news program *60 Minutes* with correspondent Scott Pelley and repeated to the masses what he had previously said only to other over-educated policy wonks.

"The banks have accounts with the Fed," Bernanke explained to the camera, "much the same way that you have an account in a commercial bank. So, to lend to a bank, we simply use the computer to mark up the size of the account that they have with the Fed. It's much more akin to printing money than it is to borrowing."

"You've been printing money?" Pelley asked.

"Well, effectively."[72]

The Old Financial Order was over and, yes, the revolution was televised for all to see.

I think I spent all of Monday watching the interview over and over. The market wasn't moving. Yet eventually people got the message. For those who bought into the market on Tuesday, March 17, 2009, the S&P 500 was up 55 percent within the next year.[73]

Our understanding and investment around the US government's new interventionist policy to pump liquidity into the system paid off handsomely for Sonic. Macro investing surely warranted more than three minutes of my time per year.

WHY THE GAME CONTINUES

I joined UBS in 2011 to create an asset-allocation investment process for its Global Wealth Management division.[74] This is what I have learned in the interim: the correlation between government intervention and market direction has only grown in importance.

My eyes were opened to this fact in 2014, the year I became UBS's global chief investment officer and had to fly to Asia to address a highbrow financial conference. I found Timothy Geithner, the former US secretary of the treasury, in the greenroom.[75] We were both waiting our turn to speak to the well-heeled audience.

Naturally, we began talking, since I was eager to thank Mr. Geithner personally for the Citigroup bailout that turned the tide for me and the markets.

Geithner told me in private what he and Bernanke had said on the record in media interviews.[76] Given the tools they had, they could not have saved Main Street without first saving Wall Street. The nation needed companies that could hire workers, and, yes, a rising tide lifts all boats. His hope was that the government could later fix some of the imbalances created with a more progressive tax policy, presumably including the enacted 3.8 percent Net Investment Income Tax (NIIT).[77]

Hearing it in person—that the former top official in a Democratic Party–controlled White House believed the only way forward was to use the existing financial system to lift all the boats and use taxes as the way to redistribute capitalism's excesses[78]—was a big deal for me as a historian and an investor. This notion cut down the risks for long-term investors.

For much of the Democratic Party's history, the party has sided more with workers and against capital, and it argued for changing the system. But the Obama White House not only sidestepped the long-cherished notion of nationalizing the nation's banks—an idea that was energetically revived by some Democrats during the Global Financial Crisis[79]—it had actually *bought shares* in them.

In other words, the Obama administration invested taxpayers' money in equity for a profit, a very different vision of capitalism from that which the Democratic Party had long clung to. It was clear that the party's plan was no longer to change the system, only to address some of its worst negative consequences.

Rightly or wrongly, that shifted America's entire political-economic debate to the right and reduced the long-term risk for those with capital to invest.

Furthermore, I knew from my work at UBS that governments around the world remained fully committed to pumping liquidity into the financial system, even though the worst appeared to be over and markets had already rallied strongly in 2009 and 2010.[80] In fact, in 2012, we witnessed ECB president Mario Draghi giving his famous "whatever it takes" speech to save the euro,[81] and one of the financial tools that governments were then using to intervene—to catapult economies out of the deflationary cycle they perceived we were in since the financial crisis—eventually came to be known as *quantitative easing.*[82]

In late 2008, shortly before Bernanke publicly announced the government's change in economic policy on *60 Minutes*,[83] the Fed began buying "risk assets" for its own balance sheet,[84] following similar actions from the Bank of England.[85] (Risk assets are everything from commodities to equities,[86] but in this case the Fed was heavily buying mortgage-backed securities.[87]) In 2010, the Bank of Japan had also started buying stocks through ETFs,[88] and in 2014, when I was at this Asian investment conference, the Fed and other central banks were still going strong, buying more and more each month.[89] In fact, a 2017 effort to reverse this asset-purchasing process (known as *quantitative tightening*) was quickly reversed during the pandemic, and the Fed would not significantly start slowing its purchases again until June 2022.[90] Geithner confirmed that no matter what you called it, supporting financial markets with taxpayer money was the plan.

I realized during that talk with Secretary Geithner that governments didn't see any other option than to buy risk assets until the rising tide lifted all boats, and since so many people didn't have any capital to invest, it was going to take a *lot* of buying to lift Main Street. But if you did have investment capital, you could buy what the government was buying and profit, as government drove asset prices higher with yet more buying.

Back in the conference's greenroom, I was tapped to speak next, and as I walked the short distance to the stage I suddenly knew what I had to say.

I stood before the podium.

"Ladies and gentlemen, the fix is in!" I announced to the audience. "This is a great time to buy risk assets, because the Federal Reserve and other central banks are buying risk assets, and they aren't going to stop until they are 150 percent sure we are out of the crisis."

Buy what the government is buying.

I confess, I did not feel great about making such a brazen pronouncement. I knew that many people in the world did not have capital to invest and were afraid because they didn't understand what the government was doing. But I made a bold statement because I knew many of our clients in 2014 were still so traumatized by the Global Financial Crisis that they refused to hold stocks, and I knew that I had to convince them that, given this government support, equities and risk assets broadly remained the best game in town. The government, through its buying of assets, was trying to encourage higher prices as a matter of policy.

That scenario is precisely what unfolded. While the S&P 500 rose 77 percent between 2010 and 2014, and another 59 percent during the next four years, it rose 203 percent in the eight-year period between January 2014 and 2022[91]—when the Fed again started reducing its balance sheet in the summer of 2022 by slowing its purchases of securities.

The Global Financial Crisis changed our way of governing, how global markets functioned, and even the very nature of capitalism itself.

If you're looking for further proof, reflect on how COVID-19 was handled. We watched governments first shut down the global economy and then abruptly change course, jolting it all back to life again with massive subsidies. As the chart in chapter 1 illustrated, this was World War II levels of intervention. We at UBS ran the "buy what the government is buying" playbook again in the aftermath of the COVID-19 sell-off, when the Fed rolled out its financial-crisis tool kit in a matter of days. By August 2021 the S&P 500 had doubled off its COVID-19 low, the fastest bull-market doubling in history (354 days).[92]

This bears repeating: the thing about the buy-what-the-government-is-buying thesis is that, from the Citigroup bailout to Bernanke being on TV to Japan buying equities to the Fed's COVID response to the Biden administration's Inflation Reduction Act, you didn't need insider information to front-run such major economic policies. They were all announced as national news, and there was still time to invest and make money *after* the public announcements.

That is as true today as it was then.

Buying what the government is buying as a strategy is not based on a crystal-ball prediction about major market turning points in the future. Yes, if you do a lot of work to understand the real chokepoints and excesses created by government's carrots and sticks, you may have insights into when the next financial crisis will happen and what assets will be hardest hit.

However, this strategy is not about trying to predict the future. It is about responding to events by following the government's money (yes, I know it is taxpayers' money) after the commitment has been publicly made.

Now, I am not saying that the current version of this approach will work the same way forever. Nobody knows how long governments—looking at you, USA—can use increasing amounts of government debt to buy the behaviors and outcomes they want by doling out carrots and sticks. Eventually, the current version of "buy what the government is buying" may become a victim of its own success, with the "bond vigilantes" requiring much higher interest rates to lend money to highly indebted governments.

Yet, if push comes to shove, like it did in the Global Financial Crisis, governments are likely to use the same tools to prop up the existing system with taxpayer money. We as investors must stay attuned, listen hard for any nuanced changes in policy, but so far neither the US nor Europe has fundamentally addressed the problem, which is they cannot seem to help Main Street without first helping Wall Street. I am not saying this is right or wrong. I am just pointing to the constraints that governments have with this existing tool kit.

Let me underscore this point by again following the money. One of the biggest changes in the US financial system in the last half century is that the defined-benefit pensions that retired workers like my grandmother Nan enjoyed have been replaced by defined-contribution retirement plans like 401(k)s. That powerful shift in how we finance our elderly years raises this question: Who is capital and who is labor today?

According to the Fed, as of 2019, 58 percent of American families held public stocks;[93] a more recent Gallup poll found 61 percent of American households owned equities in 2023.[94] Some will argue that's immaterial to making policy decisions because the majority of those shares are owned by the rich. Tell that to the elected officials who have their eye on the voters. While the wealthy do own the largest concentration of shares, that doesn't mean that voters with a modest amount of stock care less about their equity holdings. Quite the opposite. As a percentage of what they need to get by, those shares are proportionally more valuable to them than they are to the rich, so it's logical to assume they'll also care deeply about those shares.

With that 61 percent statistic in mind, it's easy to see why US politicians at some level are biased toward protecting stock prices: to protect American families. We don't hear this directly in national political rhetoric, but it is revealed indirectly in their actions. How often do we hear government officials coming out and urging calm after a significant stock market sell-off? Or that the "wealth effect"—the reduction in confidence consumers have when they see the value of their assets fall—is doing the central banks' work for them as they fight inflation?

This process of understanding how markets and government intersect started for me while I was at university, but at this point in my life, I want *you* to understand how profoundly the financial system has changed and, more importantly, how we must all adapt to this new world by building robust portfolios under new rules that can sustain the inevitable shocks that are coming.

Bottom Line

Most people should increase their allocations to equities versus bonds, compared to how they invested in the past. Inflation and high government debt loads are making historically "safe" bond investments far less of a sure thing than in the past. Conversely, we've learned from the financial crisis and other historical ruptures in financial markets that the government's objective to save the current system of equity ownership is rooted in a "whatever it takes" determination, and over the long term that makes risk assets like equities a more attractive asset class from a risk-reward standpoint.

But it's equally important to note that I am not repeating here what your traditional investment books advise, which largely tell you how to buy individual, low-priced stocks with a margin of safety when they are out of favor, and then sell them when everyone is euphoric again about their prospects. That is a great idea in theory and will always pay rewards for select individuals with world-class talent and focus. Yet this strategy, as you'll shortly see, has never been as easy for real people to follow as the stock-picking books made it out to be.

What I am saying here—and this is crucial—is that while it's important to understand that the macro forces driven by government intervention have in the long run made equities more attractive than bonds as an asset class, that same heavy-handed macro intervention can make traditional value investing in individual stocks hazardous to your financial health.

In today's markets, microplays are often irrelevant and will routinely get swept away by the Big Money flows sent this way and that by governments' shifting macroeconomic policies, all amplified by the torrid amount of private-sector capital that rushes in afterward to chase the government-offered carrot—or conversely withdraws when the sticks come out.

In other words, do macro or macro will do you.

That's why equity funds, as a general category, have seen a big shake-out, with winners and losers. By the end of 2023 investors globally had over the previous five years pulled a net $150 billion from stock-picking hedge funds, the largest outflows seen since the Global Financial Crisis.[95] Despite some outperforming funds, as a group, hedge funds investing in stocks have underperformed the US stock market in nine out of the past ten years; in other words, even pros are finding it hard to pick stocks.[96]

My advice: change your approach.

RULE 4

DON'T PICK STOCKS.
ALLOCATE ASSETS.

The first plane hit the North Tower of the World Trade Center at 8:46 a.m.[1] It was September 11, 2001, and I was sitting in my office in Boston, looking at screens and talking to my partner, Larry.

I watched in horror.

"Check this out," I said, unsure as to what I was watching.

The plane had hit before the markets opened, but the futures started to react immediately.

Then the second plane hit. It was 9:03 a.m.

Larry instantly said, "It's a terrorist attack."

Before I could process the news, Larry had shorted the S&P 500 via the futures market, and our trade went through in the few minutes the exchanges stayed open, after the second plane hit the towers.

When US markets finally opened again on September 17 and the Dow fell 7.1 percent on its first post-9/11 trading day,[2] the world seemed different, and we mourned our colleagues who lost their lives. Yet Sonic was also in a strong financial position. We had our insurance policy in place in the form of the stock market short, and we could calmly assess the opportunities and risks that subsequently unfolded.

It was an eye-opening moment.

Larry reversed course in a nanosecond and executed a game-changing trade; I was still watching the screens with a dropped jaw when Larry sent his order through. Maybe I would have gotten there eventually, but by then it would have been too late.

Some people I tell this story to are disgusted that we were focused on markets during these terrible events. At the time, none of our shareholders wrote to tell us that, though some did write to commend Larry's cool head and actions to protect their capital. I acknowledge both sides of this coin. Here again I am trying to be open about some of the hidden psychological costs of a moral person trying to actively trade in amoral markets.

At the time, my professional thinking was not philosophical; it was focused on facts. Like the fact that I was not and probably never would be as good a trader as Larry, who had just proved in real time that he was among the best in the world. According to the cockroach theory, it also meant there were probably a lot of other people out in the world who were better than me. And while I could have possibly convinced myself I could get better at trading, my understanding of objective risk led me to see something entirely different in this situation.

No one, not even Larry, could always win in these kinds of situations, because if you weren't at your desk at that precise moment the world-altering event was happening, you could not make the trade. Even if you spent every waking moment in front of the screens and only took time off to sleep, eat, and go to the bathroom, over the course of a lifetime of dedication, you would still miss 30 percent of these critical trading moments. If you aspired to do more in life than trade, eat, sleep, and poop, then the odds were even worse.

From that moment forward, I couldn't unsee what I had seen: if your investment strategy depended on always being at your screen to make the right call at the right time, you were facing a mountain of risk too tall for anyone to realistically climb. But I buried this concern deep. At that point in my life, all I wanted to do was research stocks, eat, sleep, and poop. Furthermore, our strategy was deep research into stock valuations and longer holding periods, so like many at the time, we weren't worried about the macro or daily trading.

I knew we had a shot at making our future in the hedge-fund world. The stock market was the greatest professional challenge I had found in life. I was going to give it my all.

Flash forward to 2007.

I had just cashed out of the hedge-fund industry at age thirty-six, before the Global Financial Crisis hit. I was sitting at home in Virginia, semi-retired, watching after our newborn daughter. I didn't know that we were headed into a financial crisis, but by the end of 2006 I knew it was getting harder for me to pick stocks, and we wanted to start a family. Even if I didn't exactly know why, I recognized I needed a change.

That need to change crystalized further on a particularly bad day in 2007. My much-loved grandmother Nan had just died, and a deal I was working on was falling apart before my eyes, as the financial crisis started to unfold. I was sad, anxious, and restless, when I went next door to check in on our baby girl. She instantly grabbed my finger and smiled up at me— and everything changed in the epiphany of that moment.

My daughter suddenly made me realize I had lived my whole life completely focused on the future: building my résumé, focusing on the next great trade, saving for the future, moving toward an ever-expanding list of goals. This worldview—and a lot of help from others—was of course instrumental in whatever material success I had experienced so far in life. My unwavering devotion to compound interest and delayed gratification had paid off.

But it had also cost me a whole lot of happiness in the here and now. I had spent nearly my whole life climbing a mountain toward a summit, only to find a higher summit in the distance. I thought that retiring would mag-ically draw a line under all of that, but of course it didn't change anything.

I finally got it: If I wanted to be present in that room with my daughter and share her joy, I had to stop encouraging my brain to get so excited about some pot of gold at the end of a distant rainbow. I needed to make a concentrated effort to change *my entire relationship to the stock market.*

I really wanted to be there in the moment with my daughter. So I changed.

I should also add I was in a different phase of life. I had enough savings to "retire," and investing was no longer just about making money. I wasn't a student anymore; I had a young family, so I had to start thinking about *maintaining wealth*, not just making it.

As a result of these thoughts, I picked up *The Intelligent Asset Allocator: How to Build Your Portfolio to Maximize Returns and Minimize Risk* by William Bernstein.[3]

When the student is ready, the teacher appears.

This book took me back to the importance of **asset allocation**, the pedestrian act of deciding what percentage of a portfolio should be invested in, say, fixed income versus equities.[4] As I started to read more books about asset allocation, courses I took in college started to come back to me.

Most vividly, I remembered Professor Burton Malkiel. In the early 1990s I was at Princeton, lucky enough to be in Malkiel's classroom. The professor famously wrote *A Random Walk Down Wall Street*, a book that has sold millions of copies and is now in its fiftieth anniversary edition.[5] The book "proves" that few if any professional investors can beat the real-world investment returns of a low-cost, well-diversified stock fund, for any sustainable period. (For a list of books that changed my life and shaped my approach to investing, see the appendix.)

Professor Malkiel was saying that trying to pick stocks was a waste of time. Yet Professor Malkiel was a wise man who had my number. He didn't hesitate to address the elephant in the classroom. I am paraphrasing him, but he basically said with a smile, "You smart Princeton kids. You are going to take my class, get an A in it, and forget everything I said and go out into the world and pick stocks. Probably for a living."

Malkiel knew people had trouble following his advice, and he sweetly chided us on what was likely to be the outcome. The good professor was not rooting against us making it in investment management; he genuinely wanted us to be among the few great investors who worked hard enough and were smart enough to beat the market. But he also wanted us to know that the evidence indicated many of us would try and few of us would succeed. (In the latest edition of his book, Malkiel again made his case but said many people find it too "dull" to just do asset allocations and so still pick stocks.)

At the time, I took all of this as a challenge to channel my money fears and fuel my ambition. As you know, I went on to cofound the Sonic Fund and later became a managing director at Matrix Capital Management, one of the fabled Tiger Cub funds.

The point: I know the excitement of the stock market and its appeal. But I converted later in life, and I am recommending you skip the drama of the stock picking and go straight to asset allocation. My experience, as a recovering hedge-fund manager and someone who has worked with hundreds of fund managers, is that good active fund managers are like Olympic athletes. They have natural talent, and they devote nearly all their waking hours in the pursuit of the "gold." The real question most of us need to ask is this: *How do I become a successful investor despite the fact I will never commit myself to trying to compete at that Olympic level of investing?*

The answer to this question has several parts. First, you have to stop doing what doesn't work. Then you have to start doing what *does* work. But third, you need to address the fact that without strategies and a team to keep you disciplined, most people find it impossible to stick with a winning strategy.

If you are absolutely convinced that you have no interest in being an active investor in the stock market and are completely sold on asset allocation as the best way to invest, I'll shortly explain how we think about asset allocation when building portfolios. But I offer my perspective now on why being focused on the stock market, or any other single asset class or investment, can be hazardous to your financial health. To be fair, we have many clients who love to pick stocks and there are still lots of books promising to teach you how to be an active investor picking stocks or other assets with just a few hours of work a week.

There even is some academic research to support that this is possible. An article in the *Journal of Financial and Quantitative Analysis* from September 1987 made the then-controversial claim "that a well-diversified portfolio of randomly chosen stocks must include at least 30 stocks. . . . This contradicts the widely accepted notion that the benefits of diversification are virtually exhausted when a portfolio contains approximately 10 stocks."[6]

To me, looking at how the world has changed, it is almost laughable that investment professionals thirty-five years ago believed that diversification benefits could be fulfilled by a portfolio of ten or even thirty individual stocks. But the big problem has nothing to do with what the academic research shows is technically possible. The real issue is that people are largely incapable of acting "rationally," the way the classic textbooks assume they do. I learned this out in the world working with investors, because the academic field studying how people's psychology affects their financial decisions really didn't get going until after I left school. It still isn't even at the core of many investment plans.

In the past thirty-five years, the evidence for an asset-allocation approach for real-world investors has piled up. Let's start with your personal role and the importance of self-knowledge in the investment process.

Warren Buffett, discussing how he hired staff, once said that he generally looks for "integrity, intelligence, and energy. And if you don't have the first, the other two will kill you."[7] Yet the research suggests that the person who lacks integrity, the person slaughtering your finances, is the person staring back at you in the mirror every morning.

Morningstar's annual *Mind the Gap* report revealed that investors on average underperformed the returns of the ETF they invested in by 1.7 percent a year in the ten years leading up to 2022.[8] The culprit was badly timed trades in and out of the funds, which means lay investors lost almost 2 percent of their returns simply because they thought they were smart enough to time the market or were panicked into selling at the worst moment.

Dalbar Inc., a leading research-service provider to the financial industry, has been running a "Quantitative Analysis of Investor Behavior" study since 1994. That study measures the effects of investors' decisions to "buy, sell and switch into and out of mutual funds over short and long-term."[9] Dalbar's 2024 study showed that over the past thirty years the average equity-fund investor earned around half of what they would have earned by simply buying and holding an S&P index fund.[10] What that means in real terms: The $100,000 that the average equity-fund investor invested in the market in 1994 would have been worth $1,009,064 by 2023, after all their moves in and out of funds were factored into the results. But the same $100,000 invested in an S&P 500 index fund and forgotten about would have been worth $1,817,754.

Sit with that for a moment.

Investors earned roughly half of what they would have earned if they blindly put their money in an index fund and forgot about their investments. It's a hard truth that needs to be taken in. Most investors *add zero value* to their investment process; worse than that, their investment decisions *cost* them money. That means they are wasting time and money that they could best be deploying and enjoying elsewhere.

The Dalbar study also turns on its head the arguments some investors make about the costs of having an advisor. It's cheaper and wiser to be self-directed, they figure. Well, the Dalbar data suggests that isn't necessarily true. Going it alone can be *very* costly.

Here's some evidence about relative costs drawn from our own in-house analysis, as we probe ourselves to make sure we're delivering what we promise our clients. For US dollar clients with "yield" strategies, the median self-directed clients' returns were 8 percent lower than what UBS managed-solution clients earned over five years ending in June 2024. Over the same period, for those with "balanced" strategies, the go-it-alone clients on average underperformed by almost 13 percent, and among "growth" strategies, the soloists underperformed our managed solutions by almost 19 percent.

Most investors' buy-and-sell decisions are not driven by investment logic but by emotion, which is a polite way of saying they make investment decisions based on their personal money issues—greed, fear, lack of self-awareness, not following a disciplined investment process executed by a professional team.

The Dalbar headline numbers ratchet a bit this way and that over the years, but human behavior doesn't really change whether we're in a bull or bear market or muddling through a particular epoch. As Dalbar once succinctly put it, "No matter what the state of the mutual fund industry, boom or bust: Investment results are more dependent on investor behavior than on fund performance. Mutual fund investors who hold on to their investments have been more successful than those that try to time the market."[11]

Investors do not only struggle picking the right funds or stocks. Even if they are handed the best fund in the world, they still underperform when driven by their own greedy impulses to buy the fund's shares at the top of the market, when the herd is in a feeding frenzy, or equally self-sabotaging, sell the fund's shares shortly after some external shock has sent the markets into a freefall and triggered their worst fears. Most investors are unable to detach themselves from those emotional money issues that are sandbagging their results.

Arrogance, too, plays a role. Few people with a fully developed prefrontal cortex believe they could read a book or two on Formula 1 racing, take a few laps around the racetrack for practice, and then set out to compete in a Formula 1 race. Most people understand that if they tried to stay on Lewis Hamilton's bumper as he went around the Monte Carlo circuit, they would end up in a fireball.

It's not just his world-class reaction times you're up against; it's his training, the equipment he uses, and the support of his ace Formula 1 backup team. Yet every day you read or hear countless newspapers, TV shows, magazines, and books selling you the lie "You, too, can be Warren Buffett!" Just google "How to invest like Warren Buffett" and see what the "wannabe-Warren industry" spits back at you.

You and I will never be Warren Buffett. Make this truth a part of your investment strategy.

If you want to ignore my advice and remain solely focused on buying one asset class, equities, know that the data overwhelmingly suggests you're probably not a good enough stock picker to succeed; and even if you were a decent stock picker, focusing on one asset class is just not going to get you where you want to be. This is the advice you need to hear: get to a place where you are managing your wealth, not your stock picks, and that process starts with investing in multiple asset classes, as we professionals do.

To get you into the right frame of mind, let me share with you the dirty secret of the money-management industry, which most of you probably aren't aware of—or, if you're like me, have spent half your life ignoring and suppressing: **studies reveal that over 90 percent of your investment returns in the real world come from the asset allocations you make, not from picking stocks**.

A seminal long-term study by Brinson, Singer, and Beebower— "Determinants of Portfolio Performance II: An Update," published in the Spring 1991 issue of *Financial Analysts Journal*—revealed a truth that all investors need to be aware of. By analyzing the asset allocations and individual security picks of eighty-two large pension funds made in the decade between 1977 and 1987, the authors determined that getting the asset allocations right contributed by far the most to a portfolio's overall returns. Turns out, asset allocations might not be as sexy as the high drama of picking individual stocks or bonds, but it's this panoramic vision and effort that impacts your investments most. It's the "putt for dough" not the "drive for show" of the investment world.

The Brinson, Singer, and Beebower study discovered specifically that individual security selection accounted for just 4.5 percent of the overall returns earned; market timing, 1.8 percent; a catch-all of factors called "other" produced another 2.1 percent.[12]

Asset allocations accounted for 91.5 percent of the total returns earned.[13]

The more I read about the importance of asset allocation to the returns of professional investors, the easier it was for me to give up my former identity/addiction to being a stock jock. If Brinson, Singer, and Beebower were right, and over 90 percent of my returns as an investor came purely from my asset-allocation decisions, it meant that *all the hard work and time I had spent painfully picking individual stocks or bonds had, in the end, only amounted to 10 percent of my total investment returns—at best.*

Perhaps it's no surprise, then, that I asked myself, *What if I forced myself to let go of the details of each security and instead just worked on the big asset-allocation decisions? Would I be okay with that, or would I prefer to work eighty hours a week for the chance of either losing 10 percent more or making 10 percent more?*

If you are a professional manager overseeing big bundles of money, the answer will probably be *No, I won't leave that opportunity on the table,* because 10 percent compounded over time potentially adds up to serious dollars and that is your day job. But for most individual investors wanting to spend more time making money at a "real" job or with family and the causes they love, the logical answer to this question is *Yes, losing that opportunity is well worth the better quality of life I can achieve.*

Weighing all these factors, I decided, as we headed into the financial crisis, I would no longer use my time trying to go bottom-up as a stock picker but would instead follow the research and think about macro themes, which was my natural intellectual bent, learning how to make money off big trends by investing top-down through asset allocation. Despite my newfound commitment, I still had psychological trouble rebalancing my portfolio during the depths of the financial crisis, so I know how hard it can be to follow a disciplined investment strategy. While I will always be a recovering stock market addict, over the years it has gotten easier as I have seen how asset allocation works in my own life and with our clients.

What surprised me as I dug deeper into asset allocation was that it was neither simple nor boring nor for losers. It is none of those things if you like protecting and growing your wealth.

That's why it is core to everything we now do in the UBS chief investment office. We have found that asset allocation, coupled to a practical method of applying the knowledge that flows from behavioral finance, are the keys to delivering consistent long-term investment results in the real world.[14] In the rest of this chapter, I'm going to address the first part of that equation by walking you through the theory behind asset allocation, how the "science" works, and how this corner of the wealth-management business has developed over the past twenty-five years.

THE THEORY

Everyone will benefit in real ways by switching their mindset from buying stocks to allocating assets. A simple version of asset allocation might be putting 10 percent of your portfolio in cash and 90 percent in a broad basket of stocks, and rebalancing when your cash levels get to 5 percent. Or it could be putting 40 percent in cash and bonds, with 40 percent in stocks, and 20 percent in alternative assets.

Simple asset-allocation portfolios like these you can certainly build for yourself on your kitchen table, or even task a low-cost robo-advisor—a fintech service that uses technology to automatically recalibrate allocations—to build one for you.

UBS's in-house expertise and economies of scale bump this basic version of asset allocation up to a different level of execution, and we'll get to that shortly. But for now, I want you to understand the universal benefits that come from an asset-allocation approach to investing, regardless of how sophisticated the universe of asset classes at your disposal, and why this method of portfolio management will get you closer to your end goal.

Let's start with the act of picking a portfolio weighting and rebalancing when markets move and those percentages change. Once the portfolio is constructed, most of the benefit comes from the discipline an asset-class approach imposes on the portfolio. If you remember one thing from this book, let it be this: **when trying to hold each asset class to a defined percentage of the portfolio, it's impossible to ignore when a portfolio is out of balance**. It's clear-cut when it happens, and the purpose of an asset-allocation system is to periodically rebalance assets back to the chosen allocation. Yes, people have written books on the optimal way to rebalance, but optimal rebalancing depends on a lot of personal factors that could include capabilities, taxes, and transaction costs, which go way beyond the point we are trying to make here.

Whether you do it daily, weekly, monthly, or yearly, the rebalancing process means you will *automatically* be forced to sell high and buy low, when most people are emotion-driven and do the opposite, losing about half their returns over thirty years, as the previously quoted industry study revealed. The process takes the emotion out of the equation, and I have seen, time and again, how the discipline imposed by asset allocation has saved clients from themselves.

Our client Max* was an antique-car dealer who built a formidable business and then sold it all for several million dollars. He was gifted at handling vintage cars, hard assets that are rare and have their own mercurial financial attributes, but when it came to investing, a completely different skill set, he became our early-warning system.

If Max came to us full of trepidation, pushing us to sell a declining asset class in his portfolio, we knew instantly that the asset-allocation system would shortly be instructing us to *buy* the beaten-down asset class. Conversely, if some hot market benchmark took off, and he came imploring us to get him a piece of the action, our asset-allocation system would promptly tell us to sell some of our existing holdings and realize profits. We routinely sit down with Max, gently remind him why we are doing what we are doing, urging him to trust the system. He eventually calms down and falls in line. Asset allocation has saved Max from his worst investment impulses many, many times over.

Asset allocation will save you from yourself as well.

There are many benefits to this approach. First, consider the fact that entire asset classes tend to move much more slowly than individual securities, which means following the market 24/7 is less important—and that lends itself to a better quality of life. You won't be on a constant knife-edge, nervously checking price moves every ten minutes, all while you really

---

* Names and some personal details have been changed to protect identities.

should be investing in the things that are proven to help you lead a longer and healthier life.

More importantly, however, unlike individual stocks, which are often unpredictable, in-depth analysis of historic data shows that asset classes move, in the long run, in a more predictable way. **Asset classes can act erratically in the short term, because of external shocks or momentary supply-demand constraints, but over the long term they return to their historic norm**.

To illustrate what I mean, let's go back to our US equities allocation. The bellwether S&P 500, and its predecessor S&P 90, have lived through multiple boom-and-bust cycles over the past two centuries. The US stock market fell on average 26 percent a year between 1929 and 1932, and in the stagflation years of 1973 and 1974, the market fell 17 percent and 30 percent, respectively. Conversely, during the final years of the 1990s, the stock market jumped on average 26 percent a year in the five years leading up to the millennium celebrations.[15]

But study after study shows that over the long term, whatever period you take, the US stock market tends toward about a 7 percent return on an annualized basis. The average annual returns (inflation adjusted, dividends reinvested) for the US stock market was 6.9 percent over the past 150 years; 7.4 percent over the past 100 years; 7.3 percent over the past 50 years; 7.7 percent over the past 30 years; and 7.1 percent over the past 20 years.[16]

Translation: If you make an allocation to US equities and then just let the investment run over a long time frame then you will likely earn some 7 percent a year after inflation on that equity allocation. A version of this long-term pattern repeats itself in asset class after asset class.[17]

There is no magic to the 7 percent number. I have no idea if stocks will earn an inflation-adjusted 7 percent over the next ten or twenty years, although I think it is a good bet. But what is even a better bet is that stocks, which have more risk than other things like your savings account, will earn a relatively higher yield than the savings account because, human nature being what it is, on average, people demand more reward for more risk.

So while using historical returns to predict the exact value of an asset allocation in ten or twenty years is risky, counting on the stronger performance of a carefully crafted asset allocation that has tested better than others is a more reliable approach.

Which brings us to one of the greatest asset-allocation benefits of all: **diversification**.

In this age of tumult, simply trading stocks in one asset class is dangerous to your financial health. Conversely, spreading out that concentrated position by investing in multiple asset classes radically reduces the odds that you'll get wiped out.

If you hold baskets of diversified investments that are spread in a thoughtfully weighted manner across different asset classes (cash, equities, fixed income, real estate, commodities) and different sectors (energy, construction, tech, travel and leisure, health care) and different geographies (emerging markets, Europe, China, the Americas), some of which are uncorrelated (which means the asset classes consistently move in different directions from one another), then you will wind up with a diversified portfolio that is robust and better able to withstand even the nastiest of market shocks.

There is, in fact, nothing like a portfolio of diverse asset classes to absorb the punches to the face that the markets deliver, and I got a hard-to-forget lesson in this during the Global Financial Crisis. No matter how good you were at picking stocks based on fundamental research, all stocks were being sold during that terrifying period. Between the start of 2007 and the end of 2008, the S&P 500's total return (dividends added back in) fell by 34.5 percent.[18] Quality bonds, however, moved in the other direction. The ICE US Treasury 7–10 Year Bond Index rose 21.5 percent during the same period.[19]

In other words, a diversified portfolio built on smart and well-balanced asset allocations cut the massive equity losses of the financial crisis down to more digestible amounts. That is the general principle behind a well-diversified portfolio invested in a wide range of assets: **even if part of your portfolio is tanking, other investments uncorrelated and sometimes in other parts of the world can rocket up, offsetting your portfolio losses**.

Diversification, as they say in our trade, is the only free lunch in the business. It's one of the few investment truths you can reliably bank on.

So take a deep breath and let go of what you have been taught by the wannabe-Warren industry. Your goal as an investor—and my goal, as UBS's global chief investment officer—is to earn the best returns possible *with the lowest amount of risk*. Asset allocation is the key tool for professionals and amateurs alike to achieve that result.

Sound portfolio management is never about chasing the hottest-performing benchmark, as so many amateur investors try to do. Rather, it is instead all about judiciously making allocations by holding the right-sized positions in a widely diversified basket of assets, and then rebalancing to the chosen weighting when the markets move significantly in any direction.

That's how you make money over the long term.

THE PRACTICE

There are more than one thousand professionals working with me in the UBS chief investment office, spread across Zurich and in eighteen other workshops around the world. This guild of financial professionals tracks 450 asset and sub-asset classes around the globe, which are of course the building blocks of a well-diversified portfolio.

If you follow the principles I outlined above, you or your robo-advisor can build a diversified asset-allocation portfolio that will outperform most individual stock picking on a risk-versus-reward basis. However, let me now show you how UBS uses its economies of scale and in-house expertise to lift the basics of asset allocation to a different level of execution, while also making significant improvements around the edges of the game.

Those 450 asset classes we track range from the common (US equities or EU fixed income) to the exotic (Indonesian equities or green bonds). An asset expert, usually a battle-hardened industry veteran who has lived through multiple boom-and-bust cycles, is tasked with overseeing each of the 450 asset and sub-asset classes we track and is backed by a specialist team drawn from the two hundred analysts we have in-house.

The first step of building a modern portfolio starts with what we call **capital market assumptions**, complex risk-and-return projections for each market. These calculations serve as the backbone of every allocation we make in a client's portfolio. The capital market assumptions not only determine what the expected returns are in that asset class over different time frames but also quantify how confident we are about our estimates. Remember, over a long time frame, asset-class returns coalesce around their historic average, so the farther out we go, the more confident we become in our capital market assumptions.

These capital market assumptions are continuously revisited and updated as market forces and geopolitics and technology disruptors and rocketing inflation rates and unexpected interest rate moves come at us from all angles and force us to constantly tweak or change our earlier projections.

Those market assumptions about how an asset class will behave in the coming years stand at the heart of our **strategic asset allocations**, the process that decides how much we should allocate to each asset class, in a range of "model portfolios" of varying investment objectives and risk tolerances. We do this so that clients can earn the highest expected return at whatever risk level they can tolerate.

The strategic asset-allocation system is overseen by an investment team, which I am a part of. When we review the hard data and historic trend lines that largely determine how our portfolio models are constructed, we periodically call in the experts in, say, US equities or foreign currencies or convertible bonds, to give us additional market insight. It's a bit like the US Supreme Court judges calling in lawyers to make oral arguments, which they then probe, to get their own thinking straight before making a final ruling.

In this methodical way, we create model portfolios that range from low to high expected return and volatility. These model portfolios are then matched to the client's particular risk tolerance. Once these standardized portfolios are taken off the shelf, they are adjusted, reworked, and buffed to the clients' specific requests or needs or life goals, all of which we'll demystify in the next chapter.

The process of building model portfolios not only involves picking the right asset classes but also focuses on the optimal weighting in each asset class, to squeeze out the best return possible for our clients' specific risk levels. That's done through both quantitative analysis (mathematical or statistical formulas based on extensive historical data) and qualitative analysis (input from our asset-class experts).

In other words, the mathematically calculated predictions that are based on historic data are fine-tuned by our experts and their analysis of the market-moving or volatility factors they see on the horizon of that particular asset class. For example, the historical data can't account for large events like Brexit, which may impact future projections.

There's yet another filter used in our process, and it lies at the heart of diversification and its benefits. Covering 450 asset and sub-asset classes across the globe allows us to not only grasp the individual quirks and characteristics of what's out there in the investment universe but also equally importantly to closely watch their co-movements—how the asset classes dance with or around one another—to determine their **covariance** (the direction in which asset classes move; in other words, in tandem with or inverse to each other) and **correlation** (which measures both the strength and direction of that linear relationship between the two variables).

That intelligence then helps us create the **optimal portfolio**, that spread of asset classes where the risk-reward within a portfolio is ideally balanced to a client's unique risk-tolerance level. As part of the portfolio optimization routine, we make use of **Monte Carlo simulations**, an algorithm-based technique that uses past data to predict the probability of unexpected outcomes. Every night at UBS we run portfolios through fifty thousand possible what-if scenarios to determine if we have the best possible risk-versus-reward allocation mix over the largest number of scenarios.

Put all these various covariance data points together and you have **covariance matrices**, a staggering mix of data variables in a multidimensional space, allowing us to get a complex picture of how a client's portfolio asset allocations are likely to respond in all kinds of worldly scenarios, given the client's particular level of risk.

It's terrifically complex, I know. But bear with me.

You keep hearing me say that diversification is the best safeguard against the ravages of a financial meltdown, because, if done right, a clutch of asset allocations that are "uncorrelated" to each other will reduce portfolio risk by offsetting each other during a period of volatility. That's a subject again of heightened importance in portfolio management, as the historic covariance of equities and bonds has, in recent years, reversed its long-term trend, moving more in tandem rather than inversely since inflation's return.[20]

We might, in such instances, consider an allocation to high-yield catastrophe bonds, which are bonds uncorrelated to traditional asset classes. Their payout is unrelated to classic bond variables but tied to predefined insurance-risk events happening, such as a major earthquake.[21]

Now, you don't have to understand all of this in minute detail unless you want to become a professional, but it does help to have a solid grasp of the sophisticated science and thought going on behind the scenes at a top-drawer firm managing your wealth through asset allocation. Never invest in something you don't understand.

But I'm hoping this description of our backroom efforts does more than that. I hope it sheds light on what we do to build portfolios that not only take on all the classical investment theories but update them for our complex global world.

Of course, some of you financial sophisticates will know all this already and might find my advocacy on behalf of asset allocation a little pedestrian and even outdated. The method is now commonplace in the industry. All true, but it's still not self-evident for the millions of you still building a portfolio by picking individual stocks and mutual funds. Nor was it at all commonplace when I first learned about asset allocations twenty-five years ago. In fact, it didn't feel like a core value of the wealth-management industry when I arrived at UBS almost fifteen years ago.

ASSET ALLOCATION AND THE FINANCIAL SERVICES INDUSTRY

As far as I know, when I arrived in Zurich fifteen years ago, there was no such thing as a chief investment office in private banking. In fact, the

Financial Times publication *Professional Wealth Management* didn't create an award for the world's best chief investment office until just a few years ago.[22]

Historically, the Swiss Bank Secrecy Act of 1934 made it a criminal offense for Swiss banks to share their clients' account information with anyone.[23] While Switzerland's neutrality, stable currency, and efficiency made it a great place to keep your money safe, particularly if you lived in a politically unstable part of the world, it was bank secrecy that dominated the local industry's reputation.

Luckily for me, UBS and Jürg Zeltner, who headed the bank's wealth management division from 2009 to 2017, were not basing the division's strategy on secrecy or stereotypes but rather on investment advice. Jürg wanted to get out in front of all the changes brought about by the financial crisis, and his idea was to hire a big-name chief investment officer to signal that UBS wanted to rebuild trust with private clients after the crisis, and that the bank was serious about protecting and growing their wealth. It pained Jürg personally that the honorable profession of Swiss private banking he had entered at age sixteen had fallen in respect. He wanted to get some of its mojo back.

That's why Jürg hired an old college friend of mine, Alex Friedman, as UBS's first chief investment officer. Alex had been the CFO of the Bill & Melinda Gates Foundation,[24] arriving just after Warren Buffett made his historic donation pledge.[25] If Alex was the man Bill Gates and Warren Buffet trusted, well, that was the kind of aura UBS wanted to build around its wealth-management business.

While Alex was in discussions with UBS, he asked me to join him as wealth management's head of investments. I was finally ready to go back to work and jumped at the opportunity to build on an industrial scale all the ideas that were percolating in my head about asset allocation. Alex further rounded out our team by hiring Mona Sutphen, who had just left the Obama White House as a senior policy advisor.[26] Mona became our head of macro, advising us on government policy. Like me, Alex realized that government policy would play an important role for investors post the financial crisis.

We moved to Zurich in the spring of 2011.

$\sim$

A few months later, Alex and I were sitting in the lobby of the Four Seasons Hotel that looks out on Kowloon across Hong Kong's harbor, waiting for the car that would take us to the airport and our next destination. We had been traveling the world, getting to know UBS's global business and its clients. In the process of conducting eighty internal interviews and thirty external meetings with clients and peers, we mapped out in our heads what was involved internally from the point an investment idea made it through the investment approval process to how it was acted on in a client's portfolio.

While many of our clients entrusted us with trading authority over their portfolios so we could act quickly (discretionary assets under management), other clients kept control of their trading and decided when they wanted to act on our advice, only after reading our research or talking to their advisor (nondiscretionary assets under management). The problem was that the existing system for approving investment ideas involved a complex hierarchy of four hundred people in multiple locations and time zones, with ideas filtering through a global investment committee, a global advisory committee, and then numerous local advisory committees.

Upshot: persuading internal colleagues and then the clients about the merits of an investment idea took way too long; often, the opportunity had passed before clients had a chance to allocate their capital.

I grabbed a napkin and sketched out for Alex the streamlined process I was imagining.

First, we would cut down on the number of meetings to shorten our investment cycle. But on a higher level we would change the investment management philosophy. The hedge-fund industry where I came from ran on the star system. Once a hedge fund's charismatic founder died or moved on, the fund usually collapsed. Successful funds are rarely passed on to a second generation. Furthermore, most hedge funds stick to one investment method and do that relentlessly—whether it's long, short, or what have you—and in most cases decisions are made in a secretive "black box" process that even fund investors are never let in on.

I wanted to get as far away as possible from this unhealthy hedge-fund model and create for UBS a more inclusive and transparent investment system built on asset allocation. Once again, my compulsive reading paid off. Charlie Munger, the late vice chairman of Warren Buffett's Berkshire Hathaway, drew a lot of his inspiration from Carl Gustav Jacob Jacobi, a nineteenth-century German mathematician known for solving the most difficult math problems of his day.[27]

"*Man muss immer umkehren*," Jacobi was fond of saying, which roughly means "Always invert." Munger applied Jacobi's topsy-turvy approach to the investment process, noting that "many problems can't be solved forward" but in fact "are best solved when they are addressed backward."[28] An example of this sort of thinking in the finance industry might be something like this: "Avoiding stupid investment decisions, rather than continuously seeking to come up with brilliant ones, is a lot easier to do and can produce better results."

We decided we should invert the investment process at UBS by flipping the entire hedge-fund methodology on its head. Instead of one person being the investment star, we would make our investment "system" the star, with a professional investment team overseeing decisions on strategic asset allocation—and its cohort, tactical asset allocation, which are short-term asset trades around an anticipated macroeconomic shift—during a well-documented and open process. No investment decisions were going to be made in a "black box" vacuum by a mercurial guru.

I said to Alex, "We're not running these investment meetings. We're going to have other people run the meetings, so people are not just waiting for the right answer."

I was also eager to remove any salespeople from the investment committee process, though their inclusion was common at the time. We would insist that the investment process be labeled "research," an industry term with a very specific meaning. For ideas to be labeled research, the law requires that the investment team's key performance indicators are not driven by sales. Every quarter, each of us would have to sign a document that said our ideas were put forward because we believed they would help clients, without regard to thinking about potential fees.

This was what we sketched out on the napkin.

The new centralized chief investment office we imagined would not only focus on asset allocation—the horror!—but it would also front-load the trust building into the investment process so that once decisions were made, everyone was willing to act faster. We would do this by building a more transparent process in which people could watch the sausage being made in the factory and even contribute. (We set out filming our decision-making and regularly invited financial advisors and their clients to witness our process.)

Alex instantly got it.

However, understanding group dynamics better than I, he also recognized this intellectually rigorous system we were imagining would require we kick the UBS CEO at the time, Oswald "Ossie" Grübel, out of all future investment meetings.

Ossie was a legendary trader who had saved UBS during the financial crisis. While we needed his advice, his sheer force of personality and thundering baritone would dominate the meetings. Luckily, Alex had studied and written about groupthink in organizations and was keen to avoid sheeplike thinking seizing up our new investment process, and I breathed a sigh of relief that Alex felt he could handle Ossie for us.

Our car arrived.

We grabbed the napkin sketch, and while we were on our next four-hour flight, this one to Singapore, we wrote up our proposal as a formal memo. We sent the memo to Jürg Zeltner when we landed, then immediately went to see him once we got back to Zurich.

Alex told Jürg that this was what it would take to fix things. Our plan would dramatically change the bank's investment process and people's roles, and if he didn't want us to do that because it was so disruptive, we understood. But then we should leave.

Jürg looked up and said, "No, this is exactly what I want."

I won't tell you what this radical operational reinvention involved at a conservative Swiss wealth-management firm then overseeing $2.1 trillion in invested assets[29]—that's a management book in its own right—but I'll just say there was a lot of internal skepticism about what those "crazy Americans" were up to. It was vitally important we quickly establish our credibility as well as that of our new asset-allocation system.

Fortunately, in summer 2011, there were some big trades to be made.

When we got to reviewing our strategic asset allocations, we found most of the clients' portfolios were heavily skewed toward Europe. Yet when we made our forecasts about what asset classes were going to produce the best returns in the near future, what stood out was the yield available to investors in US high-yield bonds.

In part due to the US government recapitalizing its banking sector during the financial crisis—something that did not happen in Europe—the US economy was rapidly rebuilding. But the credit markets were slower to react to what was happening in the real US economy, which was responding quickly to all the stimuli. That's why we were seeing pricing anomalies, which means prices were trading outside of their historic norms, in the sub-asset class of US high-yield debt.

Of course, no one wants to hold high-yield debt as a severe global recession starts rolling in. Companies paying abnormally high finance rates, because they look like a subpar risk to investors, are going to be the first to burn to the ground when the financial wildfire starts sweeping through the landscape. But when an economy is on the rebound from a hard recession and gearing up for a period of fertile economic growth, the risk of bankruptcy retreats at the surviving companies still issuing high-yield debt. As we built out our economic outlook, our work showed that if you bought US high yield that summer, you could pick up a very high yield at very low risk.

But here's the beauty of strategic asset allocation: you didn't have to make any economic predictions to make the right investment here. US junk bonds, the street name for high-yield debt, were then yielding 10 percent, some 8 percent higher than US Treasuries. That difference was way out of the historic norm; for much of the 1980s and 1990s, US high-yield spreads between Treasuries of similar maturity were in the 3 percent to 5 percent range.[30] That meant that by 2011, the price of high-yield bonds had fallen relative to other assets—which, if you didn't rebalance, would have reduced the percentage of high-yield bonds away from what our models showed was the right percentage. In short, high-yield bonds were due for a rebalance to a larger allocation in the portfolio. So we did it. And the spread fell back to the historic norms as the price of the bonds went up, driving returns for our clients.

From 2011 on, we made robust strategic asset allocations the core of our investment process. Alex and Mona left UBS within a couple of years, and I became the bank's chief investment officer in 2014. A decade later the chief investment office is a team of more than one thousand employees investing clients in our asset allocations around the globe. As more clients have come to trust our advisors, process, and firm, UBS has accumulated $4 trillion in private client assets that we actively manage or advise.

Bottom Line

If you want to earn better returns over your lifetime than the average personal investor, you've got to put aside your thrill-seeking efforts to trade stocks, unless, that is, you are genuinely one of those rare trading talents—which few of us are. Repeated studies show that individual investors sabotage their returns by not sticking to a disciplined investment strategy.

Now, are you so convinced about asset allocation that you now think you don't need to take in the first three chapters on how the world has changed? I would advise against thinking that way. Understanding the change and growing complexity of the world also helps us build better asset allocations, and it's why we look at 450 asset classes today, not just simply stocks and bonds.

Bear that in mind and follow this advice: convert your investment portfolio from a grab bag of individual stocks or bonds to a well-diversified asset-allocation portfolio. The genius of this anxiety-lowering asset-allocation technique is this: when asset classes are assigned a specific percentage of your total portfolio, you will be automatically forced to sell high and buy low when the predetermined percentages veer off and a rebalancing is required. Most investors need this discipline imposed on them. Still, as we will cover shortly, people often need some of the "hacks" we have developed over the years to help them keep up that discipline.

KNOW YOURSELF AND YOUR DEEPEST MONEY ISSUES

Carl* sold his business for $100 million.

He's seventy-ish and he's financially sophisticated. But even though he is savvy enough to know better, he won't organize his affairs smartly from an estate and tax perspective. Politically, he's the type who under normal circumstances would rail at the very idea that the US federal government could grab 40 percent of his hard-earned wealth in estate taxes after he dies. But that is exactly what is going to happen if he doesn't act soon.

His health has started to deteriorate.

We're not entirely sure what's going on here. His second wife died, as his first wife had done some years earlier, so it could be he's stricken by a profound and immobilizing sadness. Or he's been swallowed by the quite common issue of refusing to face his own mortality. Or both issues are hitting him at once.

---

* Names and some personal details have been changed to protect identities.

For whatever reason, we cannot get him to manage his financial affairs in a prudent manner, even though, every now and then, we gently remind him to do so.

Carl can't take the next logical step in his wealth journey because he won't face his internal block. Whatever is happening inside him is so powerful, not even his normal self-interest is engaged, and he simply refuses to deal with whatever deep issue is seizing him up.

We are at an impasse. We can't help him because he can't help himself. He smokes his cigarettes, drinks his wine, and looks out the window.

Both strategic asset allocation and the UBS Wealth Way, which we will discuss in the next chapter, are wealth-management techniques. But they depend on the investor doing their part, which is learning what makes them tick, understanding what triggers their fears, and practicing strategies to counteract such destructive forces.

As Carl's story makes clear, even the most effective portfolio-management systems only work for people willing to overcome their own internal obstacles interfering with their wealth management. This is not just a truth that the wealthy like Carl need to hear; it's equally true for a twenty-five-year-old in his or her first job, as it is for everyone else, no matter where they are in their wealth journeys.

Every time mortals like us buy or sell an investment, house, car, or just about anything else, our hopes, fears, values, emotions, and history are powerful forces driving events just below the surface of our decisions. Knowing yourself and mastering your inner money issues, especially when relatively young, is the single biggest way you can massively increase your investment returns. It is also extremely difficult. This is probably the most challenging and painful lesson to digest of all the professional wealth-management tips I am imparting in this book. The problem isn't understanding the concept of, say, buying a stock low and selling it high; the problem is in getting yourself to do it. Maybe you breezed through the last chapter, because you know all about asset allocation. But when is the last time you systematically rebalanced your portfolio according to plan?

Let's start with your gifts as an investor.

As I have said, a primary reason none of us will ever become Warren Buffett is because we harbor money-related emotions that unconsciously rule our investment decisions. Warren Buffett's folksy charm, humility, generosity, and wisdom make him sound like he's just like the rest of us, but trust me, he knows what separates him from the rest of us mortals.

One of the differentiators is his ability to control his emotions. Warren Buffett and his mentor Benjamin Graham were always crystal clear on this subject and what it takes to become a world-class investor. It is never about "beating others at their game," they warned, but about "controlling yourself at your own game."[1]

In fact, in the nearly thirty years since I began my career in the hedge-fund world, I have spent enough time with the investment greats to know that books about Warren Buffett and Peter Lynch and other amazing stock pickers are *dangerous* to your financial health. They give you a false sense of security and glamorize investing. True, picking stocks is arguably one of the most interesting, challenging, and highest-margin big businesses in the world. For those very same reasons, however, the financial industry hoovers up many of the greatest minds, machines, and support teams and then hones their skills with a Darwinian efficiency.

Every time you make a trade, you need to have a healthy fear that the smartest stock picker in the world—backed by a tailored AI model, an army of high-quality researchers, and a bank of ultrafast computers—is sitting on the other side of that trade, staring back at you.

But go ahead—you're feeling lucky and have read a few books.

The best investors, your market counterparts, are special people who have either an almost inhuman disconnect from their emotions or an almost inhuman level of discipline to get themselves into a zone where they can drive emotion out and away from their trades. In most cases they have some of both.

If you want to entirely beat those emotions away, rather than learn to work with and around your emotions, be careful what you wish for. It's a slippery slope from emotionless investing to anhedonia—an inability to experience any form of joy—to outright depression. I have seen this progression unfold many times in hard-driven investors.

I am not diagnosing Warren Buffett, but if the Buffett biography *The Snowball* is to be believed, the abilities that allow him to invest with such skill also cost Mr. Buffett a marriage he greatly valued.[2] What separates the Warren Buffetts of the world from the rest of us is not just emotionless investment decisions. It's the seemingly effortless ability to focus for hours, even days, on a problem with near photographic recall of all aspects of the issue.

I first saw this at work while at Harvard, where I watched dumbstruck as students calmly sat in the dorm lounge and played chess—in their heads. They didn't need a board because they saw the whole game playing out in their minds. Whatever their prodigious innate talents are, the real investment legends then up the ante further by practicing an almost religious discipline to get even better at what they do. Those are the type of financial professionals you are trading against when you buy or sell a security.

This was vividly brought home to me twenty years ago, when I was invited to a private lunch for hedge-fund titans at the University of Virginia, an event hosted by Blue Ridge Capital's founder, John Griffin.[3] It was a beautiful spring day in Charlottesville, the magnolias were bursting everywhere, and out on the grassy lawn, we sat at a round table surrounded by folding chairs under a small white catering tent.

John's circle of friends gathered that day included the hedge-fund heavyweights Julian Robertson, who famously seeded that generation of brilliant traders called "Tiger Cubs";[4] Daniel Kahneman, the Nobel Prize–winning economist[5] and author of the must-read *Thinking, Fast and Slow*;[6] and Paul Tudor Jones,[7] to my mind one of greatest traders in the world.

Paul first became famous by calling the 1987 stock market crash, which he warned, a year before it hit, would look like an "Acapulco cliff dive."[8]

That day in Charlottesville, Paul told us that he trades only at certain times of day.

For more than a quarter of a century, Paul reportedly paid the life coach Tony Robbins $1 million a year to act as a kind of therapist, trainer, and advisor.[9] Paul told me that the most important thing he did over the years was relentlessly track everything in and around that peak state of mind where he made his best trades. What time he made the good trade; what he ate and drank that day—everything. He studied equally hard the times he made bad investment decisions. Paul said he rarely traded during market hours anymore, because the stats showed his best trades were made when the markets were closed—and he was relaxed.

This disclosure was a preface to him asking Professor Kahneman if there were any successful studies of what can predict who will be a good trader and whether someone could be trained to be a good trader. Paul said (and this was twenty years ago) he had already spent millions of dollars collecting and studying trade statistics to answer these questions and had seemingly given up.

There was still something special that certain people had, which you could not reverse engineer from the data. Daniel Kahneman, not a dumb guy, amusingly spent the rest of the lunch pitching to get access to the data and pick up Paul's research project. That sure was fun to watch. As far as I know, that research, if it ever happened and led to conclusions, has never been published.

But talking to Professor Kahneman got me interested in **behavioral finance** and the need for people to get in touch with their more primal selves, the base impulses sometimes called our *inner caveman*, to become better investors. This is something that has become terribly important to the work we now do with UBS clients.

The kicker to this unforgettable lunch was an observation by Julian Robertson. He mostly sat and listened with his affable smile, but at one point he drawled, "Well, the most important investment decision I ever made was who I chose to marry." (Picking the right spouse is another subject close to my heart.)

Here's the point of recalling this event: if Paul Tudor Jones thinks it matters whether or not he has a glass of orange juice before he trades, this stuff matters. While Warren Buffett can make smart investment decisions after chowing down McDonald's meals and five cans of Coke,[10] even Paul Tudor Jones didn't trust himself to follow suit but went out of his way to watch what he ate and always made sure he was in a calm mental state before making important investment decisions.[11] To hear him talk with humility and honesty about the process he goes through to make good investment decisions was sobering, liberating, and inspirational.

It was sobering because I suddenly knew that even one of the greatest traders of all time needed to work hard to create a short period in the day during which he trusts himself enough to make good investment decisions. To get there, he had to start with basics, such as what he drank that morning or how he slept the night before. Nothing was too small to look at, and it was all based on his deep desire to know himself better and lift his game.

The conversation was liberating because it meant that I, too, could admit to myself I was a human being with flaws, and part of becoming a successful investor was understanding and working around the quirky features of my personality, not ignoring or wishing them away.

Finally, what he said was an inspiration because it meant that I didn't have to be a one-in-a-million natural talent like Buffett, Lynch, or Tudor Jones to improve my investment decisions. I just had to keep working to improve my investment *process*, ideally reaching a similar place where I was able to make disciplined investment decisions not swayed by the yo-yo of everyday emotions. Physical fitness became my route and the key to my mental discipline, but Paul's words that day ultimately sent me in two productive directions at once.

Like Paul, I realized I had to find an investment strategy that wasn't trying to emulate Warren Buffett, but that worked well with who I was as an imperfect human being. This was how and why I eventually settled on asset allocation as my investment method. But the other direction Paul propelled me was toward a deeper understanding of all the neurotic impulses I had tied up in my financial decisions. I wanted to better master my emotions in my personal and professional life, which is precisely the subject of this chapter.

I won't pretend what follows wasn't painful to write. But I need to work every day to keep this stuff out of the room when I make investment decisions, so it also feels good to drag it all into the open and publicly acknowledge my squirrely money issues. To encourage you to bring your own personal money quirks into the light, so you can see them clearly and deal with them honestly, I am going to share with you some of my personal issues around money and wealth.

THE ANGST IS PLANTED

"Mark, get out of the car and behold the downfall of America."

That's what Dad yelled at me as he banged on the back-seat window of our 1972 Chevrolet Kingswood Estate Wagon.

It was 1978 and I was seven years old. We were on a family outing and had stopped for gas. Outside the car, Dad was frantically beckoning me to come take a look. I reluctantly opened the back door and crept out.

I looked back and saw that my embarrassed mom was sliding ever lower in the front seat. Mom was a big believer in middle-class decorum and proper comportment, so my dad's public theatrics that day were her idea of hell. My four-year-old sister was, in contrast, blissfully ignorant and playing with her Raggedy Ann doll.

Dad was still cursing and pointing at the "grim reaper" bringing civilization to its knees.

I looked in the direction of his finger and discovered the pale rider who had come for the American dream was . . . the gas pump.

There were two major energy crises in the 1970s. In 1973 the Organization of Arab Petroleum Exporting Countries imposed an oil embargo on the US, after it resupplied the Israeli military during the Yom-Kippur War; and then again in 1979, when the shah of Iran was overthrown during the Iranian Revolution and that nation's oil and gas industry was shattered in the process, squeezing global supplies.[12]

Those faraway geopolitical battles between governments and the energy markets were being felt in real time in our cloistered suburban-American world. On that day, the gas price stood at sixty-four cents a gallon, and our family station wagon could manage ten miles a gallon at best.[13] As gas prices steadily rose through the 1970s, you could hear my dad grumbling, but sixty-four cents a gallon was his line in the sand.

I think that day, Dad finally realized higher gas prices were not a temporary crisis but a permanent fixture in our economic life going forward, and gas prices did in fact continue to rise for the rest of the decade. Forty years later, when I thought about describing what inflation feels like to colleagues who hadn't ever lived through it, this memory came back at me like it was yesterday. It was so vivid that I realized there was a lot more going on for me personally that strange day in 1978.

The most important thing that transpired in that bizarre father-son moment was in fact happening at a micro level and invisible to others. That day my father's public outrage and my mom's private cringefest somehow fused inside of me. Dad was conveying to me all his anxieties around money: his angst about its scarcity and that he didn't make enough; about the World Order that seemed to be hurtling itself self-destructively toward the rocks; that the repeated energy crises of the 1970s meant oil was running out and there weren't enough natural resources on earth to satisfy humanity's appetites.

There just wasn't enough of anything we needed.

Scarcity ruled my world.

In short, I had picked up my "inheritance" from my father, the whole white-knuckle gamut of financial anxieties that he successfully passed on and that I have spent a lifetime dealing with ever since, in all their emotional complexity.

When we got back in the car and started to drive away, my mother was still cringing; my dad was still raging about the things he couldn't understand or control; and my sister, cuddling her doll, was still playing happily, as I had been a few minutes before.

But I was sad, unsettled.

It may have led me to overcompensate.

I don't think it's too much of an exaggeration to say that this gas-station moment likely sealed my professional destiny and led me to become the chief investment officer of UBS Global Wealth Management. Of course, you can't draw a straight line from that day in American suburbia to sitting in the desert with sheikhs eating a sheep eyeball or discussing how to pass on a family business over tea in Beijing, as was to come. But, from then on, I ached to get back to feeling good, and to do so over the coming decades I unconsciously and continuously strove to return to that gas-pump scene and address all the things my deepest self wanted to understand and resolve but didn't have the maturity or life experience to figure out.

Those questions and issues ran the gamut, from how I could comfort my mother to how I could reach a place where I felt I had "enough"; to distinguishing what I had control over from what I did not; to understanding how the world really worked and what the geopolitical and economic forces were that had impacted those gas prices.

I might not have been able to articulate all of this at the time, of course, but I really wanted to be free of my father's issues and wanted answers to all these questions, including what great insight I was missing and should be aware of.

Only much later in life did I finally realize what that missing epiphany was: if everybody in the world aspired to a Chevy Kingswood Estate Wagon or was driving a car that got ten miles to the gallon, we were all in serious trouble.

THE MONEY-COMPLEX "INHERITANCE"

Our complex relationship to money is not only picked up by osmosis during childhood, as in my experience at the gas station; it is also, to some degree, inherited from our ancestors. My dad passed on to me his worries about paying the household bills and the state of the world because of what *he* picked up from his father.

My paternal grandparents—who adored my sister and me and made us feel priceless—started life poor. They came from a tiny village in Swabia, Germany. The unofficial motto of Swabia, which was framed and hung on my grandparents' wall, was *Schaffe, spare, Häusle baue,* or "Work, save, build a little house."[14] Such nice sentiments don't always help. When the 1920s rolled around, my machinist Opa couldn't find work, and the jobs he did secure were made meaningless by the fact that Germany's monthly inflation rate hit 29,500 percent in October 1923.[15]

When I was a kid—and we were chowing down a platter of Oma's Christmas cookies around the kitchen table—Opa would tell me about what it was like coming of age in the wacko Weimar Republic. When he got paid on a Friday, my grandfather had to buy everything he needed right away, because by the time Monday rolled around, he could no longer afford the same groceries. It was hard to get my little head around this notion, and I suspect Opa's lurid tales about the Weimar Republic played a role in my later fascination with economic history. So did the fact that rather than staying around to fix the Weimar Republic, my grandparents ditched all they knew and in 1926 bravely headed to America to start a new life.

In 1938, on the eve of World War II, Henry Haefele, my dad, was born stateside. The by-product of preparing for that war was of course that the US economy was itself picking up and coming out of the Great Depression. Opa found work as a machinist and bought some land in Ringwood, New Jersey. The town is now a New York bedroom community, but at the time it was more like Hillbilly Appalachia. Like the Swabian maxim on the wall said, my grandfather built their little house from scratch. He built fires around boulders and then poured cold water on the rock to crack them into more manageable chunks to build with.

They couldn't wire their house for electricity when America needed supplies for the war effort, so my dad and his parents lived in their modest house for nine years without it. They lived by kerosene lamp; well water was drawn from a hand pump in the kitchen. They cut firewood on a circular saw attached to the car axle, and one day it cost my grandma her finger.

When kerosene leaked into the well, they lowered my pint-size dad down a rope so he could skim the slick off the water's surface. A pressure tank Opa installed eventually allowed for running water, and the house was finally wired for electricity in 1951. Dad, an only child, had two beagles, and as a kid he put food on the table by hunting rabbits and squirrels in the surrounding woods.

So it's understandable why my dad was triggered by sixty-four-cents-a-gallon gas in the stagflation 1970s. Inflation had powerful, life-altering consequences for my grandparents, and my modest German immigrant family experienced real economic hardships. Here's the point: families do pass on a profound sense of hunger or entitlement or middle-class satisfaction or frustrated rage or underprivilege or louche excess, from one generation to the other, depending on the myths that have been built out of the family's life experiences and their subsequent narratives.

And that family story is another powerful inner force that investors need to understand and master in themselves in order to up their game.

I've spent half a century on a journey with the good and bad of the legacy I inherited, so I can get back in that Chevy and drive to Enough Town, that mythical place in my imagination where we all feel sated, content, and anxiety-free. Sometimes, on a good day, I get to visit Enough Town, which is sweet enough, but it is my fervent hope that eventually I'll get to move there on a more permanent basis—and that you'll meet me there too.

Let's be clear: my money complexes are part of my DNA and make me who I am. They have been a negative force, at times unconsciously consuming me and making me anxious and curtailing my enjoyment of life. But when they were understood and prodded in a new direction, they equally became an enriching source of investment ideas and smart market plays when I most needed them.

You can't and won't ever eliminate your deep-rooted money issues, but you can become conscious of them, understand how they manifest, and perhaps redirect their powerful force in a positive direction, as you will later see our most successful clients are doing for themselves via impact investing. But that reimagining is solely a by-product of the self-knowledge that flows directly from reflecting on some uncomfortable childhood memories.

In the summer of 1978 our family drove down to Disney World in Orlando in the Chevrolet Estate Wagon. I was still in first grade, and it was a big deal, since this was shortly after Dad's gas-pump hissy fit. We stayed at seedy motels along the highway where we weren't allowed to touch anything until my mother had gone over the room with a can of Lysol spray.

One day we treated ourselves to the buffet at Disney's Polynesian Village, where a monorail threaded its way through the building and colorful big-eyed totems stared down at us through the ferns. The adults drank from carved-out pineapples sporting umbrellas. The child's buffet back then was eight dollars, or thirty-nine dollars in today's money, which means Disney was as expensive in the 1970s as it is today for middle-class families scraping by but still wanting to treat their kids to a special vacation.[16]

I know the buffet was eight dollars because of my sister.

At five, she was going through a period where she was a picky eater, and my dad completely lost it when all she would eat from the Polynesian buffet was black olives. "Eight dollars for this buffet and all you're going to do is eat black olives! I hope you choke on those black olives!" It was an awful family moment, and seeing Dad worked up and railing at my innocent little sister triggered my own angst. I began piling food on my own plate and crying, "Look, I'm eating my food! I'm eating my food!"

This is how scarcity takes root in a soul.

To this day, I have a thing about not wasting food. It is a challenge not to clear my plate, no matter how full I am. I reuse teabags and eat items well past their sell-by date, even after this habit has badly upended my internal plumbing system. My tell-it-as-it-is Scottish wife informs me I pack underwear for a business trip like I am planning to poop myself twice a day.

I don't want to claim any of this as genuine hardship, because I grew up in an emotionally rich and loving family, surrounded by doting grandparents and relatives, a cool and funny sister, and devoted parents who unquestionably adored their kids. I felt loved. Even then, I knew I was lucky to have DisneyWorld problems, in a world full of much larger problems, or at least I knew that everything I had was easier, better, newer, bigger, and more climate controlled than what my grandparents and parents had had.

And things got a lot better for our tight-knit family shortly after this Disney trip because my mechanical engineer Dad got a great job at a company called Liquid Metronics, where he stayed for twenty-three years, after years of rotating jobs and occasionally getting laid off. From age seven onward, I lived with my family in a substantial house with a pool in the Massachusetts village of Stow, just outside Boston.

I guess the point of these stories is their banality. I could fill this book with entertaining stories about dinner at a six-seat *omakase* restaurant in Tokyo or a private event where I was served filet mignon while Janet Jackson performed fifteen feet away from my table. But that stuff is not important. What is important, as far as this book is concerned, is what I figured out about myself: every time there is a plate of food in front of me, if it's the most exquisite haute cuisine—or worse, a plate of fries—I am instantly transported back to that Polynesian Village buffet. I now know I can never go on an all-you-can-eat cruise ship, and I have made peace with that. It is an important insight I have acquired on my personal journey to wealth, and it's why you're going to hear me say the same thing again and again.

Know yourself. Know your triggers.

OUR MONEY ISSUES NEVER DIE

If you still think this emotional stuff is mere fluff, touchy-feely ephemera that has nothing to do with wealth creation, I strongly recommend you rethink your position. It certainly isn't considered fluff by the billionaires I work with. Untangling emotions from wealth is some of the most profound work we do at the UBS chief investment office.

One of the greatest investors I know, a UBS client, once said to me, "Mark, I have known success with money for many years, but I failed three times working on my estate plan. We have started again. I am still not confident about what I am doing."

I had spotted something earlier in the day, so I politely joked with the client that some of the difficulty might be his self-acknowledged preference to talk about "if" he died, rather than "when" he died. It was that hard-to-swallow reality, mortality, that was stirring up a lot of angst and denial and the feeling that we weren't talking about money when we talked about money. Once this fear was acknowledged and addressed, the brilliant billionaire was able to move forward, and we were able to help him build a stronger investment plan on solid emotional foundations.

Managing wealth continuously teaches us lessons about ourselves, no matter where we are in our journey. Hank* was a self-made entrepreneur with over $400 million in his portfolio. After he sold his manufacturing business, he had reached that stage in life where he finally had the time and means to actively engage with philanthropy.

One day, Hank was sharing his portfolio decisions with a group of similarly wealthy entrepreneurs in New York, and when he came to his charitable efforts, he proudly informed this self-help group he was donating $250,000 to the educational opportunities of underprivileged kids.

He expected to be lauded.

His peers tore into him.

They ridiculed his efforts. They correctly pointed out that as a percentage of his total wealth, his charitable giving was miserly. He could and should give far more.

The centimillionaire was both hurt and stupefied.

It was only when his peers started interrogating him that they collectively came to the source of the problem. Hank had a very tough

---

* Names and some personal details have been changed to protect identities.

upbringing, was literally dirt poor and starving at certain points of his early life, and though he was now wealthy, his mind was still trapped in the emotions of his childhood poverty.

Hank believed that giving away a quarter of a million dollars to charity was *incredibly* generous, something he never dreamed he would ever be able to do. It was a small fortune to an impoverished child, which was what he still felt like inside, and it was only his peers' virulent reaction that made him aware that relative to his wealth, his adult philanthropic efforts were underwhelming. After being made aware of his issue, he gradually overcame his internal obstacles and gave away increasingly larger amounts of his sizable wealth.

The emotional money issues of childhood never go away. They are with us, always, as we climb the ladder of wealth. If you want to be free of the fear and greed that rules most of your money decisions, so you can really enjoy the "richness" that can come with wealth and wise wealth management, you must do the hard work on yourself.

Bottom Line

Your deep-seated complexes around money are unconsciously driving your financial decisions, every time you book a family trip, buy a car, or invest your hard-earned wealth. They are also behind all those self-destructive buy-and-sell impulses that erode your investment returns, as we've talked about earlier in the book. If you want to up your game as an investor, you need to have a solid understanding of your deepest money issues so you can firmly put them aside when managing your wealth. Strive to create a state of mind where you can make calm and wise investment decisions. Eventually you might even be able to redirect these powerful emotional forces in a more enlightened direction, as you will see our clients are doing when we get to the chapters on impact investing.

Often one of the most valuable services we help clients with is connecting them to peers so they can together talk through such issues. Reflect, peel the onion, recall family stories and childhood scenes that shaped your financial outlook, and try to become conscious of what's going on when the attendant emotions of your complex start rearing their ugly heads—particularly when you're sitting down to make finance-related decisions. As Ben Graham, Warren Buffett's mentor, reminds us, investing is all about "controlling yourself at your own game."[17]

CREATE LIQUIDITY, LONGEVITY, AND LEGACY BUCKETS

Shortly after I arrived in Zurich in 2011 and started working with UBS's wealth managers and their clients, long-forgotten financial lessons from my maternal grandmother, Nan, came flooding back to me. The lessons Nan unconsciously passed on about money were very different from what I picked up from my high-strung dad and his financially insecure family.

There was always something noticeably different about Nan's way of living, and when I was ten and having a sleepover in her apartment above our family's garage in Stow, Massachusetts, I straight-out asked the big question about this strange aura she had.

"Nan, are you rich?"

"No," she said. "But I am comfortable."

I discovered, then, that Nan had something nobody else seemed to have. Nan had a widow's pension. I didn't know what a pension was, but it sounded like winning the lottery.

It wasn't just money. It was *steady* money you got every month for the rest of your life.

Nan, who grew up poor and never finished high school, received a policeman's pension after my grandfather died. But Nan also had her own modest pension from Bendix Corporation, where she worked for many years winding armatures for electric motors.

Furthermore, she received inflation-indexed Social Security payments, plus was earning at the time high rates of return from her certificates of deposit (CDs). Many of you below a certain age won't probably know or recall this curiosity, but in 1981—the time this "Are you rich?" conversation with Nan was taking place—Federal Reserve chairman Paul Volcker had raised short-term rates to 20 percent in his battle against that era's runaway inflation.[1] As a result, the average three-month CD in the US in May 1981 was offering a stunning 18.3 percent return.[2] My grandmother was getting more interest than ever simply by rolling over her CDs.

Of course, looking back, I now realize Nan was hardly rich, living as she did over our garage and driving a Chevy Nova, but she had an aura about her so distinct that even a ten-year-old spotted it. Nan knew with certainty how much money she could spend every month and stuck to it, and because she lived within her means and most of her income stream was guaranteed by the government, she never worried about money and had a lightness about her.

Nan was the person who opened my eyes to the fact that you could have a completely different relationship to money than the fraught relationship I had absorbed from my dad's side of the family. She had her money working for her, rather than working for her money, and as a consequence, was at peace.

In short, my grandmother lived in this mythic place that I call Enough Town, a wondrous place where contented souls live free of money worries. Enough Town is a state of mind where our decisions are made from a mindset of abundance, not scarcity, and though we live deep in the heart of capitalist society, thoughts about making, spending, and saving money do not devour us on a daily or hourly basis.

Enough Town was my goal, but unfortunately I had picked up my father's anxieties about money. While I found my way to studying the finer points of asset allocation, I had been less successful at converting that airy knowledge into greater mastery of my personal finances at ground level. My emotional money issues were still getting in the way.

I was missing something. There was a disconnect.

In a way, all that math was holding me back.

Modern optimization theories are all well and good, but they miss a lot of what the industry has learned in the past thirty years while interacting with real clients. Nan might have said, "All that book learning lacks common sense," and she would have been right.

I needed to find my way to her state of mind.

Computing your ideal asset allocation, and then starting to rebalance your portfolio toward it, can take a lot of emotion out of buy-and-sell decisions. But I eventually discovered, in my own life and while coaching others on their wealth management, the asset-allocation system was not enough on its own, for all the emotional reasons mentioned in the previous chapter.

Wealth management requires dealing with real people and their futures, and people do not, as we've established, act rationally or scientifically. That is why a wealth-management system that integrates your personal money issues into your investment process is so crucial. It's a key step toward improving your investment returns and moving away from the narrow lens of investing toward a wide-lens and more holistic form of wealth management.

The previous chapter might have given you the impression that the self-knowledge I acquired about my own money issues came in a clap of thunder one day, but in fact it came painfully in fits and starts and at different stages of my life.

A big piece of the puzzle only came to me after I was at UBS and saw how our best advisors ran an introductory client meeting. I would show up at these meetings, ready to help clients invest. I wanted to talk capital market assumptions: *Let's get down to asset-allocation percentages.*

Instead, the advisors led with questions like these:

What do you want to accomplish in your life?
Who are the people who matter most to you?
What do you want your legacy to be?
What are your main concerns?
How do you plan to achieve your life's vision?

Where is all this going? I wondered. *Are we going to hold hands and sing songs?*

No, we weren't. This was the **UBS Wealth Way**, a technique our bankers use to understand a client's personal money issues, intimate knowledge they then use to build a portfolio tailored to the client's material and emotional needs.

This is where the "art" of our financial craftsmanship starts to temper the "science" of the asset-allocation methodology—and creates something special in the process.

THE THREE LS

Hans-Heinrich,* an entrepreneur from Hamburg, flies to Zurich. He has just sold his shoe brand for EUR 200 million, and he arrives at our Bahnhofstrasse headquarters with his wife and teenage daughter by his side. He tells us he is out of the shoemaking business. His job, going forward, will be to manage their new wealth.

An old way of being has died for Hans-Heinrich and his family, and a new way is being born. But it quickly becomes apparent that the entrepreneur has had his head down obsessively building his shoe company his entire adult life, and as a result he knows little about markets and investing, which is why he and his family have arrived for their meeting. They earnestly want to transform themselves into good stewards of their wealth.

---

* Names and some personal details have been changed to protect identities.

We first spend considerable time getting to know what the clients want in life. Their dreams, needs, fears, passions—the whole gamut. At this stage, we're trying to understand who they are and what they want to happen; we want to know about their lifestyle and running costs; where they ultimately want to get to; and how much risk—portfolio volatility—they can comfortably handle to earn decent returns.

In our early "compass" conversations, which help us get our directional readings from the client, we discover the family does not want any of their wealth invested in fossil fuel and weapons stocks; they would like to own a second home in Greece one day; and they are extremely fearful of losing their wealth, almost to the point of phobia, because both sets of grandparents and great grandparents lost everything during Europe's great wars.

A basic plan would arrange for them to take some wealth-management literacy classes and to build a low-to-moderate asset-allocation portfolio. This is a huge step in the right direction and a profound shift away from the way they have managed money in the past. The next level of advice uses all the personal knowledge we've just accumulated, subdividing their portfolio into at least three subportfolios, known as Liquidity, Longevity, and Legacy Buckets.

The concept behind 3L, our informal in-house name for the UBS Wealth Way, is both simple and genuinely profound. It is about figuring out how your wealth—no matter the current level—can help you be happier today, happier tomorrow, and make others happier when you are gone.

When it comes to your journey to wealth, there is not one prescribed route that you and everyone else must rigidly adhere to. Quite the opposite. You must find a path that is *personally relevant* and leads you directly to your goals and objectives in life.

Otherwise, the wealth-creation process, no matter how successful it becomes, may never get beyond serving a survival instinct. You have no chance of connecting your wealth to a higher cause, like realizing your deepest dreams and passions so you can become fulfilled while on this earth.

When I first heard about the 3Ls, I was extremely skeptical, because, schooled in traditional investing and finance where "money is fungible," the idea of mentally separating my money into artificial philosophical buckets seemed irrational. At first, I had to translate the 3Ls into my own version of "Econ-Speak," by calling them "individual intertemporal marginal utility maximizations,"[3] so I could sort of wrap my mind around them. But I am not someone who worries about theories when I see results. In addition to seeing the effect on clients, I experimented by floating the 3L concept with my family and saw how much better the ideas made them feel about their wealth.

Here's how it's done: The **Liquidity Bucket** helps you master your near-term money concerns. Counterintuitively, we have found that by securing your near-term spending plans, you might be able to *increase* your near-term spending abilities without increasing your worries about running out of money later.

The **Longevity Bucket**, meanwhile, is meant to help you fulfill your lifetime goals and is designed to cover all your long-term spending goals, including retirement. We've learned that the more confident you feel about being well prepared for the good and bad you will face throughout your lifetime, the more energized and excited you will be to think beyond your own lifetime's spending needs.

The **Legacy Bucket** is for that purpose and is composed of asset allocations that aim to maximize the wealth that will be available to support the people and causes closest to your heart, after you've left this earth.

A conventional financial plan helps you quantify your objectives and understand your spending needs, and then figures out your chances of meeting those objectives, all under various economic and market scenarios. The UBS Wealth Way does all of that and then kicks everything up another notch. The system is designed to get under the hood of your personal psychology and aims to *exploit* your mental accounting bias, which is your unconscious tendency to use money differently depending on the income's source and its intended purpose.[4]

But the most important thing to note is that behind the entire UBS Wealth Way framework stands that singular truth I keep repeating to anyone who will listen: wealth benefits flow liberally from knowing yourself.

It's not just for defensive reasons this is important. Knowing your objectives and what you're prioritizing in life helps you as an investor understand *why* you are investing your wealth in a certain way. Your asset allocations should always be structured to support what you are trying to achieve in life.

During the financial crisis, when I knew I had to stop picking stocks and was rediscovering asset allocation, I kept asking myself, *Why are you investing?*

That's the same question you need to ask. Why you invest is key to becoming a good investor because it shapes everything that follows, and for many people I work with their why of investing changes over time. Early on, it can be to earn enough money to have a certain lifestyle; later, it can be to maintain a lifestyle without stress. Increasingly, I work with clients who want to use their wealth to positively impact the world. (Then again, I also meet people who want to chase lottery-ticket investments they can brag about at cocktail parties.)

Thinking about how much money you need to save for everything you want to achieve in this life can be overwhelming, which is why it helps to break this big problem down into these three separate buckets. Since the Liquidity Bucket is focused on just the next few years, it is a simpler concept to wrap your mind around and solve.

Once you know that your short-term liquidity needs are taken care of, you will be less likely to freak out and panic-sell when the markets are nosediving and the anchors on television are screeching at us that we're all hurtling toward financial Armageddon.

The simple act of not reacting emotionally and impulsively during a financial sell-off—which is a known and documented by-product of our 3L system—will massively boost your investment results over time, which is the subject of the Longevity Bucket.

THE LIQUIDITY BUCKET: INVESTING FOR THE NEXT THREE TO FIVE YEARS

The Liquidity Bucket gathers all the resources needed to pay your family's cash-flow needs over a three-to-five-year period. There is good reason for organizing your finances this way. If the worst happens in the global economy, and we collectively spin off into a prolonged period of market turmoil, you never want to be in a position where you are forced to sell assets into a fast-collapsing market because your income and expenses are suddenly out of whack. Selling off your portfolio to meet day-to-day expenses will lock in catastrophic losses, and those are virtually impossible to recover from.

In short, your Liquidity Bucket is a reserve held in liquid instruments with high price stability—everything from cash to high-quality sovereign debt. These resources can cover your household expenses over the choppy years ahead.

Think all this through carefully, by going through various what-if scenarios. If, for example, there is a chance you could lose your job in a downturn because your employer is showing signs of instability even during a boom period, then you've got to rely to a higher degree on investment assets being earmarked for ongoing expenses. But then remember to add back into your Liquidity Bucket the unemployment insurance you might receive during the time you're out of work.

This three-to-five-year time frame is deliberately picked to bring about peace of mind. Global recessions and depressions over the last 150 years have been studied ad nauseam.[5] Though they tend to be brutal, they also tend to be relatively short lived, before markets inevitably start to recover and begin their long march back to health.[6] **Studies repeatedly show that well-diversified and well-balanced portfolios usually *recover most or all their losses* during this three-to-five-year window.**[7] The Liquidity Bucket is designed to carry you safely through the flash flood of this kind of market turmoil, allowing you to arrive on the solid ground on the other side of the riverbank without ever having taken a bath.

Your Liquidity Bucket resources are drawn from regular income flowing from an employer or a pension; investments that have been set aside for expense purposes; and, sometimes, loans safely taken out during this rough financial period. Remember, during times of intense economic turmoil interest rates usually fall, so some people may feel comfortable using judicious amounts of lower-cost borrowing against other assets to shore up their Liquidity Bucket.

When you calculate what you need to set aside in your Liquidity Bucket, be thorough and honest about what your expenses amount to. Add in everything needed to maintain your current lifestyle, including all your taxes and vacation plans and whatever school bills are coming due. Don't shortchange yourself.

The key factors shaping your Liquidity Bucket strategy are (1) how thoroughly your regular income covers your expenses; (2) the risk of not receiving your regular income during this difficult period; and (3) the possibility you could be hit by an unforeseen expense. In all cases, you're trying to avoid a disconnect between your ongoing expenses and the market-to-market value of your Liquidity Bucket reserves.

You can of course further subdivide the assets in the Liquidity Bucket to improve the risk-reward. Most of us think of our checking account as our Liquidity Bucket. That's a good place to start when covering your monthly expenses. For emergency funds and a vacation six months away, a savings account or CDs can also become part of your Liquidity Bucket and deliver higher yields. Yet with further planning, you can add other income-producing assets into the Liquidity Bucket.

This is where a bond "ladder" can play a role. A ladder of bonds of different size and duration, maturing over the next several years—and matched to bigger expenses coming due—can enhance returns in the Liquidity Bucket.

If, for example, your daughter's private-school tuition is due in $10,000 installments in the spring and fall every year for the next three years, then you can ladder bonds to pay out around the time the six tuition payments are made. The goal is to earn the best possible return over the next three years while materially calming your inner angst about meeting those bills—all while everyone else less organized is freaking out about the financial crisis.

"Stability and reliability" is a core principle of these expense-covering reserves, which is why you might start discussing with your adviser if a 60 percent allocation to cash and a 40 percent allocation to bonds is the right starting point for you. Consider, too, you're still going to have to liquidate some investments in a bear market, when it comes time, say, to pay for the house's $25,000 roof replacement. That's why it's important that you're invested in vehicles offering a lot of price stability. Also, don't forget to consider currency or country-risk exposures in your Liquidity Bucket, if you're jet-setters with a foreign abode or have kids in overseas schools.

How much of your total income you should save to build up a Liquidity Bucket, and how much you should put into longer-term savings, will change over the course of your life. The more pretax money you can stash into retirement funds when you are just starting out, the better. But a hard look at your financial personality may lead you to shift your priorities a bit, say to boost your shorter-term savings and reduce your long-term savings, so you feel confident that you can get through an emergency or a financial downturn on the horizon.

My purpose here is to get you to think strategically and to realize there is a lot more to a good UBS Wealth Way plan than filling out an online questionnaire. Earmark a portion of your wealth to *defensively* cover all your known and unknown expenses for the three to five years that history shows us is what it takes for markets to bounce back from a meltdown. You do that precisely so you can go on the *offensive* in the next bucket.

THE LIQUIDITY BUCKET: HOW IT PAYS FOR ITSELF

In February 2020, COVID-19 was starting to shut down the global economy. One of our financial advisors was traveling through the Rocky Mountains when the virus hit. The S&P 500 started its lightning-quick 34 percent freefall, and the advisor's cell phone began to ring while he was driving to visit clients in Colorado's hinterland.[8]

One call was a client from back East, a retired widow in her late sixties. Let's call her Susan.* She had $2 million in assets in her portfolio, enough to cover her Liquidity and Longevity Buckets, but not yet enough, based on her age of sixty-seven and her lifestyle, to finance a full-fledged Legacy Bucket. But in that moment, with her wealth in the process of falling 25 percent to $1.5 million (at its COVID-19 low point), Susan was frantically telling her advisor she wanted him to immediately move her money out of all securities and go to cash.

Hearing the terror in her voice, the financial advisor pulled over, called up her account, and from the side of the road walked her through her monthly costs and how many years of expenses she had covered in her Liquidity Bucket. The advisor was in this way able to "talk her off the ledge," and did so again on many more such calls over several weeks. These calming calls worked. Susan stayed the course, without panic-selling and locking in massive losses, and the Liquidity Bucket ultimately saved Susan from her most self-destructive behavioral issues around money—her internal terror that there would never be enough.

THE LIQUIDITY BUCKET: HOW IT SAFELY LETS YOU HAVE FUN

Jack** sold his Maryland manufacturing business three years ago for $20 million. He promptly went on a buying spree, purchasing a $4 million home in a sunnier state and putting down $1 million on two other water-side condos yet to be built.

That was for starters. Jack's advisor convinced him to sell one of his many vintage Alfa Romeos for $325,000 to shore up his Liquidity Bucket, but then Jack used that money to buy a diamond necklace for his wife. "He hasn't got to the other side yet," said his advisor.

The advisor was referring to the fact that many clients go on a buying binge shortly after they've sold their businesses. That's when they start

---

* Names and some personal details have been changed to protect identities.
** Names and some personal details have been changed to protect identities.

snapping up things like private-jet cards and overseas homes, all the baubles they think rich people have.

After a sudden liquidity event, the human mind needs time to adjust to being "wealthy," particularly when the person was born into modest circumstances and that's still how they perceive themselves internally.

This binge-buying phase usually lasts a few years, until they realize that all the acquisitions they've made didn't improve the quality of their life, but rather just made their life more complicated. Finally in a place where they can listen and start learning how to manage their wealth in a more wholesome, fulfilling, and sophisticated way, the client then frequently turns to their financial advisors for help.

But it is precisely during this early phase of the wealth journey—*woohee, I'm rich!*—that a well-financed Liquidity Bucket again proves its worth. Jack's experienced financial advisor, having seen this behavior many times before, knows to prepare his clients for the first years of their post-sale life by setting aside far more cash and cash equivalents in their Liquidity Buckets than what the clients think they need, precisely to cover these sorts of impulsive acquisitions.

Many entrepreneurs don't fully grasp how much their post-sale lives will cost them, because many lifestyle expenses that were previously running "unseen" through their businesses—items such as medical insurance, club memberships, and sports tickets—are suddenly coming out of their household expenses instead. If you are similarly blessed by fortune and these are your "problems," know that good advice and a well-structured Liquidity Bucket will allow you to safely go mad for a few years, without your Longevity and Legacy Buckets—aka your long-term needs—waking up later with an unrecoverable hangover.

THE LIQUIDITY BUCKET: HOW IT PROVIDES PSYCHOLOGICAL RELIEF

Bernardine Williams Rosenthal,[9] a retired nurse and mom of three, was bereft when her beloved husband, Mort, died after a long bout of cancer. Bernardine confessed to her children she had "lost her compass."

Like a lot of women of her generation, Bernardine had let her late husband manage their finances, as she felt ill-equipped to make wealth-related decisions. She was raised dirt poor in a Chicago tenement during the Great Depression, had been deeply affected by the experience, and was, as a result, severely risk averse. In contrast her husband, an esteemed eye doctor in New York, had a feel for undervalued assets and when to take a calculated risk.

When they were young parents, still scraping by, Mort convinced Bernardine they should buy a sprawling ten-bathroom Victorian mansion on the shores of Nassau County, Long Island. Below the chipped paint and rotting wires, Mort saw what the white elephant could be, and his lowball offer, the most he could afford, was eventually accepted. It was 1964, and the couple spent the next decades raising their children and grandchildren and lovingly restoring the sprawling property with forty-foot living rooms.

Flash forward to 2002, the year Mort died. The impeccably restored mansion facing the Long Island Sound was now surrounded by billionaire neighbors. It was extremely valuable, and after Mort's funeral, a relative offered to help her with her financial affairs and introduced Bernardine to a UBS financial advisor. Bernardine knew little about finance, but she was smart, and her advisor taught her about the Liquidity, Longevity, and Legacy Buckets of the UBS Wealth Way. As he walked her through the process, he asked the spry seventy-six-year-old what her goals in life were.

Bernardine wanted a simpler existence; the massive house in Nassau was too much for her at this stage of life. In 2004, backed by her financial advisor, Bernardine took on the formidable task of selling the mansion before the housing bubble burst, a successful liquidation full of tax- and estate-management ramifications. She then moved to a full-service apartment complex near LaGuardia Airport, with doormen and security and eldercare help to assist her as needed.

When the markets imploded during the financial crisis, Bernardine was full of angst, the ghosts of her Depression-era upbringing coming back to haunt her. But her financial advisor regularly called and reminded her she had enough funds in her Liquidity Bucket to comfortably sit things out until calm in the markets was restored.

He was able to distract Bernardine from the fears and dark mental forces that had long ruled her relationship to money. He further prompted her to do some soul-searching and write down her thoughts about her life in a letter to the family. Through this process, and the comforts of the Liquidity and Longevity Buckets, Bernardine began to make decisions about her Legacy Bucket. She wanted, while she was alive, to pass on her wealth tax-efficiently and smartly to the family she and Mort so loved, including their five grandkids. One day Bernardine announced to the family she was paying half of every grandchild's college education. She took the family on memorable vacations to Paris and steadily signed over to them the tax-free savings Mort had stashed away in various IRAs, tasks she diligently performed, even in the ambulance on her final trip to the hospital.

But, more importantly, Bernardine worked on herself through the twilight of her final years. She devoted herself to the literary life she always craved but never had time or money to pursue. She took charge of the book club at her beloved Hadassah, the Women's Zionist Organization of America, and did exhaustive research and compiled book reports and hosted fundraisers. She even invited acclaimed authors, such as Jamie Bernstein, daughter of the late conductor Leonard Bernstein, to read from their works.

Bernardine then joined a group of retirees at Hofstra University's continuing education program and pushed herself to learn more about the world. She wrote her memoir and in 2020 self-published *Under the Noodle String*, a remarkably well-written and moving work about growing up poor during the Great Depression.[10]

By structuring her wealth around the 3L buckets, Bernardine was first able to contain her scarcity fears around money and then fulfill her long-held dreams and goals. The Liquidity Bucket in particular tempered her financial angst, even during tough economic times, and it allowed Bernardine to have a spiritual renaissance in her eighties and nineties, a time of life when most people feel they have fewer, not more, prospects. "My mother reinvented herself," her daughter told us. "She was full of life."

We love to hear such stories, because the 3L bucket system is designed to achieve just that—liberation from the money issues that interfere with your enjoyment of life.

THE LONGEVITY BUCKET: INVESTING FROM FIVE YEARS TO END OF LIFE

In broad strokes, the purpose of the Longevity Bucket is to ensure that within your lifetime you have enough savings to meet all your goals, aspirational and otherwise. Well, if not *ensure*, then at least raise the probability that you can meet those goals. As a rule, when you and your advisors run through various macroeconomic scenarios, you want your chances of successfully meeting your lifetime financial needs at 85 percent or better. The risk here is of course that of shortfall, which means you either outlive your wealth or you don't achieve the investment returns you needed to tick all the boxes on your wish list.

Once again, this process starts with knowing yourself and what you really want to achieve in life. Is early retirement a goal? Do you want to relocate or travel for a good chunk of the time you have remaining? Do you need seed capital to start a new business? Is a second home, or even a third home overseas, the thing that's seized your imagination?

Once those goals are identified, it's then time to think long and hard about your investment process. What's your tolerance for risk? How much can you safely set aside in your Longevity Bucket without shortchanging the Liquidity Bucket? How much time does that money have to compound and grow before you need it? How much of that pool of capital should you assume will be eroded by inflation?

Once you have settled on a Longevity Bucket program, both your goals and investment presumptions should be reviewed and adjusted on a yearly basis. Goals are likely to morph as you age, and an investor's plan needs to be fine-tuned as employment opportunities fluctuate or there are unexpected interruptions in earlier income assumptions.

That's important. You want to finance your Longevity Bucket with enough resources to self-insure against a string of poorly performing investments. Even then, if things don't pan out as planned, there's always the great fallback: trimming your immediate spending so the likelihood of meeting your financial goals still stands a good chance of success.

Because you're investing in this bucket to meet your long-term needs, it's wise to load up your Longevity Bucket with equities. That might mean asking your advisor if 85 percent in equities is appropriate. If you're based in the US, you might ask if 45 percent US equities and 40 percent international equities is the right split for you.

Studies repeatedly reveal that a basket of equities outperforms most other asset classes over the long run. A 2022 McKinsey study, for example, calculated that, since 1800, US equities have on average delivered an annual 6.5 percent to 7 percent return after inflation.[11] As to the remaining 15 percent of the longevity portfolio, you and your advisor might consider, as a starting point, parking 5 percent respectively in cash, fixed income, and so-called nontraditional assets (hedge funds, private equity, real estate, etc.).

Here's where it gets interesting.

Let's go back to our scenario of the virulent financial crisis. **Because three to five years of your daily expenses are *defensively* covered by stable and reliable holdings in your Liquidity Bucket, you can now go on the *offensive* when investing in your Longevity Bucket.** Your entire investment psychology has gone through a profound change due to the 3L bucket system. Instead of experiencing terror and panic, you now have your expenses comfortably covered in your Liquidity Bucket. Where others experience fear, you can now focus on the buying opportunities that will fortify your Longevity Bucket. It's the moment when you buy beaten-down assets on the cheap, positioning yourself for the big portfolio win when markets finally rebound.

Remember Susan, the client who wanted to sell all her positions and lock in her losses when the market crashed during COVID-19? By rebalancing and buying equities in her Longevity Bucket during the 2020 market crash's low points, she considerably *increased* her wealth when the markets bounced back.

As Susan's story illustrates, you don't have to do a lot of extra work to refill the Longevity Bucket. **If all you do is stick to your asset-allocation plan of keeping set percentages of cash and bonds versus riskier assets, you will automatically be buying stocks when they are cheaper.**

Buying lower-priced equities is not the only game in town during such moments. These can also be moments of personal fulfillment. Let's pretend you've always dreamed about that second home on the lake. Well, maybe this is the time to use your Longevity Bucket's cash and nontraditional asset allocations, coupled to one of those low-interest-rate mortgages on offer during this crisis, to finally buy that lake home that is suddenly on the market at a distressed price.

You get the general idea, but to add some extra clarity, let me share some stories about how Longevity Buckets can materially help clients navigate the vicissitudes of late life or, as we say in the business, "the go-go years, the go-slow years, and the no-go years."

THE LONGEVITY BUCKET: THE ULTIMATE RETIREMENT-PLANNING TOOL

Bill Sowles,[12] seventy-one, was talking to his wife when it suddenly dawned on him that retirement had stealthily crept up on them. For all intents and purposes, they were *retirees*.

It came as a shock.

Sowles had run a successful two-location car dealership in New England for decades, and the couple's transition to retirement had started unwittingly some fifteen years earlier when they sailed their boat down from Maine to the Bahamas. They eventually set up a second home base in Cape Coral, Florida. The couple started working ten days a month remotely from Florida during the winter months but found themselves there full-time during the COVID-19 years.

"I woke up one morning and said, '[Oh, man,] we're retired.'"

Well, not quite. Bill had three kids, with two sons working in the car dealership they would eventually inherit but weren't yet ready to run. Bill bought the business from his father's estate in 1998—it was his father who originally founded the Volkswagen dealership in 1955—and Bill spoke for a lot of family-business owners when he said, "I didn't want somebody to take this legacy business and drive it into the ground. I mean, you've heard the expression 'Rags to riches to rags in three generations'? That's what I was worried about."

Luckily, his advisor at UBS was a specialist in such business transitions and "nudged" Bill to get his affairs in order. The big question on both their minds was this: How could Bill and his wife maintain their lifestyle during their retirement years while Bill gracefully extracted himself from the business his sons would one day run on their own? Bill's medium-term business goal, as he put it, was to "manage the car dealership as if I was already dead."

A well-structured Longevity Bucket allowed him to do just that. The first thing they did was reduce Bill's CEO salary at the dealership so he could increase the salaries of his two sons and the brother who had worked loyally by his side these many years. This salary shuffle was done in such a way that the net expense to the business remained the same. He could do so largely because the dealerships were built on real estate that Bill and his siblings owned separately, and that real estate business generated reliable cash flow.

Bill had always been New England–style financially prudent; he was never a big believer in debt. That was why Bill and his wife could comfortably afford their Florida lifestyle on his much-reduced salary, plus the cash generated by the family's debt-free real estate holdings, the occasional S-corp disbursements coming from the car dealership, and the cash flow generated by his liquidity and longevity portfolios at UBS. His assets overall also included an inheritance that he had received more than twenty years earlier from his grandmother, which had been compounding untouched ever since.

Bill recently pulled off the last shoring up of his Longevity Bucket. The couple owned two homes in Cape Coral, and Bill just sold the second house to pay down the modest debt financing on the house they currently live in. (He did not take out a mortgage but partially financed the new purchase with a bridge loan from UBS.)

Back at the business, meanwhile, Bill has his stalwart general manager mentoring his sons as they mature into their leadership roles, while he dials in from Florida once a week to listen in on the management discussions. He said he is learning how not to interfere and to let his sons and their mentor figure things out on their own.

Longevity thoughts can quickly turn into legacy thoughts, particularly when you're dealing with a family business and all its attendant emotion. That's why Bill has, among other things, set up trusts and tax-efficiently passed on his 85 percent share of the dealerships to his wife, sons, and daughter. Bill also gave his brother, who previously owned 15 percent of the business, 5 percent of his shares, so that each of the key family members now owns 20 percent of the dealership.

Is this how things will remain? "It's a work in progress," Bill said. "When I first talked to UBS about this, years ago, we decided on one thing. Then we reviewed it five years later, and I made other decisions. In another five years, I'll probably make another change again."

And so he should. Goals and needs change as life progresses. Your Longevity Bucket should shift and change accordingly.

THE LONGEVITY BUCKET: HOW IT PROVIDES COMFORT TO THE VERY END

Jimmy* came with his father to hear our financial advisor's pitch and kept on noting in the meeting that UBS was "charging fifty basis points, when your rival is charging thirty-eight basis points." The financial advisor finally responded, "Is that what you are looking for? Are you shopping for the lowest cost? Is that how you buy things in life?"

Jimmy, an entrepreneur from New Orleans, sheepishly agreed that

---

* Names and some personal details have been changed to protect identities.

going after the lowest-cost provider was not always the best way to proceed, particularly when it came to something as important as his wealth management, and he ultimately decided to transfer his assets to UBS. Not long afterward, his father was diagnosed with the early stages of Alzheimer's.

As Jimmy and his advisor were discussing his goals, he aired his worries about his much-loved parents. Picking up on that angst and weighing up his total financial picture, the financial advisor earmarked some funds in Jimmy's Longevity Bucket, and said, "This is for your father if he ever needs it."

Years later Jimmy's father was in a memory-care unit that cost $11,000 a month, and Jimmy's parents had gone through their life savings. All their IRAs were gone. But the fund that was earmarked in Jimmy's Longevity Bucket was now worth $500,000, and he was able to keep his father in the Ritz-Carlton of memory care until he finally passed.

That's exactly what the Longevity Bucket is designed to do—keep you and your loved ones in dignified style until the final curtain comes down.

THE LEGACY BUCKET: INVESTING FOR BEYOND YOUR TIME ON EARTH

Thinking about a Legacy Bucket may seem like a champagne problem for people richer or older than you. I disagree. It's important for everyone. After all, even if we are living paycheck to paycheck, we should still make time to think about how we can help others. But this is not a book about philanthropy; this is a book about investing and gaining mastery of your wealth to live a better life, and that's what we're going to focus on.

Once you have built your Liquidity and Longevity Buckets with emergency money and are beyond living paycheck to paycheck, it is important to start thinking about your legacy and how you can help others—not for them, but for you.

In prosaic terms, the purpose of the Legacy Bucket is to pass on assets tax-efficiently to the next generation of your family, or to mark your time on earth by having some sort of positive impact on society, either through philanthropic gifts or through impact investing, a method of investing with social or environmental causes specifically in mind. (We'll discuss impact investing in depth in later chapters.)

Because the investment horizon we're talking about here is longer, usually beyond your lifespan and with no need for imminent payouts, the risk profile of this bucket is going to look different from those of the previous two buckets. You can afford in this pool of capital to take higher risks and have even less liquidity than in your Longevity Bucket.

The ideal investment vehicles in the Legacy Bucket are a mix of equities with hedge funds, private equity, and infrastructure and real estate investments. Why? The additional illiquid instruments can pay a premium to investors to compensate them for the fact they can't get their money out at a moment's notice.

The same sort of allocations that are made in the Legacy Bucket can also be made in the Longevity Bucket, but here's the difference: instead of public-equity markets, you might discuss with your advisor if you want to increase your allocation to illiquid private-equity investments that don't trade on public exchanges. Based on our 2024 capital market assumptions, we are predicting private markets should outperform public equities by 1 percent to 3 percent per annum.[13]

There is also a little-discussed benefit to private-market investments in a bear market. Less frequent valuations tend to smooth out risk-adjusted returns, which means the value of your investments doesn't ratchet up and down on a daily basis, the way publicly traded holdings do, and so it takes less of a toll on your psyche during volatile markets.

Finally, one of the themes of this book is that you are not going to master your wealth or be a good investor if you are operating from a mindset of fear or greed. Working through a plan of how you want to use your wealth to help others forces you to think outside of that negative mindset. In fact, I have seen people improve their overall investing track records simply by working on legacy portfolios.

THE LEGACY BUCKET: HOW IT CAN TURN YOU INTO A BETTER INVESTOR

Gary* had worked a long time in the family business. Helping others was a natural part of his life and part of his family's deep-seated ethos, but that was philanthropy, and philanthropy had nothing to do with investing.

Years ago, when Gary had built up some personal savings, he got hooked on investing. I got to know him over the years and knew he was very smart and learning rapidly about markets. Still, I noticed he was overly afraid of losing money, which was why he primarily stuck to ultrasafe bonds.

Over time, I started to think there was a disconnect between Gary's intellectual development as an investor and his emotional development as an investor. When he dabbled in equities, he agonized over losses or missed opportunities and traded a fair bit too much. In my view he was spending a lot of time and energy on his investments, and they weren't generating a sufficient excess return for what he put into them.

Then something happened that changed everything: at fifty, Gary had his first children—two boys.

Like any parent, he naturally started to think about the what-ifs. He thought about how he could help his children into adulthood and beyond, especially if he were no longer around. That's why he started building a legacy portfolio. It was only once he had set up an account for his boys' future that he started to follow what he knew to be good advice—invest via asset allocation, tilt the portfolio toward equities (he had private markets covered through the family business), and don't look at the portfolio every day.

Gary was astonished by how things unfolded.

Because he had mentally and physically designated this bucket "money for the boys' future," he could use his wealth there differently than he could the wealth in his own portfolio, where so much emotion about losses or fear of failure played an outsized role. That's the mental accounting bias, which,

---

* Names and some personal details have been changed to protect identities.

you'll recall, is the way the mind is prepared to deploy money differently depending on how it was earned or what it is earmarked for.

Once he had made the journey to a Legacy Bucket for the boys, he then had the distance to look at the way he was managing his own money. By identifying the issue, he was halfway to solving it.

What is doubly interesting about Gary is that he and his family wouldn't think twice about the need to work with wealth managers or legal and accounting teams to pass on the family business to the next generation, but he was initially wary of doing so with his personal wealth.

For over a hundred years advisors have helped families provide for the next generation and pass on their businesses, not just with tax efficiency but in a way that also passes on the family values that made the business prosper in the first place. Yet before Gary forced himself to think from the perspective of the Legacy Bucket, he had mentally separated most of his personal investing from this professional know-how.

Every family transfers its wealth differently. One time we convened twenty billionaires at an event in Beijing. We focused on wealth transfers in several of the sessions. It was very emotional. No family did things the same way. Some tried to micromanage the succession planning and the splitting of assets. Others passed it all to one child with the obligation to look after the whole family, *Godfather*-style. Still others planned to sell everything and have trustees manage the wealth on behalf of their children. All the billionaires found value, however, in talking through their various ideas with their peers. No matter what your wealth level is, wealth transfers always require better family communication and involve a lot of work.

THE LEGACY BUCKET: HOW IT CAN FORCE YOU TO GROW AS AN INVESTOR

A client was constantly complaining to his UBS advisor how his private-equity investments in his Legacy Bucket weren't "doing anything" and were in fact "lousy."

His advisor, a straight shooter who was close to his client, finally said, "I don't care what happens with that bucket, because it's not your money.

It's going to be left to charities and your children. If it goes up 20 percent or down 20 percent, who cares? But I assure you, it's going to be your best-performing sector over time. That's what history tells us. So I don't want to hear about it."

Shortly thereafter, when everyone was shopping online during COVID, one of the client's private-equity investments "doing nothing" unloaded its Amazon-style warehouses, and the client got a five-times return on his money. He was stunned, saying, "Oh, man. Wow," finally realizing the private-equity investment was never "lousy." It just took a while to monetize the value that had been created.

MORE "HACKS" THAT CAN WORK FOR YOU

The 3L bucket system works because it mixes the "science" of asset allocation with the "art" of behavioral finance, and the resulting portfolios we craft deliver dependable emotional and financial returns relevant to our clients' lives.

Two partners in a firm sold their business for $100 million in 2019. The partners split the sale proceeds evenly. Wealth-management firms came in to see whether they could win their business, and one partner, after listening to our conservative Swiss pitch about the UBS Wealth Way, decided to go with us. The other partner went with a fabled US financial institution promising him access to their hot IPOs.

Then COVID hit. Our client came through the market tumult with flying colors and did extremely well using his Liquidity Bucket to finance his day-to-day expenses, while his Longevity and Legacy Buckets snapped up equities and other depressed assets that were temporarily underwater. That's when our phone rang. Two years after that initial beauty pageant, the other partner brought what was left of his $50 million over to UBS as well. I'd be hard pressed to find a better word-of-mouth example about the benefits of 3L.

Asset allocation and the 3L framework are powerful ideas to transform your relationship to your investments and move toward managing your wealth in a way that serves your life. Still, in the real world, working with clients, I have come to learn that ideas are nothing if you can't find a way to execute them. Even with the knowledge of the 3Ls, many clients still struggle to stick with the program. So, here is a "hack" advisors use to help clients who want to change their relationship to investing but still don't want to entirely give up trading stocks. These clients think they still have the ability to profit from trading, no matter what facts we show them about the averages. I sympathize, of course, because I have been there.

My advice if that description fits you as well: Don't eliminate the excitement, but limit its potential for derailing your long-term goals. Consider another set of buckets, which are "core" and "satellite" portfolios. Your core portfolio includes the things described in this book: your asset-allocation system and your 3L sub-asset allocations. Your satellite investment portfolio is the portion of your wealth you have set aside to add in short-term trades, where you can exercise your fear and greed demons without endangering the wealth you are managing according to the goals you figured out on your UBS Wealth Way journey. Some people think of it as entertainment money, or educational money, or money they are willing to lose—either on going for a big investment win or on buying short-term insurance if they have become convinced, for example, we are headed for an imminent crash.

Having a satellite portfolio isn't an official rule, because you don't need one to invest in our turbulent times or to understand the future of investing. There is also no right allocation to a satellite portfolio. It is, however, another practical tool to use on your wealth-management journey.

Bottom Line

I've just given you a window into what really goes on in a great wealth-management relationship. The UBS Wealth Way is a system that powerfully marries your personal money issues and evolving ambitions with an asset-allocation portfolio. The process of organizing your wealth around Liquidity, Longevity, and Legacy Buckets lowers anxiety about money, improves cash flow and returns, and can set you up nicely for long-term gains. Also consider if a core/satellite approach is something that might help you better manage your personal fear and greed.

ONCE FINANCIALLY SECURE, MASH UP THE RULES TO BECOME AN IMPACT INVESTOR

If you visit the Picasso Museum in Barcelona, Spain, you're immediately struck by how the artist first mastered, when just a young boy, all the classic techniques of drawing and painting, before he went on to reinvent art in the twentieth century. His father, his first teacher, was an academic painter.[1] It was only after perfecting all the basic techniques of painting under his father's tutelage that Pablo Picasso, at age twenty, began his Blue Period (1901–1904)[2] before creating, at age twenty-six, the never-before-seen painting style known as Cubism (1907–1914)[3]—smashing all previous definitions of art.

There is an investment equivalent. Many of our most sophisticated investors who have worked and invested their way to wealth are now finding great satisfaction in mashing up all the investment rules in this book and, in the process, creating the investment "Cubism" of our age.

It's called **impact investing**.

As the writer William Gibson famously said, "The future is already here. It's just not evenly distributed yet."[4] I see more and more of our ultra-high-net-worth clients thinking about moving toward impact investing, and this trend is something that can influence the way we all invest in the future.

There are a lot of definitions floating around to describe this way of investing. We, and many people I respect who do this for a living, define impact investing as making investments with the deliberate intention of generating positive social and environmental impact—that you can measure—alongside an investment's traditional financial return.[5] This definition is clear to me, unlike some other more nebulous terms like *environmental, social, and governance (ESG) investing.*[6]

ESG investing is usually explained as investors consciously directing their capital to what they perceive are companies that are responsible in their approach to environmental, social, and governance issues. Fair or not, ESG investing has become a term loaded down with ideological and political baggage. *Impact investing*, meanwhile, often takes place in private companies where investors can personally help drive game-changing outcomes beyond what otherwise would have happened.

Rozett Phillips is a director at the GIBS Business School at the University of Pretoria in South Africa.[7] Roze, in her early fifties, is a futurist, a strategic thinker in that nexus where human ingenuity and technology meet, and she is fully committed to a portfolio 100 percent devoted to having a positive impact on the world. The exception to her rule, she said, is the legacy holding she owns in her former employer, Accenture, the global IT consulting firm.

How did she become a fully signed-up impact investor?

Roze grew up in Cape Town, South Africa, on the wrong side of the tracks during the apartheid era. "I was Black, a girl, African, and poor," she said. "The first years of my life, I thought I was cursed. I couldn't tolerate my lack of choices."[8]

But she was blessed with an unusual father, a self-trained soil technician who helped farmers earn better crop yields. Extremely bright but with little formal education of his own, and even fewer prospects, her frustrated father became an alcoholic, explaining why to this day his oldest daughter doesn't drink. But he was also a good man, determined to help his children advance beyond his own limits. "My father never ordered me into the kitchen, as so many fathers did," Roze said.

In fact, no matter what drinking occurred the night before, her father took her every other Saturday to the local library so she could find her own escape route out of the strictures of apartheid. Books and the joy of learning became Roze's means of escape, and through hard work and scholarships, she fought the odds, crossed the tracks, and finally reached the land of opportunity. Roze became a medical doctor. After a few years in practice, she changed course and earned an MBA and an advanced diploma in futurism and wound up having a significant corporate career in South Africa.

Roze worked almost twenty years for Accenture's local company before losing out in a power struggle to become its next CEO, then went on to become the head of human resources at the pan-African bank Absa while also serving as a member of the financial conglomerate's executive committee. Her father, until he died prematurely from alcohol-related diseases, always took great joy and pride in Roze's professional and personal accomplishments. "His last words to me were 'Thank you,'" she said.

Roze's journey in life—toward choice, toward opportunity, toward Africa's future, toward the empowerment of women—inexorably and logically led her to becoming 99.9 percent invested in an impact portfolio. It's what makes the most sense to her, emotionally and intellectually.

But the futurist in her also insists it's a smart financial move.

Roze likes reminding impact investors and fellow thought leaders that 60 percent of the world's arable land is in Africa.[9] Furthermore, the continent has the globe's youngest population, with 70 percent of sub-Saharan Africa under the age of thirty.[10] These geographic and demographic truths mean that there are real economic opportunities for the people of the continent, regardless of what images the news headlines evoke.

Anyone analyzing where to invest in the *future*, not the past, must have Africa on its radar, Roze insists. That is why she has, in part to honor her father, created a program that teaches local farmers how to use smartphone data to reduce the risk of crop failure, through monitoring weather patterns, learning about the latest yield-enhancing crop technologies, and tracking global commodity prices. The program is meant to significantly increase the farmers' chances of survival and help them earn the highest possible financial returns. "Food security is so important for the world," Roze pointed out, "and yet security for farmers is terrible."

Other investment opportunities in Africa are to be found, she said, in building green infrastructure projects, such as solar-driven power plants and other renewable energy so the continent can leapfrog the legacy energy infrastructure hampering developed nations; and in investing in local medical and health-care companies, particularly those doing research in the frontline field of viruses. She is also passionately committed to investing in women-run businesses, empowering and unleashing the thwarted human capital sitting at the heart of her beloved Africa.

Roze's portfolio is similarly invested in what she calls "future-focused industries," largely through equity investments. Specifically, she has invested in renewable energy; in biotech and companies using technology to address issues of aging and related health-care services; and in emerging technologies shaping the future of agricultural production.

Meanwhile, in her philanthropic endeavors, Roze uses microloans, grants, and mentorship programs to empower women entrepreneurs and the young, but even here she finds interesting crossover investment opportunities. She has, for example, provided some pre-seed capital to young Black entrepreneurs incubated at IBM. In exchange for her early financial support, she is entitled to a 30 percent discount on IPO shares, should this group of young dreamers one day get their business off the ground.

Pretty clever. Roze is using all the sound financial principles we've already discussed. She is investing in the big themes of our age, and she is investing in the issues that governments have prioritized and where they are investing public money. But she then mashes things up and *harnesses* her own emotional and behavioral-finance issues—the opposite of removing those trigger points from her investment process, as we've been advocating—to drive in a disciplined way some measurable real-world change alongside healthy financial returns, which together give her a psychic "do-good" ROI.

Roze is basically using the techniques we identified in our UBS Wealth Way described in chapter 6—using her personal and emotional particulars to up her investment game—but she's doing a supercharged version through impact investing.

HOW WE GOT HERE

I am who I am—a history buff—which is why I'm going to use this space to explain how this twenty-first-century investment phenomenon came about, while also showing how I went from being a harsh critic of impact investing to a convert.

As I've emphatically stated, I am fully committed to asset allocation, because it prevents an investor from messing up their portfolio results with emotion-driven impulses. But having dealt with their emotional baggage through a sound investment system that steadily ratchets up their wealth over time, as we have outlined, the people who can then put the emotion *back* into their investment process are pointing to the future of investing for all of us.

There is a major difference between what these sophisticated clients are doing and what many of us do when we allow money-related emotions to rule our investment decisions. Most of us allow negative and self-destructive emotional impulses to *unconsciously* dictate our investment choices. **Our impact investor clients are, in contrast, *consciously* channeling their emotions to invest wisely and for positive impact, all within the context of a clear investment strategy.** Within the UBS Wealth Way process, you can think of them as having mastered the Liquidity and Longevity Buckets and now are focusing their excitement on their Legacy Bucket.

I now know that those who take this route to investing graduate from managing their portfolio to managing their wealth, and that delivers a whole different kind of return on investment.

Well, this dummy didn't get it at first.

I was initially highly critical of impact investing, which seemed "feel good" and charity-driven more than a serious means of professionally and successfully managing money. But my forward-thinking clients forced me to rethink my position and eventually opened my eyes to the powerful ideas underlying this market approach. As result, I had one of the most rewarding experiences of my financial career.

IMPACT INVESTING ARRIVES ON THE SCENE

Since my UBS job includes serving our ultra-high-net-worth clients, it has always required a lot of one-on-one conversations with the most accomplished wealth creators around the globe. One of the first things I noticed in my new role: when I asked billionaire clients if they wanted the equivalent of chocolate or vanilla ice cream, they often replied, "Why not both?" Billionaires really do have a different mindset, and I filed that observation away in the back of my head until I needed it—which arrived sooner than I imagined.

In January 2015, seven months after I became the chief investment officer, I went to the World Economic Forum in Davos. I had due diligence to perform in my new role, and I specifically wanted to learn more about the UN's Sustainable Development Goals[11] that were in the process of being publicly announced and rolled out with much fanfare.

The UN's Sustainable Development Goals are seventeen objectives to provide everyone, particularly the disenfranchised, with economic opportunities all while supporting economic growth broadly—including closing the gap on social needs in education, health care, and employment—but doing so with as little harm as possible to the environment. The stated end goal: stamp out poverty and protect the planet by 2030.

Honestly, I thought it was crazy that the UN had highlighted seventeen goals ranging from climate change to income equality, while stating these goals needed *trillions of dollars of investment a year* from the private sector to hit the UN's targets.[12] My gut reaction: that was way too many goals to drive effective action, and the amounts of capital necessary to achieve these goals was simply beyond any nation or group of nations to provide.

While the markets could not care less what the UN thinks about climate change,[13] they do care, as we've noted, about what governments are subsidizing and what people want to buy. A UBS study we conducted at the time revealed that 69 percent of consumers were willing to pay more for products from firms with strong ethical practices that matched their personal views, while 71 percent were consciously avoiding products from firms with negative ESG reputations.[14] This was a trend I had to stay on top of.

I was just starting to learn about this area of growing interest for UBS's wealthiest clients, and, keeping an open mind, I ambled over to a small Davos gathering to hear Sir Ronald Cohen speak about impact investing.

Sir Ronald, when only in his twenties, cofounded Apax Partners, Europe's first and arguably most influential venture-capital and private-equity firm.[15] He did that until he officially retired from Apax in 2005, at age sixty, but, in truth, he was simply launching his next career.[16]

Five years before retiring, Sir Ronald was asked by the UK Treasury to "look at poverty with a more entrepreneurial eye" and come back to them with his insights.[17] The question he asked himself from then on: How can capital be invested in twenty-first-century charitable organizations to help them become more effective, the same way venture capital originally unleashed our era's tech entrepreneurs? To that end, Sir Ronald cofounded Social Finance, an NGO focused on using innovative financing to tackle social problems.[18]

In 2010, Sir Ronald's nonprofit launched the world's first social impact bond (SIB). It was a strange-looking beast: the Peterborough Social Impact Bond raised £5 million from seventeen foundations like the J. Paul Getty Jr. Charitable Trust and the Rockefeller Foundation.[19] The bond's proceeds were used to finance a rehabilitation pilot program at the Peterborough prison in Cambridgeshire, an experimental project meant to cut recidivism by helping just-released prisoners build new lives.

The financial logic behind the bond was that repeat offenders cost society a small fortune. If the Peterborough bond helped rehabilitate career criminals and cut the rate of reconvictions, then some of the incarceration funds saved by the government could arguably be returned to the bondholders financing the rehabilitation effort. If, over several years, reconvictions of the one thousand released Peterborough prison inmates in the pilot project fell below the 7.5 percent reduction target set by the Ministry of Justice, then the seventeen bond investors would get back all their initial capital, plus a return equal to 3 percent per annum over the life of the investment. It was a bargain for the UK government—if repeat offending was genuinely reduced.[20]

In July 2017 the results of the Peterborough Bond came in. The prisoner rehabilitation project financed by the bondholders reduced reoffending by 9 percent compared to a control group, which comfortably exceeded the 7.5 percent reduction the Ministry of Justice had set as a minimum target. The seventeen bondholders got all their principle back, plus 3 percent per annum.[21]

HOW GOVERNMENT SHAPED OUR GIVING

There's an important backstory here, once again bringing us to that nexus where private enterprise and government intervention meet. Like many great crises in history, World War I spurred a massive increase of government involvement in the "free" economy. In the US, for example, the Revenue Act of 1918 raised the top tax rate to 77 percent to help pay for the war.[22] But it also established the tax-free charitable bequest system that has since produced the tax-exempt charitable foundations we have today.

In the simplest terms, while it levied sizable income taxes and estate taxes on the nation's citizens, the US tax code also evolved toward providing those same citizens relief by encouraging them to reduce their high taxes by donating money to good causes through a tax-free foundation. Family foundations, the vehicles wealthy families set up to channel their charitable giving, can hire and pay staff and even earn money tax-free,[23] provided they pay out 5 percent of their endowment every year to charitable works.[24]

This has led many foundations to have two teams of specialists. The first is a donor team giving the money away. The second team are investment professionals, trying to make more than 5 percent a year through the charity's investments. If they are successful year after year, adding wealth faster than the 5 percent per annum the grant team is spending on charitable projects, the charity can essentially live forever.

Recognizing that their core mission is to give money away—while also understanding they need high-quality financial management for their endowment—many charities outsource their investment portfolio to professionals and keep the grant-writing team in-house. But this split between the mission of the charity and the mission of its endowment managers can clash and sometimes badly does.

Imagine your family foundation is devoted to cleaning up the polluted seas, and one day you discover your investment-management team has invested heavily into the cruise-liner industry, often perceived as significant polluters of our oceans.[25] These sorts of conflicts happen frequently. When I was in college, there were many campus protests arguing that universities like Princeton or Harvard should force investment committees to divest from South Africa and supporting apartheid in any shape or form, even when the investment committee was trying to increase the university's endowment.

Well, that's how "screening" and ESG investing got started in the 1960s.[26] In our hypothetical foundation case, you probably would get your foundation's board of directors to change the investment guidelines so that your endowment manager could sell the cruise-liner stocks and from then on exclude from your portfolio any companies—from oil tankers to commercial fisheries—that were remotely associated with polluting, degrading, or depleting the oceans.

This passive screening out of specific sectors or stocks from a portfolio was basically what constituted the ESG industry until a decade ago, when, among other innovations, Sir Ronald and a few others came up with impact investing.

What Sir Ronald Cohen and his ilk were starting to do with impact bonds and impact investing was upsetting to many in the foundation world, because it blurred the line between the investing team and the charitable work. That was threatening for the grant-writing team, who relied on the steady income generated by the managers running the endowment. Yet, increasingly, many families began to see impact investing as a way of adding leverage to their foundations' missions.

Instead of investing in ordinary stocks and bonds, what if the investment team was making investments in companies that *also* addressed the charity's mission?

That is having both your chocolate *and* your vanilla ice cream. It's why I intuitively knew impact investing would become widely appealing, not just for billionaires with a billionaire's mindset, but potentially also for those who don't have a billion dollars to give away to charity. If done right, even a modest-sized foundation with a few million dollars in assets could, through this method, have far more impact than simply giving away 5 percent of its endowment each year.

The technique allowed the foundation to leverage its *entire balance sheet* for the causes it most cared about, by investing in goal-relevant companies or projects in a way that *also* juiced the foundation's endowment for the future. Our hypothetical marine-focused foundation might, for example, use this mindset to invest in Danish and Israeli tech start-ups creating commercial products and services from the marine bacteria that are known to thrive by eating up ocean-floating oil slicks[27]—potentially earning the foundation decent returns in the future *and* furthering its maritime cause.

Now, when I ambled across the snowy streets of Davos in 2015 to hear Sir Ronald talk, this interesting finance-philanthropy development was happening at the micro level, in a financial-service and charity niche. But it was just starting to get leveraged at the macro level.

The UN's Sustainable Development Goals were an example of that.[28] The UN directives meant that individual governments, consumers, and institutional investors would increasingly strong-arm corporations to integrate sustainability risk and opportunity considerations into their for-profit pursuits, where relevant to their business model. Whether or not I approved on political or philosophical grounds, as a wealth manager I knew this was something my team and I needed to understand if we wanted to make money for our clients and serve their needs.

My immediate observation when I entered the stuffy room in Davos was that Sir Ronald and his ideas were electrifying the audience of wealthy families, asset managers, and government officials sitting spellbound around him. They were listening with rapt attention, reinforcing my belief that we were having a "chocolate-and-vanilla ice cream" moment.

But the more I heard, the more my inner voice started squawking dissent. I was thinking, *Impact bonds are a great idea, but Sir Ronald Cohen, one of the great investors of our times, is trying to have impact launching $5 million deals at a time when the UN says we need trillions of dollars to address the issues of our age. There's a disconnect here.*

Just then, someone in the audience asked Sir Ronald if SIBs were philanthropy or investing.

"Well, it's a great thing," he said. "It's both, you know."

I winced. The comment drove me crazy.

I was in the business of investing, of making money for clients so they could provide for their families and their futures. I knew I'd never be asked to manage people's retirement money if they thought I was going to give their money away. Nobody's going to put their retirement fund into a philanthropic exercise, and I couldn't blame them for thinking that way. The idea that you could have both chocolate and vanilla was an intriguing notion in the abstract, but casually mixing investing with philanthropy would never draw the trillions of private-investment capital required to achieve the UN's goals.

I liked the idea of SIBs, but I just knew the idea was not big enough to tackle the ambitions of the UN's Sustainable Development Goals.

Back in Zurich, I started talking to people to understand what I had just seen and to help me think it through. One of the smart people I sought out for help was Simon Smiles, a friend and colleague who was the chief investment officer for our ultra-high-net-worth client services.[29] Simon and I kicked around ideas on how we could integrate UBS's existing ESG franchise with some of the big changes that were going on in our office and in the world at large.

Simon dug around and came back confirming my worst suspicions about Sir Ronald's SIBs. The average size of SIB issues was a paltry $3.2 million each.[30]

But the impact-investing movement itself was not so easily dismissed. When, in 2017, the Peterborough prison bond experiment concluded successfully, the SIB sector was officially and formally launched. According to the Brookings Institution's data, a decade after the Peterborough Bond debuted, there were 235 social and development impact bonds launched in thirty-three countries across the globe, in sectors ranging from health care to employment.

Impressive, at first blush.

But the total capital invested in all SIBs combined a decade later amounted to just $463 million.[31] That was not moving the needle on the UN's goals. You just can't change the trajectory of the twenty-first century's existential problems with $5 million investments.

So we were right to point out back in 2015 that SIB's scalability issues were a problem and an impossible bottleneck for a massive outfit like UBS, then managing almost $3 trillion in invested assets.[32]

MY LIGHT-BULB MOMENT

Around the same time, I was talking regularly with Bard Geesaman, my brilliant doctor friend whom I had met when we both lived in Harvard's Quincy House.[33] Bard called me up during this period, when I was trying to figure out impact investing, and provocatively said, "Now is the time to launch an oncology fund." Bard was not only giving me and UBS a heads-up that there were transformative breakthroughs happening in biomedics but also doing good by his employer, which was in the business of finding investors who could help finance promising new biotech companies.

Since leaving Harvard, Bard had become a serial entrepreneur who not only had launched a health-care-software firm but had also become a specialist in genome data analysis. When he called me in 2015 and 2016, he was working for MPM Capital,[34] a firm that specialized in converting research breakthroughs in academia into profitable new companies.[35] MPM Capital was among the most successful biotech venture-capital fund managers in the world.[36]

MPM's executive team knew their business. Bard reported directly to Ansbert Gadicke, a German MD who was MPM's founder and had launched a series of successful bio-medical companies.[37] George Daley, another old friend from Harvard, was on MPM's science advisory board and on the threshold of being appointed the new dean of Harvard Medical School.[38]

In these calls Bard pointed out that there was a long bubble in oncology investing that roughly ran from 2000 to 2012. Spurred by the hype that flowed from the massive project to map the human genome, which finally concluded in 2003, tons of venture capital flowed into early-stage treatments in a grab bag of diseases.[39] The hoped-for results never materialized, and the money was wasted.

But things began to change around 2012, when immuno-oncology breakthroughs finally started translating into novel therapeutics. There was suddenly a realization that targeted drugs could not only treat cancer but also *cure* cancer by activating the body's immune system to recognize the cancer cells and eliminate them.

We were, in short, at the dawn of a new industry called immuno-oncology, and large amounts of capital were needed to get the sector off the ground. This was a trend that squarely fit inside the digitalization and demographics megatrends we've already mentioned, and this sort of med-tech space was an area in which governments were seeking breakthroughs and encouraging investment. In short, the oncology fund in concept ticked all my twenty-first-century wealth-creation "new rules" boxes.

But it did much more than that.

A UBS fund that made money for clients *and* cured cancers?

This fund ticked a couple of highly personal and emotional boxes as well. The sheer possibility had me thinking of a painful death from cancer I had witnessed that had a profound effect on me, and I wondered whether getting this cancer impact fund off the ground would help turn some of my personal poisons into medicine.

But even putting these private issues aside, this was potentially my own Reese's Peanut Butter Cup moment, at least from a financial-industry perspective. This was how UBS might put the tiny finance niche known as impact investing together with the bank's massive distribution machinery to create something entirely different, just like Reese's had put chocolate and peanut butter together to create a bestseller.

I turned to Simon. "We can do this. I think this is how we can have an impact fund."

But first we needed UBS to sign off on our experiment.

I told my boss, Jürg Zeltner, about the impact-investing oncology fund we wanted to create. He was intrigued when I said that Sir Ronald Cohen got folks excited with his £5 million experiment, but we were going to add a few zeros to that.

"We want to commit five *billion* dollars of client capital to impact investments over five years," I said. "We're going to define impact investments as having a measurable bottom line on the investment side, but we're also going to set a positive social or environmental goal for each allocation ahead of time, and we're going to try to measure our impact in that space."

It would be a vanilla-and-chocolate allocation of resources, both a financially attractive investment and one that could drive meaningful social change. By putting out a $5 billion idea, we wanted to put the investment world on high alert to start developing impact-investing funds for our clients.

Jürg instantly got it, floated the idea with other UBS executives—there were no internal objections—and then he and I flew to Boston. Jürg wanted to learn firsthand whether this cancer-curing biotech miracle that MPM was talking up, and my idea of creating a UBS impact fund around this hot new sector, had a real shot at success.

MPM's founder, Ansbert Gadicke, hosted a dinner in our honor in his art-filled home overlooking Boston's Back Bay. The best and the brightest scientists in the immuno-oncology field, including Nobel Prize winners, were in attendance. Remember, I started getting involved in impact investing because it was what my clients wanted, and it was my duty as UBS's chief investment officer to deliver solutions that matched their preferences. It was not because I was an experienced impact investor, and when we flew to Boston to kick MPM's tires, figuring out how an oncology fund could become a scalable impact investment was still just a vague formation in my head.

That night I became a convert to impact investing. I experienced firsthand how this approach could not only increase personal wealth by tapping the direction markets were moving in today's social and economic environment but also "enrich" clients in a larger sense by doing well and doing good.

Ansbert made sure Jürg and I were handed glasses of wine before he walked us around and introduced us to the who's who of leading scientists, venture capitalists, and biotech CEOs filling the room. At one point, I found myself standing next to the Nobel Prize–winning physiologist H. Robert Horvitz.[40]

"Bob," I said, "if we do this fund, can we cure cancer?"

"We can cure *some* cancers," Horvitz replied.

The conviction in his voice was unmistakable. I looked around the room, took in all these brilliant and high-powered people—the scientists, tech CEOs, venture capitalists, even the head of UBS Wealth Management—who had gathered at my request.

That was the moment.

One minute I was thinking I had gotten so far over my skis I was going to fall flat on my face; and then, suddenly, I was in the right place, at the right time, with the right people and the right skills to catalyze a change, to make a difference.

To have impact.

In the small hours of the morning—when I was a young man in graduate school—my mother had released her final death rattle before dying in my arms from pancreatic cancer. In that Back Bay moment, it felt like all my life experience—the good, the bad, the ugly—had suddenly come together. I had an opportunity to create significant wealth for my clients *and* cure cancers, and I could imagine no better way to honor my mother.

It was a thrilling experience.

"Then we should do it," I said.

STORMING THE IMPACT-INVESTING BANDWAGON

We flew back to Zurich that weekend, and on Monday, with Jürg's support, I asked Simon to get going on the approval process of our Oncology Impact Fund effort. Simon was an amazing evangelist with strong UBS friendships all around the world, the perfect person to generate the internal momentum necessary for launch. But the truth is, when colleagues heard what we were doing, they loved it. So many people went the extra mile—staying late to finish the legal documents, setting up client meetings, talking to the press—all the things required to get a conservative firm to take a leap into the unknown.

In my view, MPM channeled their inner Jerry Maguire, the sports agent of the big screen, to come up with a revolutionary new way to structure a fund to appeal to investors seeking returns plus have the potential to create large-scale change.

On the investment side, Ansbert developed a hybrid public-private investment mandate, with the public-equity portion of the fund managed by MPM's Christiana "Chris" Bardon. This was designed to address some of the issues clients often have with private investments, such as the "J-Curve," which is the tendency for a fund to experience negative returns in the early years as the private investments are being deployed.

More innovative still was the alignment of the fund's structure with the targeted impact coming from the underlying drug investments. Ansbert designed the fund so a portion of the management fees that were earned (if it generated positive returns) were donated to two charities that were aiding basic research and providing access to cancer care in the developing world.[41] But the fund would also secure an agreement that if any of the drugs developed by the fund were ultimately sold to pharma companies, those firms would donate 1 percent of the drug revenues to the same charities.[42] So the sale and commercialization of a $100 billion drug would translate into a billion-dollar donation to charitable organizations aligned with the same cancer mission. What's more, this 1 percent rule could turn out to be a model that was adopted more broadly in the pharma industry, potentially unlocking billions more for positive change.

After Simon took MPM executives on an investor roadshow around the world in spring 2016, we closed the UBS Oncology Impact Fund (OIF). Clients worldwide invested $471 million in the fund.[43] Its purpose was to not only invest in early-stage cancer treatments and make money for our clients but also create impact through both the lifesaving drugs and—by means of the structural feature I described above—funding philanthropic donations.

We initially didn't think our Asian clients would be that interested in an impact fund, due to their supposed preference for short-term trading, but the oncology fund uncovered a passionate interest in the idea of impact investing, which was growing in the region. The fund was so well structured that they piled in. Raising the money was an incredible accomplishment for an early-stage venture-capital fund, let alone an impact-VC fund. It was not just the largest of its kind at UBS, but at the time the largest social impact fund ever devoted to a single cause.[44]

This single, first-time UBS Impact Fund was more capital than the entire SIB market after ten years of development.[45]

All this was possible because our Oncology Impact Fund was first and foremost a classic investment fund built to make money for our clients, but it also had a "social good" factor built into its design from the ground up.

This returns-first approach was an important impact-investing differentiator, not just for UBS's clients, but, arguably, also for the nascent sector at large.

By mid-2020, four years after launch, the UBS Oncology Impact Fund had a 63 percent rise in value, to $773 million, while its net internal rate of return (IRI), a metric used to determine a return inside of a fund, was 28 percent per annum.[46] So it was no surprise that with these results, UBS was able to successfully launch a second $850 million oncology fund in fall 2021, bringing the total investments in our impact cancer funds up to $1.32 billion.[47] Our approach to impact investing struck a chord with clients. With the success of OIF and other funds, we surpassed our vision of $5 billion in five years.

There is, alas, a bitter dose of tragedy in this story.

Both Jürg Zeltner[48] and Simon Smiles[49] died unexpectedly from virulent forms of brain cancer, in 2020 and 2022, respectively. I think of them all the time, amazed that these two men made this oncology fund happen just before they were diagnosed with fatal cancers themselves. The impact fund they were instrumental in building left a profound legacy. It gets us to the real purpose of living and investing and deciding what to do with our ingenuity and money while we are alive and can still shape events.

One of the great joys about getting older—after working hard to cover your financial needs and a little bit more—is that it seems to get easier to revisit these kinds of extraordinary life moments. You have more experience, you know more people, and you're often better at cajoling others to share your enthusiasm and purpose.

This brings us to the latter stages of wealth creation.

I don't have it all figured out yet, but I have learned a lot from the people who are farther along on this journey than I am, and I have seen a pattern that runs solidly through the talented clients I serve. Most of them, at least the high-level wealth creators I admire, eventually seek to reimagine the power of their investing so that their lives and their wealth create significant additional value. This observation has transformed the way I think about wealth and has even made me rethink the second half of my own life.

Impact investing plays a powerful role in that because it's based on the idea that our wealth is not just what we have in our bank accounts but also includes our "off balance sheet" relationships to our family, friends, work, community, and ultimately even the planet we live on. That's a modern wealth-management concept, and it brings us to our next chapter, which is how we are likely to be investing in the future.

Bottom Line

Impact investing is, for the moment, largely restricted to the upper echelons of the wealth pyramid, because the ultra-high-net-worth have the wherewithal to source and vet a portfolio of impact investments.

We in the wealth-management industry are trying to make more compelling opportunities available to a wider audience. We know from research that there is pent-up demand for quality impact-investing financial solutions. In the interest of full disclosure, I must add that UBS is playing a significant role in trying to make more socially and environmentally impactful investments available to a wider public. Our Oncology Impact Funds are examples.

Here are some of the things we are doing that you can shadow, if moving toward an impactful investment portfolio is of interest to you.

Debt. Government debt, usually in the form of US Treasuries, is the anchor of many balanced investment portfolios. In some portfolios, however, we swap out classic government debt with bonds issued by multilateral development banks (MDB). The World Bank and multilateral institutions such as the Asia Development Bank or the European Bank for Reconstruction and Development are all MDBs, and their mandates are generally to support social and economic development in developing nations, prioritizing goals like ending poverty and boosting prosperity. They do so by financing everything from producing electric cars and scooters in Vietnam[50] to building a highway across economically distressed Georgia that could serve as an East–West European logistics corridor.[51] Investing in such bonds is directly buying what the government is buying.

MDB bonds are in many ways more attractive than US debt, as they are both safer and offer a better yield.[52] The World Bank bonds are backed by the agency's 189 member states, including the G7, and have a credit rating of AAA. US government debt was, in contrast, downgraded to AA+ back in 2011. The thing to consider is that the multilateral bank bond market isn't as liquid as US Treasuries, which is why MDB bonds offer slightly more yield in compensation. But the market is still investable and on par with the corporate-debt markets. Retail investors can make an asset allocation in this MDB space by investing passively via the FTSE World Broad Investment-Grade USD Multilateral Development Bank Bond Capped Index,[53] or through four different currency versions of ETFs tracking the Solactive UBS Global MDBB USD 25 Percent Issuer Capped Index.[54]

In some portfolios, classic corporate bonds are replaced with green bonds, which are corporate bonds like any other, but whose proceeds are earmarked for a specific climate- or environment-related project. That could be, for example, a corporate-wide project to lower the firm's energy bill by installing solar panels at all its factories across the globe. The total volume of green bonds, social bonds, and sustainability bonds (collectively known as *GSSS bonds*) now stands at $4.7 trillion.[55] There are numerous green-bond funds available in the market.[56] Of course, at UBS we have our own selection process for the funds we recommend to our clients.

Equities. There is a growing universe of accessible impact-investing financial products trading in public markets, available to retail investors in the US and globally. These funds offer lower minimum investments, compelling fees, and greater liquidity. Such public-equity impact funds tend to drive positive change through engagement with the target company's management, urging them to make social or environmental improvements where there is a clear connection to improved financial performance.

RULE 8

ALIGN YOURSELF WITH THE FUTURE OF WEALTH MANAGEMENT

How will people be investing in the middle of the twenty-first century?

Pol-Lin Hsu is in the business of producing an innovative new generation of artificial hearts.[1] Not only is her work a variation of our demographics megatrend, but her approach also gets the kind of impact-investing mindset spreading among other clients as well.

She told us, "Every penny you spend is a vote toward the world you want to live in. I think investment is at one level just a redistribution of resources. Money is money and really means nothing. But if you put your money on the thing you want to happen, then the world will move in that direction, and I believe that is what my investors and I are doing."

That's an eloquent summary of the power and draw of impact investing, and just one reason why it is likely to move more into the mainstream of the financial services industry as we go deeper into our tumultuous future.

Let's be honest: the horsemen of the apocalypse—pestilence, war, famine, and death, among other things—have, in recent years, slowed or even reversed the progress we thought we were making toward achieving the UN's 2030 Agenda for Sustainable Development.

But our clients are not giving up. At the cutting edge, they build on the investment themes discussed in this book and take them to the next level by finding ways to have a measurable positive impact on society and the planet through their work and investing. I am inspired by their stories not just because of this impact but because they have cracked the code for making investing not only financially rewarding but spiritually rewarding.

They are managing their wealth, not just their investments. Unlike me when I started my investment journey, they are not adrenaline junkies riding the highs and lows of picking stocks, watching them soar and crash on a daily basis. They are instead investing for the long term, with purpose and passion. I hope their stories inspire you to move in this direction with your own wealth journey.

So here are profiles of five very different wealth creators from around the globe, figures who are all, each in their own way, pointing us toward the future. These men and women are already creating and reimagining their businesses from the ground up, so they are, in effect, impact entrepreneurs.

They are tackling the great themes of our age, investing alongside governments, infusing their money-making skills with greater purpose, changing their old way of doing business to meet the needs of the twenty-first century—and making money in the process.

INNER RESERVES

UBS client Pavle Matijevic, an oil-and-gas engineer in Vienna, loved his work but was depleted.[2] Over decades, he'd built a classic and very profitable oil-and-gas consulting business on his technical expertise in underground-reservoir management. But as he approached his sixtieth year, his inner code no longer allowed him to continue working the old way. The final straw was a 2020 McKinsey report that indicated the oil and gas sector directly or indirectly produced 42 percent of the globe's greenhouse gas emissions.[3] Given the state of the world, he felt he had to reinvent how he operated his business.

Pavle set about reimagining his beloved energy industry, where he had been working since he was thirteen, when for the first time he spent his summer vacation toiling in Libya's oil and gas fields. His dream was to turn the oil and gas industry into a hyper-efficient showcase for net-zero carbon emissions while also ushering in our green-energy future by solving one of the emerging sector's most intractable problems—energy storage.

"What the Ukraine conflict has brought to the fore is that net-zero ambitions and the transition to green energy are also about improving energy security," Pavle said. "Relying on a small number of nondomestic suppliers for energy is no longer acceptable due to geopolitical risk and uncertainty."

Pavle is a natural systems thinker, and the transformational journey at his company, PM Lucas, began when he wanted to understand where precisely the environmental damage was happening in his industry, whether that occurred during drilling, within the reservoir, or while oil and gas were making their way through aboveground pipes to a processing plant.

Using a molecule-by-molecule carbon-tracking accounting system his company invented, then constantly checking his tech-simulator results in real time through the elaborate reservoir, physical plant, and satellite-monitoring observations, Pavle and his team discovered that all the industry's flaring and drilling accounted for just 36 percent of the environmental harm being done by the industry.[4]

The biggest environmental damage, 64 percent of the total, was not from CO_2 emissions but methane gas escaping unnoticed from faulty valves and separators at the aboveground pipes and plants.[5] "It was terrifying," he said. "We had no idea how bad it was. No clue."

Pavle took this molecule-by-molecule data and designed—using new technologies and services from Siemens, SAP, and Amazon Web Services—a method of making fossil fuel extraction carbon neutral at the source while also eliminating the more serious environmental damage occurring during oil and gas's long journey to the end customer. His fully integrated high-tech system doesn't just monitor and report harmful emissions but also has verification and mitigation procedures built into its process.

His net-zero vision for the industry is this: Leaky, antiquated pipes and valves are replaced with digitalized versions that efficiently monitor and prevent from escaping the methane that is now carelessly and silently leaking into the atmosphere. The practice of flaring—a nineteenth-century technique of reducing the pressures destabilizing a reservoir by burning off excess gas in the atmosphere—is also eliminated by capturing the pressure-building gas down in the reservoir, bringing it to the surface, then selling it in the open market.

Meanwhile, CO_2 emissions produced during downstream and upstream operations are pumped back into underground reservoirs, both neutralizing today's harmful atmospheric effects and jump-starting the underground biological and chemical reactions that ultimately produce green methane, which can profitably be sold in the future.

In 2018, Pavle partnered with Germany's Siemens, itself committed to making its sprawling business a sustainability showcase. Siemens's more than twenty thousand program developers and its industrial might would help Pavle scale up his fully integrated system, he figured, and that same year the partnership began working with a troubled independent British producer operating oil and gas fields in Kazakhstan, a country where Pavle himself worked for many years and had made a name for himself as an on-the-ground problem solver.

The British firm was buried in debt and desperately needed to become more efficient. Pavle is keen to point out that reaching net zero through his system makes the producer 100 percent efficient—no oil or gas product is wasted or leaked into the atmosphere—and that should be the goal of every well-managed energy company.

It should also be the cornerstone of every government's energy-security plan.

Pavle estimates that the oil and gas industry currently has a maximum efficiency rate of 70 percent, the rest of its production needlessly lost during the extraction, transmission, and refining processes. One lesson of the

Russia-Ukraine war is that no country can afford to let 30 percent of its oil and gas supplies leak mindlessly into the atmosphere, which means net-zero ambitions and energy security are now inextricably linked.

PM Lucas's valve-by-valve and pipe-by-pipe real-time data collection of the Kazakhstan operation revealed where oil and gas molecules were escaping, raw simulator data that was physically checked at the plant and reconfirmed through satellite images. His simulator predictor worked just as he'd hoped, Pavle said, and it quickly became clear the independent British producer never would have become financially distressed if it had just been able to trap and sell all the methane its operation had been losing.

Emboldened by his proof-of-concept results, Pavle advocated for a complete restructuring and recapitalization of energy companies so that firms can meet their net-zero emission goals by 2050—not just talk about them—and become hyper-efficient.

That's no small ambition. The IEA figures that energy-industry investments in this transformation will have to rise from the $2 trillion spent annually in recent years to $5 trillion annually by 2030, before dipping slightly to $4.5 trillion annually by 2050.[6]

Such a radical industry transformation does not come cheap. But neither does maintaining the status quo. Forget the cost of fossil fuel's ongoing environmental damage. Due to the Russia-Ukraine war, the EU alone absorbed $1 trillion in higher energy costs during just the early months of the war.

Pavle is convinced the industry's tech-driven net-zero transformation will produce a handsome ROI for energy companies and their financial backers. Trapping and selling the 30 percent of oil and gas that is currently escaping into the atmosphere will alone produce trillions of dollars in additional revenue. By Pavle's calculations, just three to four years of investment, including replacing old pipe valves with state-of-the-art equipment, will eliminate 80 percent of the industry's harmful emissions. "Let me be blunt," he said. "We do not need to look for more oil. We just need to produce it and use it more efficiently."

Time will tell whether the energy industry will use its resources to reengineer its fossil fuel process, as he hopes, or whether it will use that capital to transition directly to clean energy. The picture is constantly changing. The arrival of AI is creating huge demands for electricity, as we've noted, and that demand will probably prolong fossil fuel's stay of execution. The fossil fuel industry has responded to these forces by sending a satellite into orbit to help monitor the industry's methane leaks around the world, the exact direction that Pavle wants the industry to head.[7]

But Pavle has a fallback business strategy too.

His mind constantly restless and imagining new systems, Pavle tapped his deep knowledge of underground reservoirs to solve a major problem hamstringing the transition to green energy: the battery or storage problem.

Since the Russia-Ukraine war began, the EU has been massively investing in its green-energy infrastructure. Renewable energies supplied 23 percent of the EU's energy needs in 2022, and the European Commission has a new binding target of 42.5 percent for 2030, with a goal of reaching 45 percent.[8] The engineer makes the point that in the near future we are likely to produce sufficient renewable energy to fuel most of our basic energy needs, but that solar power is produced in abundance in the summer, and wind energy when storms brew, which creates a significant operational problem. There currently is no means to store that surplus energy when it is generated for later use in the winter, when it is most needed.

Industry sources HyUnder and Ruhnau and Qvist estimate that Germany alone will in the coming decades produce anywhere between fifty-six terawatt hours and seventy-five terawatt hours of surplus renewable energy requiring storage.[9] A 2021 McKinsey report states that building this storage capacity will be a highly attractive market for investors.[10]

Of course, building industrial-sized storage batteries to take care of this alternative-energy bottleneck—triggering huge demand for mined lithium and other minerals that are in limited global supply—is not an environmentally friendly or affordable answer or even acceptable from a geopolitical-risk standpoint.

Pavle instead envisions a holistic system, monitored and safeguarded by his molecule-tracking tech service, which starts with efficiently converting surplus solar and wind energy into clean hydrogen and ammonia fuels. After recent tech breakthroughs, this is all doable. That fuel can then be safely transported and stored in depleted underground oil and gas reservoirs until the stored energy is needed in winter and fed back into the grid.

Pavle urges us to view underground oil and gas reservoirs as earth's natural batteries, encased solidly in rock and safely storing energy underground for millions of years in liquid or gas form. His proposal is to simply use modern technologies to repurpose earth's natural storage system for the green-energy revolution.

The idea is certainly compelling on paper. Austria's underground-reservoir storage capacity alone, according to E-Control, would translate into 95.5 terawatt hours, more than enough to take care of neighboring Germany's entire surplus, and would not, if so used, create the environmental damage associated with battery production. "We do not have an energy problem in the world," Pavle claims. "We have a storage problem."

It's Pavle's innovative work in the field of reservoir management that recently helped a consortium win a massive energy contract in Bulgaria. The project's purpose is to build a network of pipelines and reservoirs that will allow Bulgaria to switch its oil and gas dependence on Russia to alternative supplies coming from the Middle East, via a pipeline coming up through Greece. He has since spun all his oil-and-gas clients into a separate company, and PM Lucas now works exclusively on alternative-energy projects.

Pavle's journey brings to life at a micro level all the macro wealth-creation themes I have been discussing throughout this book. Here is an energy executive who didn't become a placard-waving protestor picketing his industry but set out to transform the energy sector from within. Doing so gives him immense personal satisfaction, materially aids the world we all live in, and will probably make him a lot of money.

Pavle reimagined his twentieth-century business for the twenty-first century by correctly reading (not resisting) the direction the multilateral institutions, governments, and consumers wanted his industry to head—which is toward a renewable-energy future.

He saw clearly that his firm's fortunes would be renewed by heavily investing in that space where government intervention and his industry were increasingly intersecting. But he also saw that he couldn't rely on government fiat to create the solution for his firm's future. He had to use his own imagination and modern technology to find a path forward for his company and did so by investing time and energy in the long-term themes shaping our age.

Finally, Pavle reinvented his business by digging into himself, by questioning his purpose, by reimagining his own reason for being as much as he reimagined his business. He had to find a new twenty-first-century way to create value in both financial and emotional terms.

IF YOU GIVE, YOU GET

Faizal Kottikollon, a sixty-year-old Indian in black-framed eyeglasses,[11] was sitting in the back of the Arts Club Dubai. He looked from the distance like a mild-mannered accountant you might find at a consulting firm, but up close I was instantly struck by the fact that he had a lightness of being about him, a twinkle in his eye, and the open and line-free face of a child inspecting rock pools along the shore.

Yet, after so many years on the job, I can instantly spot what we call *realized wealth*, and my "wealthdar" began to ding furiously the moment I was in Faizal's presence. There were also some intriguing hints, dropped here and there, that suggested I wasn't dining with your standard widget maker. "I don't start a business without a purpose," he said quietly, "and the purpose is always, 'How can we make our surroundings better?'"

Faizal was born into a Muslim family in Calicut, a city in India's southern state of Kerala, and educated in Christian missionary schools. His father was a lowly rice trader who went on to become a highly respected local businessman. The rebellious middle son, always questioning the conventional path that was prescribed for him, Faizal left India in 1989 and went off to earn a second engineering degree at Bradley University in the US.

He married Shabana, who would prove to be his ideal partner in life, and the young couple settled in Dubai, a corner of the world that was just starting to develop and where they thought they could achieve their goals. Over the next twenty years, Faizal became a serial entrepreneur. In 2011 he sold off his vertically integrated valve-manufacturing business, Emirates Techno Casting, netting him his first $400 million. After this liquidity event, Faizal and Shabana set up KEF Holdings to manage their investments and a parallel family foundation to oversee their "give back" to the world.

Faizal kept on asking himself, *What am I going to do with this money?*

Making money for money's sake was no longer possible, and the questions he began asking himself about his wealth and purpose prompted Faizal and Shabana to embark on a new kind of search. They were at a stage of their wealth journey where they wanted to create value of a different sort, and that led them to return to Mother India, to study their homeland's massive educational needs.

Public schools across the country were in a state of frightening disrepair. Classes were often held in cracked and leaking buildings, the playgrounds were dustbowls, and the fly-filled toilets were revolting. "More than the teachers, more than the syllabus, it was the whole crumbling educational infrastructure that was the problem," he said.

Faizal's and Shabana's mission to refurbish dilapidated public schools—in the two and a half months when the children were out on summer break—led to them retrofitting, with quick-to-assemble prefab technology, a showcase 120-year-old school; which led to a mass remodeling program for 966 public schools; which led to KEF Holdings' next immensely successful business. KEF Infra, created in 2014 on a forty-two-acre campus, rapidly became the world's largest integrated offsite manufacturer of prefab construction.

The KEF Infra plant, highly automated and robotics-driven, went on to build corporate headquarters, a chain of canteens, and a string of cancer centers. In 2018, just four years after he created it, Faizal sold KEF Infra for an undisclosed sum to Katerra, a US-based offsite construction firm owned by Japan's SoftBank, creating a new company that had $3.7 billion in revenues at the time of the merger.

In short, Faizal's need to give back to the world and address a major government-related problem around education created his second fortune.

The Arts Club waiter brought us our next course, and the interruption gave me time to gather my thoughts. It was clear Faizal was a visionary hardwired to upend sclerotic industries, as his KEF Holdings philosophy—"Innovation and disruption for a positive impact"—neatly summed up. This guy was a major industrialist. But though I understood he was able to see and execute opportunities that others overlooked, even in some very rough-and-tumble global industries, I couldn't help sensing there was something else going on below the surface. I kept on noticing, for example, his joyous air and something glaringly conspicuous for its absence—any sign of stress.

"Faizal, with all due respect, we aren't at the heart of it yet. There is something else special about you," I said. "What is it?"

He smiled sheepishly. "Well, I get up at four thirty in the morning, before the sun rises, and do one and a half to two hours of yoga and meditation every day. I never meet bankers for dinner, as I am doing now. I'm in bed at nine thirty or ten every night, so I can get up for yoga."

It turns out that Faizal, Muslim born and Christian educated, has for the past thirty years been practicing Vedanta, an ancient Indian spiritual philosophy of the Hindu order. His dedication to the disciplines of his spiritual and physical practice is such that he and his wife retreat every year into a Vedanta ashram, far from the digital disruptions of the modern world, which has all led to Faizal's most audacious business creation to date.

When COVID-19 hit and the world was forced into retreat, Faizal and his family were saved mentally by the health-and-wellness spa they had built into their United Arab Emirates home. With Mohammad, his personal masseuse of the past fourteen years, Faizal and extended staff spent their COVID time creatively reimagining holistic mind-body treatments, such as the hybrid Ayurveda-hammam massage, scrub, and washdown they created and that he receives at the end of the day on a heated table of his own creation. "Our mind has to be pure for us to be healthy and happy in life," he said. "Most of people's problems today is the unhappiness of a cluttered mind. So you need to remove the clutter."

That is how Tulah, which means "balance," took hold in his imagination. Tulah is a wellness center that Faizal has built in Southern India, a $100 million modernist mirage emerging from Kerala's bird-filled jungle overlooking the Arabian Sea. The complex is a twenty-first-century take on midcentury architecture, a series of cool-looking domes and waterways and Babylonian-style hanging gardens that blend in with the surrounding natural beauty. Tulah was built in Faizal's own prefab production facility, with every detail thought through to create a completely sustainable ecosystem on the thirty-acre property.

Tulah's soft launch will be in December 2024. The business has filed for global patents, including for its unique Ayurveda-hamman wash-and-scrub table, all while it refines its digital platform meant to monitor a patient's Tulah Life Index, a composite of measurements tracking a patient's various body, mind, and soul conditions.

There is more going on here than meets the eye. Tulah is part of Faizal's grand plan to disrupt the global health-and-wellness industry. He believes Tulah's purpose is to completely reimagine our approach to health, wellness, and way of being, a center of excellence where the links between psyche and soma are taken seriously in a reinvented health-care process minutely overseen by Faizal and his team of medical and spiritual advisors.

In essence, Tulah will marry the best of ancient healing practices engaging the five senses—such as the massages and herbal-oil remedies of India's five-thousand-year-old Ayurvedic medical system—with the data-driven rigors of twenty-first-century Western medicine and science.

What we are seeing here is not a rich man's folly in the jungle but a minutely thought-out twenty-first-century global business taking shape. Tulah is his haute couture line, where his best health-and-wellness ideas are invented and tested, before they are passed down to his ready-to-wear version for the street. Faizal intends to roll out mini Tulahs around the world, so that clients returning to their respective homes have a community version to visit for periodic rejuvenation stays. In other words, Faizal imagines that Tulah will ultimately become a luxurious global health-and-wellness brand producing calm minds and serious riches. The first mini Tulah will open in Dubai in 2025, and will, if all goes to plan, be followed by a center in Europe.

"Tulah is my most passionate project," he said. "It's going to change the way things are delivered in health care today. We've really got to start looking inside, at what we are doing. The world is in such crisis. The point of Tulah is to reimagine the world—differently."

On a macro level, Faizal is investing his wealth in some of the biggest issues of the age. He's investing alongside government in education and in health care, addressing megatrends ranging from digitization to demographics to climate change. On a micro level, however, note that Faizal is managing his wealth, not his portfolio.

What he is doing is something that all of us can do—which is cultivating and practicing successful work-life habits that help us create personal success and wealth—and then getting great joy from giving back and sharing that success with others, ultimately to help them with their own pursuits in life.

BUILDING A BETTER CONSTRUCTION INDUSTRY

"The construction industry is the only sector that hasn't changed," scoffed fifty-year-old Spanish real estate developer Pablo Castro Saez.[12] "We are still constructing buildings like we did three hundred years ago—with the hands, through an artisanal system. The car sector? The evolution is amazing. Logistics? It's far from what it was even ten years ago. The food and agriculture sectors? Look how they've changed. Now let's go to the construction sector. The only thing that has improved is perhaps the quality of the materials. Nothing else. A construction site today looks exactly like it did two hundred years ago."

Pablo intends to upend all of that. "Industrializing the construction sector that I love, it is, for me—putting the money aside for a moment—a great dream."

Pablo, at one point the largest real estate developer in Spain, seems to be close to realizing his dream to produce prefabricated sustainable housing in a cost-efficient industrialized process of his firm's invention.

The problem with most prefab housing modulars, he explained, is that they are rigidly and monotonously identical; the house frames are either made from wood, making them immediately wobble and shift out of positions when hoisted by a crane, or they are made of poured cement, which is a wasteful process and not remotely sustainable.

Pablo's Barcelona-based real estate group has instead invented a proprietary system that mass-builds house-frame bars that are 90 percent made with recycled steel, put together like puzzle pieces. The "sandwich" wall panels are, in turn, made entirely from insulation and compressed recycled materials. Meanwhile, his highly automated production takes place in a net-zero factory; to lower the CO_2 emissions that come with transporting a relay of prefab housing components to the building site, he uses a fleet of electric trucks.

The Spanish real estate magnate has, in other words, tried to make every step of his construction system sustainable. The factory is energy self-sufficient and doesn't use water during production, an increasingly valuable commodity that the traditional construction industry wastes with reckless abandon.

Pablo's design system is also unusually flexible. His computer software immediately reconfigures the development's footprint to the shape of the underlying parcel of land so that not a single square meter is wasted. The housing design and materials—such as the facade—can be easily customized to meet local building standards.

After designing and building a prototype prefab building on a three-thousand-square-meter property in Barcelona, Pablo realized he needed to bring his manufacturing costs down through economies of scale. "We did a proof of concept," he said. "The building was tested by the local administration, and our system worked well. The only problem was the price. It was 25 percent more expensive than doing it with traditional construction methods."

Pablo likens the next step of his company's growth to that point when, more than one hundred years ago, Henry Ford brought down the cost of his Model T from $850 in 1909 to $260 in 1924, essentially by inventing mass production.[13] Pablo's opportunity to develop a housing version of the car's production line arose, he thought, when left-of-center German Chancellor Olaf Scholz took office in late 2021, promising to build four hundred thousand new apartments every year while in office.

In that moment, Pablo saw how his wealth and business prospects would reach their goal more quickly by surfing the waves the German government's social and environmental policies would create. It's a great example of why following the money becomes so powerful a frame of reference for understanding how things work, which is ultimately what all wealth creators are trying to do—whether that be you and I as investors, or Pablo, Faizal, and Pavle as entrepreneurs.

But Pablo wasn't connected with the right people in Germany. That's when he turned to UBS for help, tapping into our network of clients. UBS put him in touch with a well-connected German landowner, and together the partners planned to produce three thousand sustainable and affordable apartments a year in several cities, starting with Berlin. The partnership was on the threshold of breaking ground on their first project when Russia invaded Ukraine. The German government's spending priorities suddenly shifted in a completely new direction, and the project was put on ice.

Pablo instantly pivoted toward the US, where he had quietly been investing since 2019, after UBS had similarly made some Miami-based introductions. He saw an opening in a new local law that permitted large-scale affordable-housing developments to get greenlighted using a streamlined approval process.

In early 2025, once the final planning approvals are passed, Pablo's US firm, HueHub, will break ground on the first phase of a six-tower, 3,233-unit apartment complex in the North Corridor of Miami-Dade. The local press is touting his West Little River twelve-acre project as the "biggest" ever development in South Florida, ambitiously aimed to be a self-sustaining city-within-a-city with everything from an Olympic pool to podcast studios on premises.[14] It also strives to be a low-cost sustainable showcase: the complex will, among other things, run on solar panels, smart thermostats, and low-emission glass panels.

This is an "attainable housing" project, the property built from the low-cost prefab, sustainable construction panels shipped over from factories in Europe, before being assembled and finished locally using local suppliers and craftsmen. Pablo's HueHub apartments, constructed in this hybrid way, are aimed at providing quality housing to policemen, teachers, and students in Miami-Dade, and the studios, one-bedroom, and two-bedroom rentals will be priced accordingly at $1,200 to $1,800 a month. Pablo's game plan: build forty thousand such modestly priced apartment units over the coming decade.

Pablo says the economies of scale that such a massive project delivers allow him to price his prefab apartment units 20 percent cheaper than traditional construction methods, besides putting him in a better position to absorb Florida's ever-higher insurance costs. Furthermore, building three thousand apartments at a time typically takes five or six years using the conventional construction process, not the one year or so that his system takes, and such time savings also provide him (and his partners) with hidden benefits.

"There is a lot of corruption in construction," Pablo said. "When the construction process is long, you can get blackmailed, and the price becomes 'negotiable.'" In his prefab production system and business model, there is by contrast little room to renegotiate prices when construction surprises try to rear their ugly heads. In this way, step by step, Pablo is finding a new way to build homes in the twenty-first century that is mindful of resources and energy efficiency. He is part of our network of real-world experts helping solve issues around demographics and decarbonization.

INDUSTRIALIZING BOTTLE RETURNS

Suchitra Lohia is the sixty-year-old executive director and deputy group CEO of Thailand's specialist chemical company Indorama Ventures.[15] She is among this new generation of impact entrepreneurs, alongside her equally committed CEO husband, Aloke Lohia, and their three adult children working in the business.

Suchitra has an interesting take on the UN's seventeen sustainability goals. "Maybe the UN's Sustainable Development Goals were unrealistic, but they've put us on the right path," she insists. "I think many of us quietly wanted to help the planet, which has given us so much abundance, and the UN's goals made us realize it was our turn to reimagine the way we do business. Many businesses are striving to become sustainable, even though it was a forced hand. Now everyone is mindful of doing as little damage as possible."

This is an extraordinary remark when you consider that publicly traded Indorama Ventures makes the raw material used in plastic bottles—to many environmentalists the very bane of modern existence and a complete industrial horror. Still, the stated purpose of Indorama Ventures—a world-leading chemicals manufacturer with $16 billion in 2023 revenue[16]—is "reimagining chemistry together to create a better world."

Polyethylene terephthalate, commonly known as PET, is a clear, strong, and lightweight plastic. But unlike other plastics, which are discarded after single use, PET is 100 percent recyclable, and is in fact "made to be remade," as the American Beverage Association snappily puts it.[17] When collected in a relatively pure state, PET bottles can be melted down and converted into flakes or pellets, which are then fed back into the bottle-making process. Typically, 5 percent to 20 percent of a new bottle is made from this recycled material, the rest created from so-called virgin PET. But recycled PET can also be spun into carpet fibers or even used in car production, and Indorama Ventures is a global leader in such recycled products too.

The firm's impact-investing journey started back in 2011, when Indorama acquired Wellman International's assets in Europe. Wellman, recycling 1.6 billion used plastic bottles a year, was a leading manufacturer of polyester staple fiber products and recycled PET flakes. That acquisition helped turn Indorama Ventures into the world's largest recycler.

It had nothing to do with the UN's sustainability goals.

It was purely a business-driven decision.

At the time, the Lohia family wanted Indorama Ventures to become vertically integrated and own the entire PET manufacturing process, from recycled flakes to new PET product, all processed for customers like Coke, Pepsi, Danone, and their bottlers. "There was a vision that at some point this all needs to be recycled and the recycling needs to be taken care of in-house," Suchitra said.

Since the UN's sustainability goals were articulated, Indorama Venture's prescient business objective has turned into a social and environmental imperative, with the EU Commission mandating, for example, that by 2025, PET bottles must contain at least 25 percent recycled material, rising to 30 percent by 2030. (Hmm, I wonder if the politicians needed a large scientific community to get those percentages and dates right, or if they did it with a stroke of a pen?) Her husband's new dream, Suchitra said, is to not "see one bottle on the ground," part of the bottling industry's grand initiative to "get every bottle back."

Becoming a leader in the *circular economy*—a fancy name for recycling and another major investment theme of the twenty-first century—is easier said than done. "The biggest issue is not technical," Suchitra explains. "The technical operations are easy. It's the collection. The world lacks the necessary infrastructure as far as bottle collection goes."

In developing countries, recycling is the business of the poor, with an army of scavengers pouring over landfills and retrieving whatever has been discarded but still has value. In Thailand, 89 percent of all solid waste is recycled, according to the World Bank,[18] and Indorama Ventures can, in theory, purchase used PET bottles relatively cheaply in such emerging economies. The problem here, Suchitra said, is the scavengers' level of education and the recycling industry's general sanitary conditions.

"The world is now trying to separate from the general waste the plastics and the aluminum and bottles and so on. That is requiring a lot of education, which is why we are working on a Recycling Global Education Program, particularly in Thailand and Indonesia."

In Thailand, Indorama Ventures is running a five-hundred-school educational initiative. "We want to educate the coming generation that these bottles are resources and not to be treated like waste. PET is not a normal plastic, it's different, something that is part of our daily life, and that we cannot wish away because there is no substitute that makes life so easy for all of us. The children listen, they agree—and they teach their parents at home."

In the developed nations, meanwhile, there is a costly industrialized recycling system in place, with municipal or privately run side-loader trucks rumbling down back alleys to empty out presorted recycle bins. In this case, Suchitra said, the collection system generally fails for logistics reasons— the collection points in the US are, for example, simply too far away from the bottle producers to be of any real value—and the economies of the stand-alone recycling plants aren't nearly of the scale needed to be competitive. For these reasons, recycled PET product is generally 50 percent more expensive than virgin PET product, according to Suchitra.

The answer, she said, is for PET suppliers like Indorama Ventures and the bottlers themselves to build their own network of collection centers closer to their PET recycling plants so they can capture profits along the entire supply chain and thereby defray recycling costs. Indorama Ventures fully intends to be at the heart of this wholesale infrastructure transformation. It has committed another $1.5 billion in investment to mechanical recycling by 2030. On target to recycle fifty billion bottles a year by 2025, Indorama has just upped its target to one hundred billion bottles by 2030, partly by building new recycling plants in India and Nigeria.

Consumers play a role too. New bottles can be entirely made of recycled PET, Suchitra said, but a 100 percent recycled bottle takes on an opaque or gray color, which until recently has been a major turnoff for consumers purchasing bottled water. But Indorama Ventures now believes that sophisticated consumers around the world are, like the "forced hand" companies themselves, overcoming their initial qualms for the greater good.

That's probably why Fiji Water, among other brands, had the confidence to announce its bottles in the US market will be 100 percent made with recycled PET by 2025,[19] which means these private-sector achievements are already well beyond the mandates of even the EU Commission and the State of California (where 65 percent of plastics must be recycled by 2032).

The Lohia family is in fact doing more than just recycling PET to reach the UN's sustainability goals. It has committed another $7 billion by 2030 to enhanced recycling and its biomass feedstock business, so that even its surfactant products—compounds used in cosmetics and cleaning agents—will increasingly be made with green materials. To that end, Indorama's Milan-based new venture-capital vehicle is scouring the world for ready-to-industrialize technologies and projects working in this recycling and bio-based feedstock space.

Meanwhile, over at the Lohia's family office, Suchitra has with her daughter created Volta Circle, a fund that invests in sustainable food systems, technologies that can reduce businesses' environmental impact, and tools that increase access to health care and education.

This is not an easy route to follow; it requires intense focus, in good times and bad. The petrochemicals company had a tough year in 2023, due to several macro issues hitting the firm all at once, and it required a muscular response from the Lohia family. In March 2024, Suchitra's husband announced the firm was, among other things, selling off noncore assets and lowering its debt level to get the firm's profitability back on track. But tough times have not shaken the family's commitment to sustainability. Quite the opposite. They're upping their goals. The firm predicted, for example, its new efficiency drive could increase value by $350 million a year simply by "leveraging sustainability innovation."

"As entrepreneurs and investors, we believe that we have to balance impact with returns," Suchitra said. "It's what our family believes—and our corporate thesis. So our endeavor, constantly, is how we percolate this [idea of profitable impact] down to our twenty-six thousand employees. It's out there for them to see and read about, but we want it to be part of the company's DNA—and that requires constant effort."

I am drawn to this story because it illustrates a market-government truth that is often overlooked. Government diktats and red-tape regulations can quash entrepreneurial advancement in the private sector; the heavy hand of the state can make it extremely difficult for businesses to operate. But it's equally true that government interventions can at times also propel industries to greater heights, as we saw happened to America's meat-packing industry at the dawn of the twentieth century and appears to be happening here too.

Government directives about PET have spurred petrochemical entrepreneurs into finding a new and better way of doing business in the twenty-first century. Will it be enough to save us all from drowning in a sea of plastic?

I honestly don't know. But at the very least it instills the idea that government subsidies and directives can catalyze private-sector ingenuity and capital toward solving existential problems, and that is probably the *only* way the trillions of dollars needed can be amassed to change the trajectory of where we are headed.

That, then, is our glimpse, through our clients, into the twenty-first century and the kinds of future-oriented businesses that stand a good chance of rewarding investors, precisely because they are buying what the government is buying and tapping the big investment themes of our age.

IT'S NOT JUST ANECDOTAL

Some might claim I cherry-picked these entrepreneurial case studies to reinforce my new-rules thesis; that the world of business really doesn't look like this. I disagree. I could in fact fill an entire book with similar client profiles.

I could share stories about Indonesia's largest construction-material supplier, an entrepreneur who—concerned for his son's future, driven by his faith to not "sin"—is systematically turning his past PVC products into a showcase for sustainable and recycled materials.

Or I could profile a coffee trader who is using digital tools to bind together a massive network of small-farm independent coffee growers across the globe, enhancing their product quality and crop yield, and then using their collective power as suppliers to get them a greater share of coffee's retail price in London and New York.

Or I could tell the story of the former Catholic newspaper editor who has restructured his financial public relations firm into a communications specialist devoted solely to purpose-driven clients.

Furthermore, dig into corporate research and you'll find survey after survey in the US—by Nielsen, the *Wall Street Journal*, Edelman, Accenture, *Forbes, Harvard Business Review,* IBM, National Retail Federation, *Fortune,* and Deloitte, among many others[20]—reinforcing this trend toward impact entrepreneurship, a force that is largely driven by consumers' strongly expressed desire to support companies positively addressing the big issues of our age.

One such seminal study is the 2015 *Harvard Business Review* (HBR) survey called "The Business Case for Purpose,"[21] which suggested that purpose-driven companies are, among other things, more profitable than their peers.

The CEOs and their companies were placed into three groups—those that already "prioritize" purpose; the "developers," who were striving to do so but with mixed results; and the "laggards," where the company's purpose was little understood or dwelled on. The *HBR* survey discovered that 58 percent of the companies that prioritized purpose reported revenue growth above 10 percent during the previous three years. Those high-growth results fell to 25 percent among the developers and 15 percent among the laggards.

In short, the entrepreneurial trends identified in our profiles above are not isolated cases, but part of a significant business movement. Nothing moves in a straight line, of course, and growth, even when in an upward trajectory, often happens in fits and starts. After such a rapid corporate push toward having positive impact, the reactionary pendulum, particularly in the US, has reportedly swung back in recent years against corporate engagement in ESG objectives.[22]

Many of our impact-investing clients think that's a good thing. They argue that this backlash can help expose the "greenwashers," companies superficially interested in sustainable labels for marketing purposes, and it has left only those firms firmly committed to purpose and impact so consumers can make better choices. But in some ways, that's all immaterial. Like it or not from a philosophical perspective, I know, by talking to UBS's most accomplished clients around the globe, that the impact-driven innovations I have described here—reimagining the energy sector, the construction industry, the petrochemical business, the health-care business—are part of an entrepreneurial groundswell and cannot be easily dismissed. They're improving products to better meet the demands of today's consumers and governments, and in so doing, they stand a chance of transforming both the profitability and sustainability of some massive industries.

Still, one of the reasons these stories are inspiring is because it is still just a small intrinsically motivated group who are able to combine their work, investing, values, and passion so effectively. But what we see increasingly is that the next generation of investors simply won't accept that; they want to be similarly inspired and impactful, even though the route to that future isn't always straightforward.

A recent study of sixty-five family foundations—ranging in size from $11 million to $16 billion in assets and collectively managing $89 billion—discovered that 92 percent of those organizations were active members of groups like Global Impact Investing Network and Mission Investors Exchange. But only 5 percent of those foundations (based primarily in the United States) were actively engaged in impact investing.[23]

Why the disconnect? The survey's sponsors, Jeff Skoll's Capricorn Investment Group and Bridgespan Social Impact, attributed this hesitancy to "beginner's dilemma." The foundations are too overwhelmed to know where to start; they feel the space is still too niche; they worry that they will have to compromise on financial returns if they pursue an impact-investing strategy. Yet philosophically, taking this approach makes so much sense; if they weren't afraid of lower investment returns, why wouldn't these foundations use their investment capital to align to or achieve many of the same goals they target with their philanthropic grant making?

In other words, the families are experiencing the same sort of early-stage skepticism and scalability issues that we at the UBS chief investment office experienced. Well, in my view, these foundations better get working, because one of our 5Ds of disruption—demographics—is coming for them.

NEXTGEN WEALTH WANTS CHANGE

What we are seeing as we advise and manage the world's billionaires is that while the impact-investing education has begun, there are still a lot of fence-sitters, as the Capricorn-Bridgespan study suggests. But dig below the surface image projected by that study and a very different picture emerges. Often it's not the current family office decision-makers who are driving this new investment approach, as we are discovering.

It's the next generation of family members poised to become decision-makers over the next twenty to thirty years who are agitating to evolve their family's portfolio management approach to a process that more intentionally incorporates impact into the equation.

This generational divide we observe among our clients is also showing up in the research data. Consider global warming. A three-year Gallup poll that concluded in 2018, probing the age gap on environmental issues, surveyed a random sample of 4,103 adults and found that a majority of Americans were worrying about climate change and global warming. When it came to those fifty-five and older, however, 56 percent of the respondents "worry a great deal / fair amount about global warming." The younger the respondents, the greater the worries: 70 percent of the respondents aged eighteen to thirty-four placed themselves in this high-anxiety camp.[24]

If you think through the financial-market fallout of this market data, and couple that with our direct client observations, it's hard not to conclude that the more we move into the middle part of the twenty-first century, as more millennials and Gen Z assume the reins of power, the more likely we are to see these large environmental and existential concerns moving to the fore of finance and getting integrated into financial products.

It's not hard to imagine, as these new generations take command, that impact investing will morph from an investment niche favored by a small financial elite to the "normal" way to invest for all of us. It's a fundamental law of the street: more demand results in more financial product, which results in more investment choices.

Let's now cross-check this impact-investing picture of the future we're painting by following the money. In this case, I'm going to grab some snapshots of our clients running family offices, which are investment offices that families with more than $500 million in investable assets create to efficiently manage their wealth. There's a reason why I'm focused on this elite group of clients. In the wealth-management business, family offices test-drive the newest products and ideas.

If new investment ideas or products are successful with the very wealthy, they then trickle down the wealth pyramid until they eventually wind up in retail financial products for the masses. Private-equity and alternative investments were, for example, originally embraced by family offices and exclusively available to the wealthy.[25] They are now available to the masses through mutual funds or ETFs investing in private markets.[26]

HOW FAMILY OFFICES ARE INVESTING FOR IMPACT

A SEARCH FOR MEANING

Laura and Lisa* are from Atlanta, scions of a billionaire family who made a fortune in the chemicals industry. The sisters, in their midfifties, inherited the family fortune from their deceased parents and are united in their family office objective: they want to have a positive impact on struggling communities in the South and address climate change. But they are increasingly using impact investing in addition to philanthropy to get their capital working toward their social objectives.

---

    * Names and some personal details have been changed to protect identities.

The sisters are focusing a portion of their fixed-income firepower on municipal bonds financing affordable housing, community development, and education initiatives in a swath of Southern communities known to be economically distressed. The portfolio concentration they have in the South is then offset by diversified investments across the globe that tackle the mega environmental and social issues of our times.

They primarily do so through passive investments or through active public-equity investments. Their public-equity investments are, for example, focused on climate-related themes and so-called inclusive businesses, which in this case partially means focusing on women-run companies in parts of the world where women are often marginalized.

Similar climate change and social impact themes, with emphasis on gender issues and affordable housing, are also the driving impact impetus for their asset allocations in private markets, where their capital is locked up for longer periods but where the sisters' returns are coming in at the high single digits to low teens.

"This family is not targeting, in climate change, say, a specific amount of emissions they want removed," said their advisor. "What they are saying is 'I want to know that this solution is going to address the problem explicitly in some way, and that the fund manager is measuring the impact in a meaningful way.'"

GENERATIONAL PAYBACK

One Indonesian family, let's call them the Alims,* has entered the billionaire class by building a real estate and industrial empire over multiple generations. This family's move to impact investing is being driven by the third generation, now in their late fifties and early sixties, and they have done so by setting up a family office that exclusively focuses on philanthropy and impact investing.

These family members have set up trusts benefiting the fourth generation, their children, that are 100 percent invested in impact investments. In

---

* Names and some personal details have been changed to protect identities.

other words, the family's transition from traditional asset management to impact investing is slow, deliberate, and thoughtful, a process that is going to take years to unfold.

Their thematic focus is on both climate change and a broader set of impact goals focused on emerging and frontier markets. Here are their impact-portfolio allocations:

- 20 percent to 40 percent in public equities (mix of active and passive)
- 10 percent to 20 percent in fixed income
- 10 percent to 20 percent in private markets with a focus on growth venture
- 20 percent to 30 percent in private credit
- 5 percent to 10 percent in private "real assets": timberland, infrastructure, and private commercial real estate
- A negligible amount held in cash

"The first and second generation might not be there, philosophically speaking," said their advisor, giving us insight into where the impact-investment industry currently is and, more importantly, where it is heading. "It's the third generation that is into impact investing, but they can't yet move entirely into the space themselves because they have legacy investments and long lockups in the private-market portion of their portfolios. But they can set up their children's trusts to be 100 percent invested for impact. That's where the mentality shifts. But that's also why it takes time generally to shift portfolios into impact investing."

NEIGHBORLY OUTREACH

Our next billionaire family, let's call them the Jacksons,* are a case study from the Northeast in the US. As the next generation came up, agitating for change, the family collectively decided to move as close to a 100 percent

---

* Names and some personal details have been changed to protect identities.

impact portfolio as possible, with a heavy focus on environmental and equality causes.

Liquid equities are heavily invested in "active multi-thematic," which means the big themes and disruptors we outlined at the beginning of the book, as well as investments in corporate leaders who are emerging as influential players in the environmental, sustainable, and good-governance space. The liquid fixed-income portion of their portfolio is, meanwhile, flowing into sustainable and impact bond issues, besides building up significant holdings in multilateral development bank bonds (such as World Bank bonds financing, say, a wind-energy plant in Latin America).

The Jacksons have invested in mortgage-backed bonds financing low-to-moderate-income borrowers, as well as multifamily properties in minority-heavy and low-income neighborhoods, with the intent of preserving housing affordability. They're also significant purchasers of taxable municipal bonds funding affordable housing and neighborhood redevelopment projects.

Meanwhile, in the illiquid private-market tranche of assets, they are focused on a range of impact outcomes, ranging from expanding access to the workforce and affordable housing to supporting "inclusive" entrepreneurship, often through venture capital and private lending.

Here's the key point: in each of these family case studies, **the underlying act of passing on wealth to the next generation was the catalyst spurring the family's transition to impact investing.**

NEXTGEN IS INHERITING BIG MONEY TO DRIVE CHANGE

That the next generation was the catalyst for each of these families' moves to impact investing becomes relevant once we revert to following the money. Research outfit Cerulli Associates estimates that in the next twenty years the United States' high-net-worth and ultra-high-net-worth citizens will, by themselves, pass on $84.4 trillion to their heirs and chosen charities.[27] It's a flow of funds so massive and market-moving it has been branded *the great wealth transfer*. The bulk of that windfall is of course coming from the wealth-creation efforts of the baby boomers. Heirs will directly inherit $72.6 trillion of the total, with the remaining $11.9 trillion still invested in the social and environmental issues of our times, but in this case via charities.[28]

This generational transfer of wealth is unfolding around the world, and occurring, counterintuitively, because of the demographics we discussed earlier in the book. A by-product of declining birth rates is a higher concentration of wealth. Imagine four grandparents funneling two sets of wealth streams to their married children, who then funnel all this concentrated multigenerational wealth down to just one child. This all adds up to Big Money, the flow of funds we talked about earlier in the book and that investors are wise to follow.

The global-warming angst among eighteen-to-thirty-four-year-olds identified by the Gallup poll has to go somewhere. When the wealthy millennials and Gen Z come to power, they are likely to insist on investing with purpose and using their portfolios to make a difference in the world, at which point it is likely that scalable impact-investing products targeted at the less wealthy millennial and Gen Z masses will also come to market in a meaningful way. Wall Street, after all, always follows the big consumer trends, since that is where the bucks are to be made.

The point is that all of these different tributaries of money I outlined above—driven by anxieties coming from different corners of the globe and from different sectors of society, but all converging and flowing in ever-greater volume in the same direction toward the sea—could potentially become a boon to early- and middle-stage impact investors.

Of course, there are many dangers that could upend this impact-investing future that we see emerging. The roughriders of the bond market could, as previously mentioned, scale the hill of government debt and bayonet states' abilities to finance the market outcomes they want—stanching a major money flow shaping the direction the markets are heading. Or World War III could erupt, which in turn would propel a new set of spending and regulatory priorities. Or a new asset bubble could inflate globally and pop, maybe even in impact investing, all because one government-stimulated corner of the market worked so well it accelerated us all off the cliff.

When we are nearer to such inflection points, smart investors will proactively rethink all the rules outlined in this book—and decide if they remain relevant or whether the investor needs to bail on them and come up with a new approach.

But for now, the risk of an impact-investing bubble inflating let alone popping is a very long way off, should it ever happen, and it's likely that many new fortunes will in the meantime be made this new Cubist way.

If you follow the money and the data, this is the picture that emerges about where the world of investing and wealth creation is increasingly heading as we move deeper into the twenty-first century.

Governments burdened by excessive debt cannot solve the big risks of our age on their own, but once a growing share of private capital sees the financial and civic benefits that result from buying what the government is buying, investing in and around the same great themes of our age, the public-private combination of investment flows are likely to reach a tipping point and become quite large. They could in fact reach the trillions of dollars the UN and others say is needed to address our existential threats.

Some of you might think, as many of our passionate impact-investor clients do, that this investment trend gathering steam provides a glimmer of hope that humanity may be able to alter some of its self-destructive habits, ideally before our collective luck runs out.

Bottom Line

As you know by now, in my role as chief investment officer, I try to separate what I think should happen or hope will happen in the market from looking at where the money is going and what are effective tools for helping clients manage their wealth better. My job is to stay grounded in the present. Having now read through this book, I hope you can see that the rules I offer are designed to separate out what successful investing is actually about: understanding the great macro forces like government intervention and learning a time-tested investment process and strategy like asset allocation and the UBS Wealth Way. They are distinct from what we often want investing to be about, which is feelings of excitement, fulfillment, or passion. In the evolving area of impact investing, however, our clients are successfully combining it all. That's why I see this trend as the future: nothing succeeds like success.

To conclude: The rules in this book are designed to help you understand the ideas, strategies, and processes that our most successful clients—regardless of their net worth—use to manage their wealth today. If you are where I was when I started my wealth-management journey, and think your wealth—or worse, your identity—is all about the excitement or terror of picking individual stocks, rules 1 to 3 are designed to let you know that it's okay to step away from the keyboard. A world in which governments control increasingly larger proportions of gross domestic product to combat global challenges such as demographics, decarbonization, and digitization has made investment much more complex and competitive for stock picking alone.

If you were already wondering what the alternative was to stock picking, rules 4 to 6 are about what techniques really move the needle for real people in the real world, based on academic research and over 160 years of experience with clients.

When you have mastered the basics of investing, rules 7 and 8 are designed to inspire you to graduate from a sound investing strategy to a wealth-management strategy. Impact investing is the way we see more and more clients finding a healthy and successful way to combine their investing with their passions and values. Finally, my bonus rule, coming next, is that extra bit of advice to help you stay grounded and on track as you pursue all the techniques mentioned in this book.

UNDERSTAND THAT INVESTING IS AN EXERCISE IN HUMILITY

Humility is among the most underrated qualities of the successful investor. If you don't want to be humbled by the market, I have a very simple solution for you: pay other people to manage your money so you have someone to yell at when the unexpected happens. But look for the ones who already have had some humility beaten into them.

Wall Street famously attracts "master of the universe" types, figures driven by excessive self-confidence. Chuck Norris, the eighties action hero, has become synonymous with a meme about the "trader who has no fear." Here are some Chuck Norris jokes that Wall Street traders find hilarious.[1]

- Chuck Norris is on the other side of every losing trade you make.
- Chuck Norris has no stop-loss, because he never loses.
- Chuck Norris determines the bid/ask when he trades.
- Chuck Norris never meets resistance in the market. It wouldn't dare.
- When Chuck Norris buys options, they never expire.

As ridiculous as these aphorisms are, they illustrate, in an exaggerated way, the hubris at work in many investors and traders.

Being humble about your abilities and being afraid of what the world can deliver can save your life and your fortune. I was not a fast learner, and some of the lessons I learned in my personal life I unfortunately had to learn all over again in the markets. So, I am going to share some painful personal stories about risky situations that informed the way I invest today. I would like to think that my formative experiences in choking on too much risk have helped me evolve and stick to the asset allocation wealth-management strategy described in this book.

LESSONS IN HUMILITY

AN ACUTE CASE OF TESTOSTERONE POISONING

It was a typical case of teenage testosterone poisoning that left me clutching at the outside of an airplane flying over Georgia. I didn't just wake up one day with a burning desire to be a paratrooper, but a succession of escalating decisions landed me at US Army Airborne School. My father, looking at the cost of college tuition, encouraged me to apply for a US Army Reserve Officer Training Course (ROTC) scholarship because it would pay 80 percent of the $15,440-per-year tuition that my first-choice school, Princeton, cost back in 1990.[2] Mom, in contrast, flipped out that I was even considering ROTC and focused relentlessly on the fact that I might wind up fighting a war. She repeatedly begged me not to join the program. But my dad had always spoken fondly of his time in ROTC and the army reserves, and it had been a lifetime (or my lifetime) since the United States had been in a "real" war. Furthermore, I had a year to try out the program for "free" before I committed. What could go wrong?

I had a great time in ROTC my freshman year. Helicopters swooped down to pick us up at Princeton and then flew us back and forth to South Jersey's Fort Dix, where we played machine-gun laser tag. I was loving the army and the army loved me. In fact, I was selected as one of the few

173

first-year Princeton cadets deemed hard-core enough to be accepted for US Army jump school over the summer.

I was thrilled. I was going to be a paratrooper.

Late in the summer of 1990, between my freshman and sophomore years, I flew down to Fort Benning (now Fort Moore), on the Georgia-Alabama border, to take the army's three-week Basic Airborne Course. Transporting from the ivory tower of Princeton to the regular US Army required a bit of a mental adjustment. It started when I was forced to trade in my name and individuality and from then on be identified only as Charlie 323, due to the "C-323" on my helmet. The first week they tried to weed out cadets through a regimen of running, push-ups, and pull-ups. We were "dirty nasty legs" trying to earn our "silver wings." I was scared as hell, sweating until there were salt stains on my fatigues, and was constantly yelled at for ten hours a day by the "black hats" (drill sergeants).

But I kept telling myself, *It's only three weeks, with free time on weekends. I can do anything for three weeks.* All in all, my Princeton ROTC colleagues had prepared me well for what was coming. At one point we practiced jumping out of a tower, a Fort Benning requirement before deploying from a real airplane. Back at Princeton I had been warned that if the black hats sense any fear or hesitation when you get up the tower, they will try to make you think they didn't clip you in right and throw you out the platform door. Sure enough, they did this to some of the legs, and after coming out of the tower screaming with arms and legs paddling at the air, they quit the program.

In this way the pointy-head Princetonian fond of reading the French philosopher Michel Foucault was systematically reduced to the "infant" that forms the basis of an "infantry," transformed in just two weeks into a mindless automaton who could, in a trancelike state, successfully execute all the steps necessary for a successful parachute jump.

The last week, jump week, the first hurtle from an airplane went as planned. They had trained me well. I was still scared but now confident I could see it through to the end. On my second 1,250-foot jump, I was last in a stick of five or six soldiers. Not a problem. I was still terrified, but when

I heard "Stand up! Hook up!" I was transformed into a robot shuffling to the door of the airplane.

Last in line, I threw myself out of the C-130 and expected the quiet floating to earth, as I had experienced before, but instead slammed full force into the side of the door, half in and half out, watching my arm flap uncontrollably outside the plane.

I didn't know what was going on or why I was in this strange state, watching my arm try to detach itself from my body and fly away, but in that moment my thinking brain shut down and pure animal fear took over.

The only thought flashing through my mind was *Live! Live! Live!*

The jumpmaster pulled me back into the airplane. I must have looked crazy scared, because he started laughing and then pointed to the red light. While I had been heading out the door for my jump, the light had abruptly turned to red as we passed the safe-jump zone, which was why he had, at the last moment, grabbed the back of my pack and why I had slammed hard into the side of the C-130.

The airplane circled back over the jump zone and the jumpmaster again barked, "Stand in the door!" Instantly, the training kicked back in. The fear was gone. The jumpmaster had successfully rebooted the computer, and I executed the program. I followed all his commands and safely landed during jump number two.

I'm making light of it now, but the truth is I had never experienced this level of disorientation and terror before. It not only vividly brought home how little I understood about how dangerous even training with the paratroopers was, but it also taught me something important about the fluidity of my own mental state. Everything but my lizard brain had shut down in an instant.

Like Ernest Hemingway's description of how bankruptcy happens— "Gradually and then suddenly"[3]—my big lessons in life-and-death risk began with deliberate and seemingly well-reasoned risk decisions, months or even years before the actual event, all of which rapidly spiraled out of control once I was in the moment. It was great to have a scholarship and do all the fun army training, but now I realized I was in way over my head.

Almost immediately after experiencing risk in this micro way, believing I was about to die for those coveted silver wings, I had to deal with a macro risk and make the most important decision of my life up to that point.

On August 2, 1990, just as I was starting my airborne training at Fort Benning, the Iraqi army invaded Kuwait on Saddam Hussein's orders.[4] Three days later president George H. W. Bush made his famous "This will not stand" speech.[5]

The Gulf War had started. The last jump I did was again on a C-130. The plane landed, refueled, and immediately took off to the Gulf to become a part of Operation Desert Shield. When I signed up for an ROTC scholarship, there hadn't been a major war since Vietnam, and now Charlie 322 and Charlie 324, standing either side of me, were being deployed into a battle zone. The danger I was in suddenly hit full force.

At the airborne graduation ceremony, the commander reminded us we were now part of an elite fraternity. He proudly proclaimed that during the Normandy invasion the US Army airborne units lost 70 to 80 percent of their men, but they still drove on to accomplish their mission.[6]

Well, even I could understand math like that.

How did I not realize what I was getting myself into?

I didn't have time to feel sick when I was flapping in the wind, but now, standing at attention, I wanted to vomit. Yet when I stole a glance to my left and right to see what Charlie 322 and Charlie 324 thought of those kind-of-terrible odds, they were filled with pride, the exact opposite of what I was feeling. As one of the smallest and weakest cadets to graduate that day, I was certain I would become one of the paratroopers found dead in France.

I was starting to understand the difference between subjective and objective risk, although not yet fully. I felt confident that my discipline and training reduced my risk when jumping out of planes; subjectively, my risks had gone down. However, the reality—the objective risk—was that the next jump could be in combat. I was hearing that the graduating seniors with college ROTC scholarships like I had were not getting sent off to the reserves, like my father was, but were getting called up for four years of active duty. When I called home after the graduation, my mother was beside herself with rage and fear that I might be jumping into a war. I think she worked my dad over, because when my father finally got on the line, I found he was no longer making the hard sell on how great the army was.

"Dad, I thought I had this all planned out," I told him. "I would go into the army reserves and get my schooling paid. But if this is a war when I graduate, I could be jumping into it from five hundred feet with no reserve chute. I think I might quit."

Dad replied, "Yeah? Well, you better do that quick."

He had a point. The ROTC paid for your freshman year, at which point you could exit the program without financial consequences, but once the army's check cleared for sophomore year, you were committed.

I reviewed my balance sheet. I was nineteen, doing well at an Ivy League college, and surrounded by a loving family. I suddenly understood how much I had, and I knew that some of the boys I jumped with had signed up simply for the extra jump- and hazardous-duty pay they could get in units like the Eighty-Second Airborne. Guys younger than me and equally scared were married with kids, and those extra few dollars a month were a big deal to their families.

I intuitively understood, even though I was not yet able to put it all into the language of an investor, these guys were selling put options on their lives, because that hazardous-duty pay was the best deal they could get. As in selling a put option in the market, they received a small extra payment today in exchange for the chance a war would be put on them later.

I had an entirely different deal lined up. The "lucky sperm club" and good report cards had bought me choices: the option to get my college paid for by the US Army and the option to exit that deal without severe consequences after the first year, even if I would have to take out student loans.

I suddenly saw something about how the world really worked, and once I saw the power of those options contracts we all write in life—and understood you must be prepared to pay up in full if the US Army or some other option buyer ever comes to collect—I could never unsee it. I never again wanted to be in a situation where I didn't understand what payment in full would feel like in the worst-case scenario, and I hoped to never climb out on a limb until I knew two or three ways of getting down safely from that tree.

It was a painful decision.

I had so many sunk costs. I was about to let down good people who had helped me, which made for some restless nights. The easy thing to do was nothing. Soon the decision would be made for me. But I finally decided the ROTC route contained an unacceptably high level of risk. Though I knew it would haunt me and leave me ashamed, I figured I still had time in life to pay back what I felt I owed the US government.

Just before I started my sophomore year, I pulled the rip cord and bailed on the ROTC, with my mom's blessing and her huge sigh of relief ringing in my ears.

At some level, I have never gotten over my decision to be a quitter when others were willing to sacrifice for what they saw as a higher purpose. It was humiliating. While some of my colleagues graduated and served honorably on peacekeeping missions in countries like Haiti, I went to Australia as a Fulbright scholar. What a wimp.

Later I realized that being a great quitter can be a world-class skill too.

As ashamed as I was and still am about this decision, it helped put my life on a different path that I am grateful for.

THERE ARE BENEFITS TO SURVIVING

Another formative lesson in humility and risk occurred in my final Princeton years, when I climbed Alaska's Mount McKinley, the highest mountain in the US, since restored to its native name, Denali.[7] The Climb for the Cure,[8] as our effort was called, happened right after I graduated from Princeton, but the journey really started four years earlier when I unexpectedly met, while on an incoming freshman orientation trip called Outward Action, a smart New Yorker named Alex Friedman,[9] the same friend who would later bring me to UBS.

Alex and I both found ourselves at Princeton's Butler College when the new term started. We shared a common love of the outdoors. One day in the cafeteria, Alex shared with me his idea about organizing a climb of Denali to raise money for HIV/AIDS research and awareness. I was stunned by the brilliance of his plan. Alex gave me my first real-life business lesson in the Reese's Peanut Butter Cup theory: put two great but established things together in a new way (such as chocolate and peanut butter) and create something revolutionary in the process.

HIV/AIDS was wreaking unimaginable horrors and havoc. Despite the huge number of deaths, the disease was still a taboo topic in polite society. Alex figured by sponsoring a group of clean-cut Princeton students climbing the highest mountain in North America, to raise awareness of the mounting AIDS health crisis, the climb could put a different face to the pandemic and help bring this tragic health issue into the mainstream.

Alex had the qualifications to pull this off—he had published awareness-raising op-ed pieces on HIV/AIDS and was an accomplished climber—and he delivered all he promised and more. He appeared on the *Today* show, interviewed by Bryant Gumbel, and was quoted in the *New York Times*.[10] It was a huge achievement.

But the considerable pre-expedition media attention also meant we were under a lot of pressure to pull off a successful climb. Whether we realized it or not, that was a mounting if hidden risk, even before we put a foot on Denali's icy slopes.

On June 12, 1993,[11] nine of us students flew to Alaska, carting everything from pasta to tents for our push up to Denali's 20,310-foot summit.[12] Just loading the two thousand pounds of gear into the plane was an eye-opening logistical exercise, which was then followed by a dramatic flight in between peaks to land at the 7,000-foot Kahiltna Glacier base camp.[13] We spent a few days at the camp, practicing and getting acclimatized, while Denali's summit glittered alluringly in the sun, a fifteen-mile-or-so climb up from where we were.

Instead of getting halfway up the mountain before learning that a major swath of climbers had died during their attempt, as happened to paratroopers in Normandy, I resolved to do some research *before* starting out on our adventure. I prepped by compulsively reading all the Denali accident reports, learning where people had been killed or seriously hurt. Only about half the people who try to climb Denali make it to the top, but the accident rate, I discovered, was much lower than that.

While some people got unlucky with the altitude or weather, a lot of the accidents seemed to be the result of taking silly risks. Or so it seemed to me while reading the accident reports at my desk. As a result, I was reasonably confident that the climb would be challenging but not deadly.

Well, that experience painfully injected important lessons directly into the marrow of my bones. Fresh, unexpected, and humbling insights into risk seemed to materialize daily out of the thin mountain air, and they influenced my later life as an investor.

For example, reading the accident reports down in the lowlands, I said to myself, *I won't make those stupid mistakes. I will manage the risks I take.* Yeah, right. Subjective risks are the calculated risks you decide to take and think you have some control over. This kind of thinking leads mountaineers to do things like cut the handles off their toothbrushes so they can move a fraction lighter about the mountain. But it's the objective risk of spending thirty days on the mountain that is the real problem. That's when your risks ratchet way up, no matter how much your toothbrush weighs.

On the mountain you experience fatigue, cold, falling rocks, and perilous weather every day. As soon as the sun went behind the mountain, the temperature instantly dropped thirty degrees, and within minutes I was shivering uncontrollably. These mountainside risks are not abstract. One day my friend Sarah Prager was clipped into the rope in front of me and punched through the snow and ice, with her feet in a deep crevasse, and it took us almost an hour to pull her out safely. Thankfully, nothing fell on us.

On another morning I looked back at part of the path we had traveled and saw that enormous boulders must have rolled across during the night. I would be dead had I still been in that spot. Then I forgot to double back and secure the belt on my safety harness, a classic and very stupid mistake that happened on the headwall above the fourteen-thousand-foot camp. It happened in a moment of exhaustion, precisely when I had reached one of the most dangerous moments in the climb.

I could picture my reaction to reading that accident report. *Idiot didn't put his harness on right! Won't do that!*

I realized that training can reduce your risks, but it won't *eliminate* them.

In fact, training can lull you into a false sense of security, because when the objective risk is high, the risks don't add up—they multiply. The experience of climbing Denali helped me realize something I would later see in investing: **if you think you are avoiding risk, you might be managing it, and if you think you are managing risk, you are probably out of control**.

The most professional mountain guides can reduce the number of near-fatal blunders they make from one hundred to three mistakes a day, but they can never eliminate them completely. And the longer they climb mountains, the greater the odds are that one day they won't make it back down alive. Scott Fischer, our superman lead guide who safely steered us up Denali, died on Mount Everest just three years after we did the Climb for the Cure.[14] Within five years, many of the professional climbers we spent time with at the fourteen-thousand-foot camp were dead on mountains somewhere in the world.

As the great Tyrolian climber Reinhold Messner said, "Mountains are not fair or unfair, they are just dangerous."[15] The same principles apply to markets and investing. Markets have risks just like mountains do. What I learned climbing Denali—and learned again later about business and markets—is that inevitably mistakes will happen and they can multiply into life-and-death situations.

You need to plan ahead for that, which is why I think the Liquidity Bucket in the UBS Wealth Way is such a good idea.

People can get so focused on how well they think they are managing the subjective risks—things they arguably can control—they fail to recognize the objective market risks they can't control are steadily rising all around them.

Let me put this another way: Hoping you won't see an economic crisis in your lifetime is not an investment strategy. Assuming you *will* experience at least one financial crisis in your lifetime, as history suggests you will, is a far better starting point for an investment plan.

Finally it was Summit Day. To reach the mountain's pinnacle, we had to climb up a steep incline, almost like an Olympic ski slope. Then we had to hike along a ridge before we hit a football-field plateau, which is the preparation for the final climb up to the summit. At this point, we were down to two rope teams. One team had turned around at a lower camp, when their experienced guide fell ill with altitude sickness and couldn't go on.

As we came up onto the summit ridge, the winds were howling and pelting us with ice. A whiteout squall came through. I could just make out Annie Howell ahead of me on the rope. I was worried she was going to stumble off the edge. If she fell off to one side of the mountain, I had to immediately hurl myself off the other side, to balance out the weight on the rope and so save everyone else from getting pulled to their deaths.

That's the theory, anyway. Good luck having the presence of mind to do that.

We were a couple hundred feet from the summit, and I remember thinking, *We've lost a guide, people are getting sick, Annie is about to stumble off the side, and there is a lot of outside pressure on us to reach the summit today. This is getting hairy. We're pushing it, and it's super windy.*

I understood we had entered a new level of danger.

When that internal voice made the risk assessment *You're no longer working with the mountain*, I was not thinking about what it takes to reach the summit. I was thinking only about what it takes to *get back off* the summit. One thing the books had taught me was that most of the catastrophic accidents happened on the way back down because people spend all their energy to reach the summit and have nothing left to get them back.

I knew I had a bit left in me to go forward—heck, I was getting pulled forward by Annie and the team—but I wasn't sure whether my reserves were enough to get me back down again. I was once again in way over my head and needed to make a snap decision about which direction I was heading, a decision that would have a big impact not only on me but also on a lot of people I cared about.

I tugged on the rope and yelled.

"Annie, please, I don't want to go on. I don't want to do this."

Annie was on automatic pilot. She didn't want to stop. She yelled back that we were so close to the summit.

I shook my head. I was adamant.

"I'm turning around," I yelled.

If one climber wants to turn around, then of course everyone tied to them on the rope must turn around as well. Word of my decision spread down the line and then on to the lead rope team that Scott was leading and Alex was on. When Alex heard the news, he was understandably upset and slammed his ice axe into the snow. It was too dangerous for one rope to go ahead on its own, Scott decided, so my decision meant that *both* rope teams had to turn around.

Annie was gracious about what I had done and told me she had been feeling sick enough to vomit. Alex, who was under intense pressure to fulfill the mission, was visibly upset. I suspect others may have been as well, but they didn't let me know directly. Rob Hess, the guide on my rope, came up to me afterward and said, "I want you to know I don't think badly of you for making that decision."[16]

His remark triggered my shame but also a slew of other thoughts.

I appreciate that you want me to feel better, Rob, because on some level I do feel bad that I was the person who made everyone turn around. On the other hand, none of the other teams on the mountain summited that day because of the way the wind picked up. Maybe we had a window, but maybe we didn't. Every other group on the mountain had a quitter that day too. I will learn to live with the consequences of a decision that upset people I care about.

True to the statistics, only half of our Climb for the Cure team successfully reached the summit on July 2. I stayed at camp four trying to stay warm as the others made that second attempt. *People* magazine later reported that Alex wrote in his diary, "The hardest 10 hours of my life. Moving beyond known limits of myself. I am too exhausted to write much now, but today I wept at the summit of Mt. McKinley. I will never forget it. I am so thankful."[17]

I can be proud of Alex's decision and achievement and accept my own. The summit ridge was close enough to the goal for me. Yes, I craved achievement, but the fun part for me was camping with my friends. Thankfully, the people I kept from the summit are still dear friends more than thirty years later.

Once again, I quit. On some level the decision still haunts me today. But I have come to learn my definition of a successful investor or mountaineer is the one who makes it back alive. Bilbo Baggins's tale is called *There and Back Again* for a reason.[18] So call me more hobbit than hard man, but the truth is that while I am on the way up the mountain, I am already thinking about how I will get back down again.

In the end, the greatest lesson from that trip was not from that climbing god and founder of Mountain Madness, Scott Fischer, but from the lesser-known guide Lee Ann Owen, who taught me her motto for climbing.

Live to wimp another day.

THE MARKETS SMACK ME DOWN TO EARTH

Unfortunately, what I thought I had learned in life, I had to learn all over again in the markets. Larry Kam and I created the Sonic Fund in our Harvard dorm rooms, and in early 1999, as soon as we were legit, I went out and about getting "friends, fools, and family" to invest in our start-up. We raised what now seems like a small amount of capital, but since it came from our not-rich families and friends, it carried the weight of a billion dollars for us.

The world at that time was gripped with a massive fear known as Y2K, which essentially was the concern that there would be a global cascade of collapsing computer systems on January 1, 2000, because computers, routinely using the last two digits as the year's shorthand, wouldn't be able to distinguish whether the 00 meant 1900 or 2000.[19]

This was uncharted territory for the computer age, and no scientist could predict what exactly would happen when the date flipped to 2000. Sounds bizarre now, but the scare was real. No one wanted to fly through the New Year, for example, in case air traffic control towers monitoring flights went out and there was mayhem in the skies.

Corporations spent billions of dollars addressing their potential Y2K problem, which the Gartner Group estimated would cost as much as $600 billion to repair.[20] A lot of money was sunk into this hole. Wall Street titan David Goel, my future boss, was at the fabled hedge-fund Tiger Management at the time, and he once told me he knew there was a bubble when he saw far too many Y2K programmers searching online for Ferraris and Porsches in their spare time.[21]

But the Federal Reserve under Alan Greenspan took Y2K very seriously, since it didn't know if the banking system would freeze up as we entered the twenty-first century. In the late 1990s, the Fed started flooding the financial system with extra money.[22]

The Fed was undoubtedly well intentioned, trying to anticipate a worst-case scenario under Y2K, but their cure hurt many of the people it was designed to help. It was another example of how cheap money for too long inevitably comes at a huge price.

So Larry and I started our hedge fund during a Fed-induced economic boom that was both fueling the internet and inadvertently providing us with an important lesson in the space where government policy and markets intersect. We may not have understood all of this the way we do now, but we were clear-eyed about the basics. The stock market was increasingly losing touch with reality, jacking up the valuation of companies with no real-world value, and people all around us were starting companies that consistently made no money at all.

Yet this is precisely what made us so enthusiastic about starting our hedge fund, because Larry had a fantastic track record for spotting the charlatans and shorting the stocks (betting on their eventual collapse) of overhyped internet companies, even while we were in a rising market. While Larry picked the stocks and taught me about markets, I did the fund's admin and anything else required, and the confidence I got from mastering accounting and business fundamentals has paid massive dividends over the years.

I learned the stock-picking business by watching Larry trace cash through a company's accounts, but then gradually found my own way, gaining us access to a new community of managers and investment ideas. One way I did that was cold-emailing TheStreet.com's cofounder Jim Cramer.[23] We started exchanging emails, and soon afterward Jim offered me a writing spot at what had become the hot tip-sheet of the digital age. This helped me build connections and increase the flow of ideas into Sonic.

Larry and I were still following the stock-picking game established by legends like Peter Lynch, and I was helping Larry by researching our target companies' competitors and understanding how they were similar or different to the companies Larry was focusing on. That way we could map out whole forests, not just single trees. In the process, I started developing my own views as to what made a good investment. Because of my academic background in economic and diplomatic history, I was always looking to connect the macro with the micro and find bigger themes.

Yet my development hit some major hurdles in the spring of 1999.

Mom was complaining of a crippling pain radiating out from her abdomen and reaching around her back. Her doctors conducted tests to determine what was happening. Soon afterward I went to work out in Harvard's Quincy House gym with my friend Bard Geesaman, who was doing his residency in internal medicine at Massachusetts General Hospital and earning a Harvard-MIT MD PhD in neurobiology.

Bard saw something was bothering me and asked straight-out, "What's wrong?" I described my mom's symptoms. He didn't tell me this at the time, but he secretly guessed it was pancreatic cancer, and a couple of days later the CT scan confirmed the worst. Mom was given two months to live.

When we got the news, a friend, Justin Cammy, skipped class to drive me home. I got out of the car and walked into our old house, where everyone was crying. I knew then life was going to suck for a while.

My old friend Mark Briggs called me up that night. "You can't control what happens," he said, "but you will define yourself by how you act and react through this period. Be there for your family."

I was blessed with good friends. Larry stepped up with lots of research and as a sounding board for me when interacting with the doctors. Bard took command of Mom's care, recognizing we were helpless to process and navigate the health-care system the way he could. Our mutual friend George Daley—later dean of Harvard Medical School and already a medical luminary—was also enlisted, and before we knew it, my mom's care had been moved from a local hospital to Massachusetts General Hospital, under the care of top cancer specialists.[24] Mom was added to a clinical trial for an experimental cancer-drug cocktail, and her cancer was miraculously reduced in size by 25 percent in the first six months.

I was, in short, learning a lot about investments from Larry while struggling to deal with our emotional family upheaval, and could only do so by becoming a raging workaholic and severely compartmentalizing my life. I worked from my childhood bedroom Friday afternoons and over the weekend, and then went back to Cambridge for the rest of the week.

It's always darkest before it gets pitch black.

Larry and I were aware that Federal Reserve liquidity and the Wild West internet were producing stock market insanities. But making it in this overheated environment was a *feature,* not a bug, of the Sonic Fund's business model. We were already making money shorting stocks as the market went higher, so our shorts would *really* make money, we reasoned, when the markets inevitably turned south.

Well, we had a failure of imagination about just how out of whack things would get in the blow-off top, just before the bubble finally popped, and it was an error in judgment that almost killed us professionally. In summer 1999, Larry found WorldPort Communications, a small but acquisitive Georgia-based telecoms company on the make.[25] In June 1998 the outfit spent some $100 million acquiring its principal asset, a Dutch telecom firm called EnerTel.[26] The Georgia company's European asset had built a fiber-optic ring around the Netherlands and touted itself as "the leading second network operator" in its home country.

Larry dug into WorldPort's financials, as he always did, and shared with me his discovery: EnerTel was meagerly profitable because it had spent way too much building its Dutch fiberoptics highway. WorldPort was overleveraged, its financing was in shambles, and it was leaning on a seriously bad business model to keep itself afloat. Larry was certain the company was going to go bankrupt. We shorted WorldPort.

"Certain" and investing are a combustible mix.

A hedge fund will fail if the management does not have strong convictions, but it will also fail if it has *too strong* convictions. Humility and fear are the friends you don't know you need. That WorldPort was going to run out of cash was certain, but that it would go bankrupt was not as certain as we believed. As the adage often attributed to economist John Maynard Keynes notes, "Markets can stay irrational longer than you can stay solvent."[27]

On November 11, 1999, Energis PLC, a British company, bought WorldPort's EnerTel for a whopping £325 million.[28] That was $570 million in 1999 dollars, or five times what WorldPort itself had paid for the Dutch company just sixteen months earlier. When the cheap-money boom ended, people finally saw Energis for the money loser it was, and the firm collapsed, proving our hypothesis right.[29] But that was no comfort to us in the moment.

Our WorldPort short blew up and we immediately lost a significant amount of our assets under management, which was of course money that had been entrusted to us by our not-rich families and friends.

As I watched the stock price ratchet up on the screen, my hands turned icy, and then the ice ran up my arms into my heart. My heart started pounding like it would burst, and I wanted to hurl up my stomach contents.

What have I done?

Mike Tyson, the boxer, said it best about these terrifying moments: "Everyone has a plan until they get punched in the face."[30]

There was no time for hand-wringing. The immediate thing we had to do was stabilize Sonic and talk to our investors, including my family. I saved the worst for last and visited my mom in the hospital. Seeing how upset she was about losing the money—how angst-ridden it made her feel on top of the angst she was already feeling due to her fast-deteriorating health—spiraled me down to a new low.

That WorldPort short was on us. We screwed up. Facing my parents and friends over the WorldPort loss became an important and early lesson in humility.

Good communication, I discovered, is key to managing market mayhem; there is an emotional component to clear communications as much as there is an informational component. In the end, all we could tell our families and friends was, "This is on us. We *will* make this right." This was one team I was not quitting. In some situations, though they may be terrible, you know you can't live with yourself if you don't keep going.

Within a year, Larry and I had almost entirely recouped our loss. Our business idea turned out to be true; when the internet bubble finally blew up, Sonic's portfolio was a moneymaker, as other investors' portfolios tanked. Unfortunately, failing to anticipate how absurd things would get before the tide turned in our favor cost us dearly, and all our first post-bubble wins went to fill the hole we had created.

I still have this hurt: my mom never saw me make good. She died before we recovered our losses.

Even now, my shame is intense.

But feeling that shame, I now realize, helped instill in me a healthy sense of fear. I needed to constantly question how smart I truly was. I began asking myself again and again, *What can go wrong with this investment? What happens if two bad things occur at once? How are my investment decisions being affected by other things in my life?*

More important than a mental checklist, though, was that *feeling*. I will never forget that feeling of the ice running up my arms to my heart.

MAYBE I FINALLY LEARNED SOMETHING

In 2004 our track record at Sonic caught the eye of the hedge-fund heavy David Goel, one of the so-called Tiger Cubs. David, already a great manager and on his way to an even bigger success, asked us to join his Matrix Capital Management as managing directors.

I was thrilled. This was an opportunity to take what I had learned about US markets and apply those lessons internationally. My new job was to seek out investment opportunities all over the world, and it required touring steel mills in Mexico, sailing up the Bosporus from Istanbul in the US ambassador's yacht, and analyzing shopping malls in India. I learned a lot about the world and had some successes.

But once again, Larry was ahead of me. In early 2006 I think he sensed a disturbance in the markets. He told me he wanted to retire from the hedge-fund world and only manage Sonic as family money. Fortunately, we were family.

Larry left Matrix and moved to a penthouse on the beach in Hawaii. He continued to run the Sonic investment process he loved, but from then on completely on his own terms and with lots of flexibility.

This was a difficult period for me. I had talked to Larry for hours on end every day for the past ten years, and now we were on different paths. I was still learning and wanted to keep going at Matrix. One of the countries that intrigued me was Vietnam, which was just starting to publicly list its state-run enterprises. It was the perfect time to parachute into the country, find some hidden jewels, and invest as new wealth was being created.

I eventually ended up in Hanoi, where a local investment firm helped arrange some company visits. After a day of meetings, the firm's management invited me to a local bar with a look and vibe I would describe as "communist chic." That wasn't the surprise. The shock was discovering six or seven people from New York hedge funds, doing their own reconnaissance in Vietnam, hanging out in the same bar. I knew them all from back home.

When I got back to Boston and told David about what had happened at the bar in Hanoi, he said, "Wow, we thought it was the frontier, but that cake is already baked."

I couldn't get David's baked cake out of my mind. That Hanoi bar was a sign world markets were overheated, and I was suddenly worried that the macro trends I had been playing in emerging markets weren't going to pay off in the end. None of my shorts were panning out, either, and I simply was no good at the domestic-growth names like Apple and Google that were the big plays during that era.

Over the New Year, going into 2007, my pregnant wife and I flew to Grand Cayman. For days I walked up and down the Seven Mile Beach and thought through my entire life. I thought about how every time I considered making a big change—be it with the US Army airborne, or in academia, or now with my hedge-fund career—somebody who loved me had encouraged me to give up the path I was clinging to for financial-security reasons. They all promised to help me make a better life, and every time I had taken that leap of faith, things *had* gotten better.

I didn't know we were heading into the Global Financial Crisis. But I somehow sensed that seeking out growth stocks, especially in emerging markets, was not going to be a successful path for me going forward. I knew from experience that trying to climb during a storm had killed better and stronger people than me, and those experiences gave me a healthy fear of how fast risk can catch up and how painful it can get.

I reflected on the way I invested and what was going on in markets and asked myself, *Can I even add value to the Matrix team and the Matrix investment process in this climate?*

The honest answer, at that point, was no.

That was the only thing that mattered.

When I flew back to the US, I walked into David's office and told him I was retiring from Matrix and the industry. I couldn't see how I could add value to Matrix anymore.

He was great about it. I packed up my meager possessions in the rented Waltham, Massachusetts, apartment, where I had been based while working for Matrix, and moved back to our home in Virginia to help raise our new family.

It was January 2007. As the financial crisis gathered steam into early 2008, I knew getting out of the business had been the right call for me.

Bottom Line

If you have to make decisions in a panic, they can haunt you for the rest of your life. While we all want to believe we get better at assessing risk over time, an increasingly complex world should make you skeptical of your ability to develop this superpower.

Investing is not just about making the right choices; it's about making those choices in the right size and at the right time. As humans, we are prone to either over- or underestimate our ability to get to the desired outcome and how we will really feel after things go wrong—and they *will* go wrong. That's why planning ahead with investment strategies like diversification, rebalancing, and the 3L strategy are proven actions to help save us from ourselves.

APPENDIX

Books That Shaped My Thinking

The Education of Henry Adams (Illustrated)
Henry Adams
Got me thinking about identifying megatrends and triangulating over the horizon of history.

The Power Broker: Robert Moses and the Fall of New York
Robert A. Caro
For me, the greatest American work of nonfiction. Bonus: an explanation of why you get stuck in NYC traffic.

The Art of Thinking Clearly
Rolf Dobelli
Dobelli's books offer practical guidance on improving life through more disciplined thinking.

The Missing Billionaires: A Guide to Better Financial Decisions
Victor Haghani and James White
Explains the intersection of sizing positions, risk, and conviction.

The Ideological Origins of the American Revolution
Bernard Bailyn
America was founded on conspiracy theories.

The Intelligent Asset Allocator
William Bernstein
A revelation about asset allocation by a self-taught investor rather than an academic.

Confessions of a Street Addict
James J. Cramer
My old boss, a brilliant writer, openly writes about the impact that portfolio management had on his physical and mental well-being.

Thinking, Fast and Slow
Daniel Kahneman
Great advice on why you need a core and satellite portfolio. Bonus: the greatest colonoscopy story ever.

Geopolitical Alpha: An Investment Framework for Predicting the Future
Marko Papic
A framework for understanding how to analyze the big issues of our times.

The Snowball: Warren Buffett and the Business of Life
Alice Schroeder
You are not Warren Buffet.

Financial Shenanigans, Fourth Edition: How to Detect Accounting Gimmicks and Fraud in Financial Reports
Howard Schilit, Jeremy Perler, and Yoni Engelhart
Helps you analyze financial statements with less chance of missing what could be lurking in the details.

Narrative Economics: How Stories Go Viral and Drive Major Economic Events
Robert J. Shiller
Because it is increasingly important to understand how stories shape reality.

No Bull: My Life In and Out of Markets
Michael Steinhardt
Taught me a lot on how to manage stress and risk.

The Americanization of Benjamin Franklin
Gordon S. Wood
A story of personal and political reinvention.

The End of the World Is Just the Beginning: Mapping the Collapse of Globalization
Peter Zeihan
What if the Americas avoided war and worked together?

ACKNOWLEDGMENTS

The encouragement and support of Iqbal Khan, cohead of UBS Global Wealth Management and president of UBS Asia, made this book possible. There are many in our industry who excel at staying on top of a bank's complex operational issues, and there are other executives who have an innate gift for serving clients, but very few can do both well. Iqbal is the world's most connected private banker, and this book is a glimpse into but a slice of his universe.

Similarly, Richard Morton—Global Wealth Management's chief marketing officer, who also happens to have been an accomplished footballer in his younger days—has been my reliable teammate since day one in my role as CIO and on this project, adroitly moving the ball down the field and selflessly passing at the key moment so the entire team could score. My sincere thanks to both these men for ensuring I could put pen to paper in this unusual way.

Heartfelt thanks, too, to the unsung heroes of this book—our clients and their advisors.

Many have shared their stories with us in unprecedented ways, and my coauthor Richard and I were genuinely honored and humbled to receive their trust in this manner. There are so many to thank, but I would be remiss if I did not single out the individuals who so generously gave of themselves on the record in the pages of this book: Bill Sowles; Faizal Kottikollon; Karen Gray sharing her mother's story, the late Bernardine

Williams Rosenthal; Pablo Castro Saez; Pavle Matijevic; Rozett Phillips; and Suchitra Lohia.

Regrettably, I cannot individually name the talented client and financial advisors who, from all corners of the globe, materially contributed their wisdom to this book, but I can thank my colleagues who organized all their storytelling efforts. They are Patrick Corry in New York, and Serge Steiner and Annegret-Kerstin Meier in Zurich.

As the readers of this book will gather, I have in the course of life been blessed by real friends, colleagues, teachers, bosses, and—most of all—a loving family who stepped in to help when I was most in need. All I can do here is note how lucky I was to have the genius brigade step in and generously offer their time to help with parts of this story. Thank you, Mark Briggs, Bard Geesaman, and Larry Kam.

I am deeply grateful to be part of the UBS and chief investment office teams. Every day I am humbled by their kindness and accomplishments. Even though I cannot name them all here, I must express my sincerest gratitude to those CIO colleagues who I not only rely on heavily in the normal course of business but who went above and beyond to help me with the particulars of this book. They are Daniela Barajas, Mark Andersen, Kiran Ganesh, Vincent Heaney, and Andrew Lee.

There are many other UBS colleagues whom I haven't mentioned by name but who were generous with their time and played an invaluable role in helping to shape this book along the way. Their guidance and expertise added immeasurably to the final result.

When you make a trade in the marketplace there is a seller and a buyer and often there is an intermediary. We were the seller, of course, and our buyer was HarperCollins Leadership. Richard and I are so grateful for the entire team at HCL, who made sure we looked good, and we hope they are all richly rewarded for their risk-taking: publisher Matt Baugher, executive editor Tim Burgard, and senior editor Meaghan Porter, backed by HCL's competent production team Kevin Smith, Lauren Kingsley, Sicily Axton, Josh deLacy, Hannah Harliss, Heather Howell, and Sara Colley. Our heartfelt thanks to one and all.

This successful marriage between UBS and HCL was all made possible because of the matchmaking skills of our talent agent, Anthony Mattero at CAA, and his assistant, Sydney Shiffman. Richard would additionally like to thank his agent, Richard Pine of InkWell Management, supported by Naomi Eisenbeiss.

Lastly, my thanks to my writing partner Richard Morais. I know there were times in our back-and-forth that he wished we had never suggested this project, but it never showed. He is a dedicated artist and professional.

NOTES

INTRODUCTION

1. *UBS Annual Report 2023* (UBS Group, 2023), https://www.ubs.com/content /dam/assets/cc/investor-relations/annual-report/2023/files/annual-report -ubs-group-2023.pdf.
2. "Berkshire Hathaway Inc Portfolio Holdings," Fintel, accessed September 11, 2024, https://fintel.io/i/berkshire-hathaway.
3. Jennifer Mossalgue, "France to Require All Large Parking Lots to Be Covered by Solar Panels," Electrek, November 8, 2022, https://electrek.co /2022/11/08/france-require-parking-lots-be-covered-in-solar-panels/.
4. Richard C. Morais, personal notes taken while attending the hotel Fontenay event, October 27–30, 2022.
5. Barry Rittholz, "David Einhorn: Market Structures Are Broken," *Masters in Business*, Bloomberg Podcasts, February 8, 2024, https://www.youtube .com/watch?v=QuGQ0LDWUt8.

RULE 1: FOLLOW THE BIG MONEY

1. Christopher J. Neely, "Negative U.S. Interest Rates?," *Economic Research*, no. 4 (2020), https://doi.org/10.20955/es.2020.4.
2. Thomas Holst, "Insight: What Negative Oil Prices Really Mean," University of Utah Kim C. Gardner Policy Institute, accessed August 6, 2024, https:// gardner.utah.edu/blog/blog-what-negative-oil-prices-really-mean.
3. Christopher Rugaber, "Higher Gas and Rents Keep US Inflation Elevated, Likely Delaying Fed Rate Cuts," Associated Press, April 10, 2024, https:// apnews.com/article/inflation-prices-rates-economy-federal-reserve-biden-f0 2b969d1b44a7ccb0385be03f766de0#.

4. "U.S. Debt Credit Rating Downgraded, Only Second Time in Nation's History," House Budget Committee, August 2, 2023, https://budget.house .gov/resources/staff-working-papers/us-debt-credit-rating-downgraded -only-second-time-in-nations-history.

5. John Mecklin, ed., "2024 Doomsday Clock Statement," Bulletin of the Atomic Scientists, January 23, 2024, https://thebulletin.org/doomsday -clock/current-time.

6. "Billions of People Still Breathe Unhealthy Air: New WHO Data," World Health Organization, April 4, 2022, https://www.who.int/news/item/04-04 -2022-billions-of-people-still-breathe-unhealthy-air-new-who-data.

7. Michael Haederle, "Microplastics in Every Human Placenta, New UNM Health Sciences Research Discovers," UNM Health Sciences Newsroom, February 20, 2024, https://hsc.unm.edu/news/2024/02/hsc-newsroom-post -microplastics.html.

8. "Explainer: Capital Crowd Out Effects of Government Debt," University of Pennsylvania Penn Wharton Budget Model, June 28, 2021, https://budget model.wharton.upenn.edu/issues/2021/6/28/explainer-capital-crowd-out -effects-of-government-debt.

9. Dan Sabbagh, "Global Defence Spending Rises by 9% to Record $2.2TN," *Guardian*, February 13, 2024, https://www.theguardian.com/world/2024 /feb/13/global-defence-spending-rises-9-per-cent-to-record-22tn-dollars; IMF World Economc Outlook Presser, IMF Media Center, July 16, 2024, https://mediacenter.imf.org/news/imf-world-economic-outlook-presser/s /f7765ca6-8a67-46e3-a368-22d0b0b626a3.

10. "Overview and Key Findings," in *World Energy Investment 2023* (IEA, May 2023), https://www.iea.org/reports/world-energy-investment-2023 /overview-and-key-findings.

11. John Egan, "Texas Attracts Big Percentage of Government Clean Energy Investment, Says 2023 Report," Innovation Map, March 18, 2024, https:// houston.innovationmap.com/texas-clean-investment-monitor-report -2667540199.html.

12. "GDP (current US$)—Greece," World Bank Group, accessed August 8, 2024, https://data.worldbank.org/indicator/NY.GDP.MKTP.CD?locations =GR.

13. Office of the Texas Governor, Greg Abbott, "Texas Leads Nation with Fastest Economic Expansion," press release, March 31, 2023, https://gov .texas.gov/news/post/texas-leads-nation-with-fastest-economic-expansion; "GDP (current US$)—Russian Federation," World Bank Group, accessed

August 8, 2024, https://data.worldbank.org/indicator/NY.GDP.MKTP.CD ?locations=RU.

14. "The Serenity Prayer and Twelve Step Recovery," Hazelden Betty Ford Foundation, October 14, 2018, https://www.hazeldenbettyford.org/articles /the-serenity-prayer.

15. Elizabeth Stanton, "Fed's Biggest-Ever Bond-Buying Binge Is Drawing to a Close," Bloomberg, March 9, 2022, https://www.bloomberg.com/news /articles/2022-03-09/fed-s-biggest-ever-bond-buying-binge-is-drawing-to-a -close.

16. Victoria Masterson and Madeleine North, "What Is 'Global Debt'—and How High Is It Now?," World Economic Forum, December 21, 2023, https://www.weforum.org/agenda/2023/10/what-is-global-debt-why-high.

17. "Federal Debt: Total Public Debt as Percent of Gross Domestic Product," Federal Reserve Bank of St. Louis, June 27, 2024, https://fred.stlouisfed.org /series/GFDEGDQ188S.

18. "Public Debt of the United States from June 2013 to June 2024," Statista, accessed July 15, 2024, https://www.statista.com/statistics/273294/public -debt-of-the-united-states-by-month.

19. Aris Folley, "Budget Watchdog Warns US Could Suffer Market Shock over National Debt," The Hill, March 27, 2024, https://thehill.com/business /budget/4560301-budget-watchdog-warns-us-could-suffer-market-shock -over-national-debt.

20. Caleb Naysmith, "Jerome Powell Says $34 Trillion National Debt Is Ready for an 'Adult Conversation'—Janet Yellen Calls Sustainable Fiscal Path 'Critically Important,'" Benzinga, February 15, 2024, https://www.benzinga .com/startups/24/02/37156426/jerome-powell-says-34-trillion-national-debt -is-ready-for-an-adult-conversation-janet-yellen-calls-s.

21. "Do We Spend More on Interest Than Defense?," US Budget Watch 2024 (blog), Committee for a Responsible Federal Budget, February 20, 2024, https://www.crfb.org/blogs/do-we-spend-more-interest-defense.

22. "Interest Costs on the National Debt Are on Track to Reach a Record High," Fiscal Blog, Peter G. Peterson Foundation, February 16, 2023, https:// www.pgpf.org/blog/2023/02/interest-costs-on-the-national-debt-are-on -track-to-reach-a-record-high.

23. "Interest Costs"; Anita Hawser, "Countries with the Most Debt," Global Finance, June 8, 2023, https://gfmag.com/data/economic-data/countries -most-addicted-debt; US Debt Clock, https://www.usdebtclock.org.

24. Eric Wallerstein, "America's Bonds Are Getting Harder to Sell," Wall Street

Journal, April 14, 2024, https://www.wsj.com/finance/americas-bonds-are
-getting-harder-to-sell-c3fde4de.

25. Abbigail J. Chiodo and Michael T. Owyang, *A Case Study of a Currency Crisis:
The Russian Default of 1998* (Federal Reserve Bank of St. Louis, November/
December 2002), https://files.stlouisfed.org/files/htdocs/publications
/review/02/11/ChiodoOwyang.pdf.

26. Karin Strohecker, Andrea Shalal, and Emily Chan, "Russia in Historic
Default as Ukraine Sanctions Cut Off Payments," Reuters, June 27, 2022,
https://www.reuters.com/markets/europe/russia-slides-towards-default
-payment-deadline-expires-2022-06-26.

27. Patrick Collinson, "Danish Bank Launches World's First Negative Interest
Rate Mortgage," *Guardian,* August 13, 2019, https://www.theguardian.com
/money/2019/aug/13/danish-bank-launches-worlds-first-negative-interest
-rate-mortgage.

28. Gerrit Koester et al., "Inflation Developments in the Euro Area and the
United States," *ECB Economic Bulletin* (August 2022), https://www.ecb
.europa.eu/press/economic-bulletin/focus/2023/html/ecb.ebbox202208_01
~c11d09d5fd.en.html.

29. "Alert on Cryptocurrency Money Services Businesses," Public Service
Announcement Alert Number: I-042524-PSA, FBI, April 25, 2024, https://
www.ic3.gov/Media/Y2024/PSA240425; "Statement by Secretary of the
Treasury Janet L. Yellen on Recent Crypto Market Developments," US
Department of the Treasury, November 16, 2022, https://home.treasury
.gov/news/press-releases/jy1111.

30. "Bitcoin Value Drops 50% Since November Peak," BBC, May 9, 2022,
https://www.bbc.com/news/business-61375152.

31. Tucker Reals, "Janet Yellen Says FTX Collapse Shows Cryptocurrencies Are
'Risky . . . Even Dangerous' Investments," CBS News, November 15, 2022,
https://www.cbsnews.com/news/ftx-collapse-janet-yellen-crypto-economy
-inflation-diesel-shortage-ev-batteries-china.

32. David Yaffe-Bellany, "Is Crypto Back? What to Know About Bitcoin's
Surge," *New York Times,* March 5, 2024, https://www.nytimes.com/2024/03
/05/technology/cryptocurrencies-bitcoin-explainer.html.

33. Jesse Hamilton, "Trump's Talk of Bitcoin Reserves for the U.S. Leaves
Industry Waiting for More Details," CoinDesk, July 29, 2024, https://www
.coindesk.com/news-analysis/2024/07/29/trumps-talk-of-bitcoin-reserve-for
-the-us-leaves-industry-waiting-for-more-details.

34. Gary Richardson, Alejandro Komai, and Michael Gou, "Roosevelt's Gold

Program," Federal Reserve History, accessed August 4, 2024, https://www
.federalreservehistory.org/essays/roosevelts-gold-program.

35. "President Invokes Gold Hoarder Law," *New York Times*, April 6, 1933,
https://timesmachine.nytimes.com/timesmachine/1933/04/06/issue.html.

36. "Government Confiscation of Gold: Understanding the Facts," United
States Gold Bureau, accessed August 4, 2024, https://www.usgoldbureau
.com/gold-confiscation.

37. Chris Colvin and Philip Fliers, "How the US Government Seized All
Citizens' Gold in 1930s," The Conversation, May 21, 2020, https://the
conversation.com/how-the-us-government-seized-all-citizens-gold-in-1930s
-138467.

38. "Mario Draghi," European Central Bank, accessed August 7, 2024, https://
www.ecb.europa.eu/press/conferences/ecbforum/previous_fora/2017
/html/biographies/draghi.it.html.

39. "Verbatim of the Remarks Made by Mario Draghi," Global Investment
Conference, London, July 26, 2012, European Central Bank, https://www
.ecb.europa.eu/press/key/date/2012/html/sp120726.en.html.

40. "Overall Cryptocurrency Market Capitalization per Week from July 2010
to July 2024," Statista, accessed August 4, 2024, https://www.statista.com
/statistics/730876/cryptocurrency-maket-value.

41. "Commercial Real Estate—U.S.," Statista, accessed August 4, 2024, https://
www.statista.com/outlook/fmo/real-estate/commercial-real-estate/united
-states#value; "Global Cryptocurrency Market Cap Charts," Coingecko,
accessed August 4, 2024, https://www.coingecko.com/en/global-charts.

42. *National Security Strategy* (White House, October 2022), https://www.white
house.gov/wp-content/uploads/2022/10/Biden-Harris-Administrations
-National-Security-Strategy-10.2022.pdf.

43. Rob Garver, "China, US Swap Trade Sanctions on Semiconductors,
Graphite," *Voice of America*, October 20, 2023, https://www.voanews.com/a
/china-us-swap-trade-sanctions-on-semiconductors-graphite-/7320136.html.

44. Peter Vanham and Nicholas Gordon, "The EBRD's Chief Economist
Wants Business Leaders to Push Back Against 'the Dangers of Economic
Fragmentation,'" *Fortune*, January 10, 2024, https://www.voanews.com/a
/china-us-swap-trade-sanctions-on-semiconductors-graphite-/7320136.html.

45. Luis Torres, "Mexico Seeks to Solidify Rank as Top U.S. Trade Partner,
Push Further Past China," Federal Reserve Bank of Dallas, July 11, 2023,
https://www.dallasfed.org/research/economics/2023/0711.

46. Charmaine Jacob, "India Wants to Become the Top Manufacturing

Alternative to China. But First It Needs to Beat Vietnam," CNBC, April 1, 2024, https://www.cnbc.com/2024/04/02/india-wants-to-become-the-top-manufacturing-alternative-to-china-but-first-it-needs-to-beat-vietnam.html.

47. Jihoon Lee and Cynthia Kim, "In South Korea, World's Lowest Fertility Rate Plunges Again in 2023," Reuters, February 28, 2024, https://www.reuters.com/world/asia-pacific/south-koreas-fertility-rate-dropped-fresh-record-low-2023-2024-02-28.

48. Feng Wang, Baochang Gu, and Yong Cai, "The End of China's One-Child Policy," Brookings Institution, March 30, 2016, https://www.brookings.edu/articles/the-end-of-chinas-one-child-policy.

49. Lee and Kim, "In South Korea."

50. Farah Master, "China's Population Drops for Second Year, with Record Low Birth Rate," Reuters, January 17, 2024, https://www.reuters.com/world/china/chinas-population-drops-2nd-year-raises-long-term-growth-concerns-2024–01–17; Michael E. O'Hanlon, "China's Shrinking Population and Constraints on Its Future Powers," Brookings Institution, April 24, 2023, https://www.brookings.edu/articles/chinas-shrinking-population-and-constraints-on-its-future-power.

51. "Republic of Korea," PopulationPyramid.net, accessed August 5, 2024, https://www.populationpyramid.net/republic-of-korea/2019.

52. "Europe," PopulationPyramid.net, accessed August 5, 2024, https://www.populationpyramid.net/europe/2080.

53. "Unites States of America," PopulationPyramid.net, accessed August 5, 2024, https://www.populationpyramid.net/united-states-of-america/2080.

54. *Leaving No One Behind in an Ageing World: World Social Report 2023* (United Nations Department of Economic and Social Affairs, January 2023), https://www.un.org/development/desa/dspd/wp-content/uploads/sites/22/2023/01/2023wsr-chapter1-.pdf.

55. *World Migration Report 2024* (International Organization for Migration, 2024), 21, https://publications.iom.int/books/world-migration-report-2024.

56. "Healthcare Expenditures as a Percentage of GDP," USA Facts, accessed August 30, 2024, https://usafacts.org/data/topics/people-society/health/healthcare-expenditures/healthcare-expenditures-as-of-gdp.

57. "Budget Basics: Medicare," Peter G. Peterson Foundation, April 18, 2023, accessed August 30, 2024, https://www.pgpf.org/budget-basics/medicare.

58. Emma Wager et al., "How Does Health Spending in the U.S. Compare to Other Countries?," Health System Tracker, January 23, 2024, https://www.healthsystemtracker.org/chart-collection/health-spending-u-s-compare-countries.

59. "The Decade Ahead," *Year Ahead 2024: A New World* (UBS, December 2023), 40, https://advisors.ubs.com/katz/mediahandler/media/611610/digital-ubs -year-ahead-2024-global-en-3.pdf.

60. "Markets Data," Bloomberg, accessed August 5, 2024, https://www.bloom berg.com/quote/SPX:IND.

61. Garver, "China, US Trade Sanctions."

62. Elizabeth Kolbert, "The Obscene Energy Demands of A.I.," *New Yorker*, March 9, 2024, https://www.newyorker.com/news/daily-comment/the -obscene-energy-demands-of-ai.

63. Andy Patrizio, "Data Centers Push into New Territory in Pursuit of Energy, Space," Data Center Knowledge, March 5, 2024, https://www.data centerknowledge.com/buildconstruction/data-centers-push-new-territories -pursuit-energy-space.

64. Patrizio, "Data Centers."

65. "Renewable Energy Directive," European Commission, accessed August 5, 2024 https://energy.ec.europa.eu/topics/renewable-energy/renewable -energy-directive-targets-and-rules/renewable-energy-directive_en.

66. "Directive (EU) 2023/2413 of the European Parliament and of the Council," *Official Journal of the European Union*, October 18, 2023, https://eur-lex .europa.eu/legal-content/EN/TXT/?uri=CELEX%3A32023L2413&qid=169 9364355105.

67. "Energy Decisions Are Influenced by Economic, Political, Environmental and Social Factors," CLEAN, accessed August 3, 2024, https://cleanet.org /clean/literacy/energy5.html.

68. "Overview and Key Findings," in *World Energy Investment 2023* (IEA, May 2023), https://www.iea.org/reports/world-energy-investment-2023 /overview-and-key-findings.

69. "Investment," IEA, accessed August 25, 2024, https://www.iea.org/topics /investment.

70. Andrew Sissons and Laurie Smith, "Too Cheap to Meter: Could Low-Cost Renewables Create an Abundance of Energy?" Nesta, accessed September 12, 2024, https://www.nesta.org.uk/feature/future-signals-2023/too-cheap-to -meter-could-low-cost-renewables-create-an-abundance-of-energy/; Office of Energy and Renewable Energy, "Why Clean Energy Matters," accessed September 12, 2024, https://www.energy.gov/eere/why-clean-energy -matters; Dolf Gielen, Francisco Boshell, Deger Saygin, Morgan D. Bazilian, Nicholas Wagner, and Ricardo Gorini, "The Role of Renewable Energy in the Global Energy Transformation," *Energy Strategy Reviews* 24 (April 2019): 38–50, https://doi.org/10.1016/j.esr.2019.01.006.

RULE 2: BUY WHAT GOVERNMENTS ARE BUYING

1. "Inflation Reduction Act of 2022," US Department of Energy, updated September 22, 2023, https://www.energy.gov/lpo/inflation-reduction -act-2022.

2. "Indxx U.S. Infrastructure Development Index," Indxx, accessed May 22, 2024, https://www.indxx.com/indices/benchmark-indices/indxx_u.s ._infrastructure_development_index.

3. "Fact Sheet: One Year in, President Biden's Inflation Reduction Act Is Driving Historic Climate Action and Investing in America to Create Good Paying Jobs and Reduce Costs," White House Briefing Room Statement, August 16, 2023, https://www.whitehouse.gov/briefing-room/statements -releases/2023/08/16/fact-sheet-one-year-in-president-bidens-inflation -reduction-act-is-driving-historic-climate-action-and-investing-in-america -to-create-good-paying-jobs-and-reduce-costs; "Fact Sheet: CHIPS and Science Act Will Lower Costs, Create Jobs, Strengthen Supply Chains, and Counter China," White House Briefing Room Statement, August 9, 2022, https://www.whitehouse.gov/briefing-room/statements-releases/2022/08 /09/fact-sheet-chips-and-science-act-will-lower-costs-create-jobs-strengthen -supply-chains-and-counter-china.

4. "iShares Semiconductor ETF (SOXX)," Nasdaq, accessed May 22, 2024, https://www.nasdaq.com/market-activity/etf/soxx/historical.

5. Hudson Lockett and Cheng Leng, "How Xi Jinping Is Taking Control of China's Stock Market," *Financial Times*, September 21, 2023, https://www .ft.com/content/f9c864c1–6cd4–405e-aa4b-d0b5e2ec6535.

6. Lockett and Leng, "How Xi Jinping Is Taking Control."

7. US Department of Justice, "Justice Department Files Complaint Alleging Environmental Violations by eBay," press release, September 27, 2023, https://www.justice.gov/opa/pr/justice-department-files-complaint -alleging-environmental-violations-ebay; Chris Rosales, "Ebay Could Owe $1.9 Billion in Fines for Allowing Sale of 343,000 Emissions Defeat Devices," The Drive, September 30, 2023, https://www.thedrive.com/news/us-sues -ebay-for-allowing-sale-of-more-than-300000-emissions-defeat-devices; Kate Gibson, "Ebay Faces up to $2 Billion in Fines over Selling 'Rolling Coal' Devices," CBS, October 17, 2023, https://www.cbsnews.com/news/ebay -rolling-coal-devices-epa-justice-department.

8. "Grammercy Provides Record Litigation Loan for Environmental Lawsuits," Hedgeweek, October 2, 2023, https://www.hedgeweek.com/gramercy -provides-record-litigation-loan-for-environmental-lawsuits.

9. "What Was the Dieselgate Scandal?," Envirotech Online, December 23, 2022,

https://www.envirotech-online.com/news/air-monitoring/6/international
-environmental-technology/what-was-the-dieselgate-scandal/59471.

10. Ivana Kottasová, "Swiss Women Launch Landmark Lawsuit in Europe
Claiming Weak Climate Action Breaches Their Human Rights," CNN,
March 29, 2023, https://www.cnn.com/2023/03/29/europe/climate-lawsuit
-switzerland-european-court-intl/index.html; Gloria Dickie, Kate Abnett,
and Christian Levaux, "Swiss Women Win Landmark Climate Case at
Europe Top Human Rights Court," Reuters, April 9, 2024, https://www
.reuters.com/sustainability/climate-activists-seek-breakthrough-human
-rights-court-ruling-against-european-2024–04-09.

11. Madeline Fitzgerald and Elliot Davis Jr., "Russia Invades Ukraine: A
Timeline of the Crisis," *U.S. News & World Report*, February 22, 2024,
https://www.usnews.com/news/best-countries/slideshows/a-timeline-of
-the-russia-ukraine-conflict.

12. "European Union Natural Gas Import Price (I:EUNGIP)," Ycharts, accessed
May 23, 2024, https://ycharts.com/indicators/europe_natural_gas_price.

13. Doug Bandow, "Allies Begin the Reckless Seizure of Russian Assets," Cato
Institute, May 30, 2024, https://www.cato.org/commentary/allies-begin
-reckless-seizure-russian-assets.

14. Jackie Northam, "A Debate Is Centered on What to Do with the $300
Billion in Seized Russian Assets," *Morning Edition*, NPR, March 11, 2024,
https://www.npr.org/2024/03/11/1237398076/a-debate-is-centered-on-what
-to-do-with-300-billion-in-seized-russian-assets.

15. Aaron Arnold and Daniel Salisbury, "The Sanctions-Busting Architects:
Moscow's Preparations for the West's Sanctions," *Lawfare*, March 4, 2024,
https://www.lawfaremedia.org/article/the-sanctions-busting-architects
-moscow-s-preparations-for-the-west-s-sanctions.

16. "REPowerEU: Affordable, Secure and Sustainable Energy for Europe,"
European Commission, May 18, 2022, https://commission.europa.eu
/strategy-and-policy/priorities-2019–2024/european-green-deal/repowereu
-affordable-secure-and-sustainable-energy-europe_en.

17. Rob Copeland, "How Does the World's Largest Hedge Fund Really Make
Its Money?," *New York Times*, updated November 2, 2023, https://www
.nytimes.com/2023/11/01/business/how-does-the-worlds-largest-hedge
-fund-really-make-its-money.html.

18. Will Daniel, "Ray Dalio Slams 'Tragedy' of a *New York Times* Journalist's
Shocking Book About Him, Claiming He Was a Bridgewater Reject Who
Wrote 'Fiction, Created as Fact,'" *Fortune*, November 29, 2023, https://
finance.yahoo.com/news/ray-dalio-slams-tragedy-york-074835620.html.

19. "Value vs Growth: Current Trends, Top Stocks and ETFs," Ycharts, December 1, 2023, https://get.ycharts.com/resources/blog/value-vs-growth-stocks-funds-etfs-investing; Björn Jesch, "Value vs. Growth," DWS, March 27, 2024, https://www.dws.com/en-us/insights/cio-view/macro/cio-special-03272024.

20. Sarah Hansen, "Will Value Stocks Take the Lead in 2024?," Morningstar, January 11, 2024, https://www.morningstar.com/markets/will-value-stocks-take-lead-2024.

21. "Germany's Renewables Energy Act," IEA, May 9, 2023, https://www.iea.org/policies/12392-germanys-renewables-energy-act; "The Germany Feed-In Tariff," World Future Council, accessed August 1, 2024, https://www.futurepolicy.org/climate-stability/renewable-energies/the-german-feed-in-tariff.

22. Kate Connolly, "Germany to Cut Solar Power Subsidies," *Guardian*, March 2, 2012, https://www.theguardian.com/world/2012/mar/02/germany-cuts-solar-power-subsidies.

23. Erik Kirschbaum and Christoph Steitz, "Germany to Cut Solar Subsidies Faster Than Expected," Reuters, February 23, 2012, https://www.reuters.com/article/idUSTRE81M1EH.

RULE 3: UNDERSTAND HOW WE GOT TO WHERE WE ARE

1. "Sean Wilentz," Princeton University, Department of History, accessed August 5, 2024, https://history.princeton.edu/people/sean-wilentz.

2. Upton Sinclair, *The Jungle* (New York: Grosset and Dunlap, 1906).

3. Lyndon B. Johnson, "Remarks upon Signing Bill Amending the Meat Inspection Act," American Presidency Project, December 15, 1967, https://www.presidency.ucsb.edu/documents/remarks-upon-signing-bill-amending-the-meat-inspection-act.

4. "United States Code Annotated. Title 21. Food and Drugs. Chapter 12. Meat Inspection," Animal Legal and Historical Center, Michigan State University, March 2024, https://www.animallaw.info/statute/us-meat-chapter-12-meat-inspection.

5. Robert W. Bray, "History of Meat Science," American Meat Science Association, 1997, https://meatscience.org/about-amsa/history-mission/history-of-meat-science.

6. Todd S. Purdum, "Walt Rostow, Advisor to Kennedy and Johnson, Dies at 86," *New York Times*, February 15, 2003, https://www.nytimes.com/2003/02/15/us/walt-rostow-adviser-to-kennedy-and-johnson-dies-at-86.html.

7. Mark Henry Haefele, "Walt Rostow, Modernization, and Vietnam: Stages of Theoretical Growth" (PhD dissertation, Harvard University, 2000), ProQuest, https://www.proquest.com/openview/4079551888ced53ed489 30482bfd0e75.

8. "Betting on the Market," *Frontline*, PBS, accessed August 1, 2024, https://www.pbs.org/wgbh/pages/frontline/shows/betting/pros/lynch.html; Jay Jenkins, "Everything You Need to Know About Peter Lynch in 8 Quotes," Motley Fool, updated October 15, 2018, https://www.fool.com/investing /2016/06/15/everything-you-need-to-know-about-peter-lynch-in-8.aspx.

9. "The Panic of 1907," Federal Reserve History, accessed August 1, 2024, https://www.federalreservehistory.org/essays/panic-of-1907.

10. "Panic of 1907," Federal Reserve History.

11. "Panic of 1907," Federal Reserve History.

12. Abigail Tucker, "The Financial Panic of 1907: Running from History," *Smithsonian Magazine*, October 8, 2008, https://www.smithsonianmag.com /history/the-financial-panic-of-1907-running-from-history-82176328.

13. "Stop 23. The Panic of 1907," audio tour, Morgan Library and Museum, accessed August 1, 2024, https://www.themorgan.org/exhibitions/online /guide/stop-23-panic-1907.

14. Alan Feuer, "For Playing Solitaire or Saving the Economy," *New York Times*, March 18, 2009, https://www.nytimes.com/2009/03/19/nyregion/19rooms .html.

15. "Panic of 1907," International Banker, September 9, 2021, https://international banker.com/history-of-financial-crises/panic-of-1907.

16. "The Gutenberg Bible," Morgan Library and Museum, accessed August 1, 2024, https://www.themorgan.org/exhibitions/online/bookmans-paradise /gutenberg-bible.

17. "J. Pierpont Morgan's Library: Building the Bookman's Paradise," Morgan Library and Museum, accessed August 1, 2024, https://www.themorgan .org/book/export/html/1381561.

18. "J. P. Morgan, the Panic of 1907, and the Federal Reserve Act," Teach Democracy, accessed August 1, 2024, https://teachdemocracy.org/images /pdf/jpmorgan.pdf.

19. "Panic of 1907," International Banker.

20. Feuer, "Playing Solitaire or Saving the Economy."

21. "United States Government Spending to GDP," Trading Economics, accessed August 1, 2024, https://tradingeconomics.com/united-states /government-spending-to-gdp.

22. "United States Government Spending to GDP."

23. Jonathan Stempel and Trevor Hunnicutt, "Bailout Buffett Burnishes 'Lender of Last Resort' Image," Reuters, June 22, 2017, https://www.reuters.com/article/idUSKBN19D2IJ.

24. Stempel and Hunnicutt, "Bailout."

25. Theron Mohamed, "Warren Buffett Injected $3 Billion into GE During the Financial Crisis. Here's a Look Back at How He Helped the Industrial Giant," Business Insider, updated January 8, 2023, https://markets.business insider.com/news/stocks/warren-buffett-invested-3-billion-general-electric -ge-2008-crisis-2020-6-1029327040.

26. "Berkshire Hathaway Invests US$5 Billion in Goldman Sachs amid the Global Financial Crisis," Goldman Sachs, accessed August 5, 2024, https:// www.goldmansachs.com/our-firm/history/moments/2008-buffett -investment.html.

27. Theron Mohamed, "Warren Buffett Plowed $5 Billion into Bank of America During the Debt-Ceiling Crisis of 2011. Here's a Look Back at One of the Most Lucrative Deals of His Career," Business Insider, January 14, 2023, https://markets.businessinsider.com/news/stocks/warren-buffett-invested -5-billion-bank-of-america-made-fortune-2020–10-1029690339; John Melloy and Liz Moyer, "Warren Buffett Just Made a Quick $12 Billion on a Clever Bank of America Investment," CNBC, June 30, 2017, https://www.cnbc .com/2017/06/30/warren-buffett-just-made-a-quick-12-billion-on-bank-of -america.html.

28. Michael Fleming and Weiling Liu, "Near Failure of Long-Term Capital Management," Federal Reserve History, November 22, 2013, https://www .federalreservehistory.org/essays/ltcm-near-failure.

29. "Case Study: LTCM," C. T. Bauer College of Business, University of Houston, accessed August 5, 2024, https://www.bauer.uh.edu/rsusmel/7386/ltcm-2 .htm.

30. Adam Hayes, "Black-Scholes Model: What It Is, How It Works, and Options Formula," Investopedia, updated July 11, 2024, https://www.investopedia .com/terms/b/blackscholes.asp.

31. Fleming and Liu, "Near Failure."

32. Fleming and Liu, "Near Failure."

33. Colin Read, *The Rise of the Quants: Marschak, Sharpe, Black, Scholes and Merton* (Great Britain: Palgrave Macmillan, 2012), 206.

34. *Systemic Risk and the Long-Term Capital Management Rescue* (Congressional Research Service, June 10, 1999), https://crsreports.congress.gov/product /pdf/RL/RL30232/3; Ron Rimkus, "Long-Term Capital Management," CFA

Institute, April 18, 2016, https://www.econcrises.org/2016/04/18/long-term
-capital-management.

35. Abbigail J. Chiodo and Michael T. Owyang, *A Case Study of a Currency Crisis:
The Russian Default of 1998* (Federal Reserve Bank of St. Louis, November/
December 2002), https://files.stlouisfed.org/files/htdocs/publications
/review/02/11/ChiodoOwyang.pdf.

36. Rimkus, "Long-Term Capital Management."

37. Matthieu Benavoli, "LTCM Crisis," Extreme Events in Finance, accessed
August 5, 2024, https://extreme-events-finance.net/resources/ltcm-crisis.

38. "Buffett's Lessons from Long Term Capital Management," *Novel Investor*
(blog), June 19, 2024, https://novelinvestor.com/buffetts-lessons-long-term
-capital-management.

39. Stephen Slivinski, "Too Interconnected to Fail?," *Region Focus*, Summer
2009, Federal Reserve Bank of Richmond, https://www.richmondfed.org
/-/media/richmondfedorg/publications/research/econ_focus/2009/summer
/pdf/economic_history.pdf; David Shirreff, "Lessons from the Collapse of
Hedge Fund, Long-Term Capital Management," accessed August 30, 2024,
Econometrics Laboratory, University of California Berkeley, https://eml
.berkeley.edu/~webfac/craine/e137_f03/137lessons.pdf.

40. Troy Segal, "Government-Sponsored Enterprise (GSE): Definition and
Examples," Investopedia, updated August 19, 2024, https://www.investopedia
.com/terms/g/gse.asp.

41. "About Fannie Mae and Freddie Mac," Federal Housing Finance Agency,
accessed August 4, 2024, https://www.fhfa.gov/about-fannie-mae-freddie
-mac.

42. "About Fannie Mae and Freddie Mac."

43. "Greenspan Admits 'Mistake' That Helped Crisis," NBC News, October 23,
2008, https://www.nbcnews.com/id/wbna27335454; Bruce Bartlett, "Who
Saw the Housing Bubble Coming?," *Forbes*, July 13, 2012, https://www
.forbes.com/2008/12/31/housing-bubble-crash-oped-cx_bb_0102bartlett
.html.

44. Mark Calabria, *Fannie, Freddie, and the Subprime Mortgage Market* (Cato
Briefing Papers, Cato Institute, March 7, 2011), https://ciaotest.cc.columbia
.edu/pbei/cato/0021652/f_0021652_17915.pdf.

45. Rosanna Lockwood, "Time to dust off that #mortgagecrisis scene from
The Big Short," X, June 22, 2023, https://x.com/Roolockwood/status/1671
855874661335041.

46. *The Financial Crisis Inquiry Report* (Financial Crisis Inquiry Commission,

January 2011), XV, https://www.govinfo.gov/content/pkg/GPO-FCIC/pdf /GPO-FCIC.pdf.

47. "Bear Stearns Collapses, Sold to J. P. Morgan Chase," History, January 19, 2018, https://www.history.com/this-day-in-history/bear-stearns-sold-to -j-p-morgan-chase.

48. "A Dozen Key Dates in the Demise of Bear Stearns," Reuters, March 17, 2008, https://www.reuters.com/article/idUSN17240319.

49. Federal Reserve Bank of New York, "New York Fed Completes Financing Arrangement Related to JPMorgan Chase's Acquisition of Bear Stearns," press release, June 26, 2008, https://www.newyorkfed.org/newsevents /news/markets/2008/ma080626.

50. Keith Fitz-Gerald, "Have We Hit the Bottom?," Money Morning, March 27, 2008, https://moneymorning.com/2008/03/27/have-we-hit-the-bottom.

51. "S&P 500 (GSPC)," Yahoo Finance, May 19, 2008, accessed August 4, 2024, https://finance.yahoo.com/quote/%5EGSPC/history.

52. Joe Hernandez, "How Lehman's Collapse 15 Years Ago Changed the U.S. Mortgage Industry," NPR, September 15, 2023, https://www.npr.org/2023 /09/15/1199321274/lehman-brothers-collapse-2008-mortgages.

53. "Ben S. Bernanke," Federal Reserve History, accessed August 4, 2024, https://www.federalreservehistory.org/people/ben-s-bernanke.

54. Ben S. Bernanke, *Essays on the Great Depression* (Princeton, NJ: Princeton University Press, 2004), https://press.princeton.edu/books/paperback /9780691118208/essays-on-the-great-depression.

55. Perry G. Mehrling, "Bernanke vs. Kindleberger: Which Credit Channel?," Institute for New Economic Thinking, October 13, 2022, https://www .ineteconomics.org/perspectives/blog/bernanke-v-kindleberger-which -credit-channel.

56. Barry Eichengreen and J. Bradford DeLong, "New Preface to Charles Kindleberger, *The World in Depression 1929–1939*," CEPR, June 12, 2012, https://cepr.org/voxeu/columns/new-preface-charles-kindleberger-world -depression-1929-1939.

57. "Money, Gold, and the Great Depression," remarks by Ben. S. Bernanke, March 2, 2004, H. Parker Willis Lecture in Economic Policy, Washington and Lee University, Lexington, Virginia, Federal Reserve Board, https:// www.federalreserve.gov/boarddocs/speeches/2004/200403022; "Review: What the Great Depression Taught the Fed," Reuters, February 4, 2015, https://www.reuters.com/article/idUS32838103.

58. "Deflation: Making Sure 'It' Doesn't Happen Here," remarks by Ben. S. Bernanke, November 21, 2002, National Economists Club, Washington,

DC, Federal Reserve Board, https://www.federalreserve.gov/boarddocs
/speeches/2002/20021121.

59. Gerald P. Dwyer, "Stock Prices in the Financial Crisis," Federal Reserve
Bank of Atlanta, September 2009, https://www.atlantafed.org/cenfis
/publications/notesfromthevault/0909.

60. David M. Herszenhorn, Carl Hulse, and Sheryl Gay Stolberg, "Talks
Implode During a Day of Chaos; Fate of Bailout Plan Remains Unresolved,"
New York Times, September 25, 2008, https://www.nytimes.com/2008/09
/26/business/26bailout.html; Liz Wolgemuth, "Hank Paulson: Kneeling
Before Pelosi," *U.S. News & World Report*, September 26, 2008, https://
money.usnews.com/money/blogs/the-inside-job/2008/09/26/hank-paulson
-kneeling-before-pelosi.

61. Public Law 110–343, 110th Congress, Troubled Asset Relief Program, US
Government Printing Office, October 3, 2008, https://www.congress.gov
/110/plaws/publ343/PLAW-110publ343.htm.

62. "About Tarp," US Department of the Treasury, accessed August 5, 2024,
https://home.treasury.gov/data/troubled-assets-relief-program/about-tarp.

63. *The Financial Crisis Inquiry Report* (Financial Crisis Inquiry Commission,
January 2011), 246, https://www.govinfo.gov/content/pkg/GPO-FCIC/pdf
/GPO-FCIC.pdf.

64. "Jurassic Park (1993)—They Remember," Anders Andersson, December 15,
2012, YouTube, https://www.youtube.com/watch?v=CvrxcR-gdQ0.

65. Dan Wilchins and Jonathan Stempel, "Citigroup Gets Massive Government
Bailout," Reuters, November 24, 2008, https://www.reuters.com/article/id
USTRE4AJ45G.

66. David Ellis, "Citigroup Plunges as Bank Mulls Next Move," CNN Money,
November 21, 2008, https://money.cnn.com/2008/11/21/news/companies
/citigroup/index.htm?postversion=20081121.

67. Dan Wilchins and Jonathan Stempel, "Citigroup Talking to U.S.
Government," Reuters, November 22, 2008, https://www.reuters.com
/article/idUSTRE4AK5D6.

68. Federal Reserve System Board of Governors, "Joint Statement by Treasury,
Federal Reserve, and the FDIC on Citigroup," press release, November 23,
2008, https://www.federalreserve.gov/newsevents/pressreleases/bcreg2008
1123a.htm; "Summary of Terms," Federal Reserve Board, November 23,
2008, https://www.federalreserve.gov/newsevents/pressreleases/files/bcreg
20081123a1.pdf.

69. US Department of the Treasury, "Treasury Announces Participation in
Citigroup's Exchange Offering," press release, February 27, 2009, https://

home.treasury.gov/news/press-releases/tg41; "Transaction Outline," US Department of the Treasury, February 27, 2009, https://home.treasury.gov /system/files/136/archive-documents/transaction_outline.pdf.

70. Eric Dash and Louise Story, "Latest Citigroup Rescue May Not Be Its Last," *New York Times*, February 27, 2009, https://www.nytimes.com/2009/02/28 /business/28citi.html; Jonathan Stempel, "Citigroup Stock Falls Below $1 for First Time," Reuters, March 5, 2008, https://www.reuters.com/article /idUSN05328477.

71. "Bank Nationalization 'as American as Apple Pie,'" NBC 4 Washington, February 22, 2009, https://www.nbcwashington.com/local/bank -nationalization-as-american-as-apple-pie/1865543.

72. "Ben Bernanke's Greatest Challenge," *60 Minutes*, CBS News, March 12, 2009, https://www.cbsnews.com/news/ben-bernankes-greatest-challenge.

73. "S&P 500 (GSPC)," Yahoo Finance, March 17, 2009, accessed August 5, 2024, https://finance.yahoo.com/quote/%5EGSPC/history.

74. UBS, "Mark Haefele Appointed UBS Global Chief Investment Officer," press release, June 2, 2014, https://www.ubs.com/global/en/media/display -page-ndp/en-20140602-message-mark-haefele.html.

75. "Timothy F. Geithner," Warburg Pincus, accessed August 5, 2024, https:// warburgpincus.com/team/timothy-f-geithner.

76. Jeff Cox, "Bernanke, Paulson and Geithner Say They Bailed Out Wall Street to Save Main Street," CNBC, September 12, 2018, https://www.cnbc .com/2018/09/12/bernanke-paulson-and-geithner-say-they-bailed-out-wall -street-to-help-main-street.html.

77. Laura Saunders, "The 'You-Make-A-Lot-Of-Money-Tax' Hits More Americans," *Wall Street Journal*, June 23, 2023, https://www.wsj.com /articles/niit-tax-strategies-net-investment-income-1c2f8e25.

78. Jackie Calmes, "Spotlight Fixed on Geithner, a Man Obama Fought to Keep," *New York Times*, November 12, 2011, https://www.nytimes.com /2011/11/13/us/politics/spotlight-fixed-on-geithner-a-man-obama-fought -to-keep.html.

79. David E. Sanger, "Nationalization Gets a New, Serious Look," *New York Times*, January 25, 2009, https://www.nytimes.com/2009/01/26/business /economy/26banks.html.

80. "S&P 500—90 Year Historical Chart," Macrotrends, accessed August 1, 2024, https://www.macrotrends.net/2324/sp-500-historical-chart-data.

81. "Verbatim of the Remarks Made by Mario Draghi," Global Investment Conference, London, July 26, 2012, European Central Bank, https://www .ecb.europa.eu/press/key/date/2012/html/sp120726.en.html.

82. "How the Federal Reserve's Quantitative Easing Affects the Federal Budget," Congressional Budget Office, September 2022, https://www.cbo .gov/publication/58457.

83. "Ben Bernanke's Greatest Challenge."

84. "History of Quantitative Easing in the U.S.," American Deposit Management, accessed August 5, 2024, https://americandeposits.com /history-quantitative-easing-united-states.

85. "Quantitative Easing," Bank of England, updated May 10, 2024, https:// www.bankofengland.co.uk/monetary-policy/quantitative-easing.

86. James Chen, "Risk Asset: Definition and Examples from Stocks to Crypto," Investopedia, updated September 29, 2022, https://www.investopedia.com /terms/r/risk-asset.asp.

87. Federal Reserve System Board of Governors, "Federal Reserve Announces It Will Initiate a Program to Purchase the Direct Obligations of Housing-Related Government-Sponsored Enterprises and Mortgage-Backed Securities Backed by Fannie Mae, Freddie Mac, and Ginnie Mae," press release, November 25, 2008, https://www.federalreserve.gov/news events/pressreleases/monetary20081125b.htm; "History of Quantitative Easing."

88. Mitsuru Katagiri, Junnosuke Shino, and Koji Takahaski, "Bank of Japan's ETF Purchase Program and Equity Risk Premium: A CAPM Interpretation," *BIS Working Papers* 1029 (Bank for International Settlements, July 2022), https://www.bis.org/publ/work1029.pdf.

89. Neil Irwin, "Quantitative Easing Is Ending. Here's What It Did, in Charts," *New York Times*, October 29, 2014, https://www.nytimes.com/2014/10/30 /upshot/quantitative-easing-is-about-to-end-heres-what-it-did-in-seven -charts.html.

90. Amalia Estenssoro and Kevin L. Kliesen, "The Mechanics of Fed Balance Sheet Normalization," Federal Reserve Bank of St. Louis, August 23, 2023, https://research.stlouisfed.org/publications/economic-synopses/2023/08 /23/the-mechanics-of-fed-balance-sheet-normalization.

91. "S&P 500 (TR) (SP500TR)," Yahoo Finance, January 2014–January 2022, accessed August 6, 2024, https://finance.yahoo.com/quote/%5ESP500TR /history.

92. Yun Li and Nate Rattner, "S&P 500 Doubles from Its Pandemic Bottom, Marking the Fastest Bull Market Rally Since WWII," CNBC, August 16, 2021, https://www.cnbc.com/2021/08/16/sp-500-doubles-from-its-pandemic -bottom-marking-the-fastest-bull-market-rally-since-wwii.html.

93. Aruni Soni, "A Record High 58% of American Households Now Own

Stocks," Yahoo Finance, October 19, 2023, https://finance.yahoo.com/news /record-high-58-american-households-225829999.html.

94. "What Percentage of Americans Own Stock?," Gallup, May 24, 2023, https:// news.gallup.com/poll/266807/percentage-americans-owns-stock.aspx.

95. Arun Soni, "Investors Have Pulled $150 Billion out of Stock Picking Hedge Funds over the Past 5 Years," Business Insider, February 7, 2024, https:// markets.businessinsider.com/news/stocks/us-stock-market-losers-dotcom -era-hedge-funds-fed-rates-2024-2.

96. Joseph Wilkins, "Hedge Funds Are Reeling from Some of the Worst Outflows Since the Great Recession and Managers Are Shunning Wall Street—Even as a Bull Market Reigns," Business Insider, July 14, 2023, https://markets.businessinsider.com/news/funds/hedge-funds-reeling -from-worst-outflows-since-great-recession-2023-7.

RULE 4: DON'T PICK STOCKS. ALLOCATE ASSETS.

1. "FAQs," 9/11memorial.org, 9/11Memorial & Museum, accessed August 26, 2024, https://www.911memorial.org/911-faqs.

2. Marc Davis, "How September 11 Affected the U.S. Stock Market," Investopedia, September 11, 2023, https://www.investopedia.com/financial -edge/0911/how-september-11-affected-the-u.s.-stock-market.aspx.

3. William Bernstein, The Intelligent Asset Allocator: How to Build Your Portfolio to Maximize Returns and Minimize Risk (New York: McGraw-Hill, 2000).

4. James Chen, "What Is Asset Allocation and Why Is It Important?," Investopedia, October 11, 2023, https://www.investopedia.com/terms/a /assetallocation.asp.

5. Burton G. Malkiel, A Random Walk down Wall Street: The Best Investment Guide That Money Can Buy (New York: W. W. Norton, 2023).

6. Meir Statman, "How Many Stocks Make a Diversified Portfolio?," Journal of Financial and Quantitative Analysis 2, no. 3 (September 1987), https://www .jstor.org/stable/2330969.

7. Marcel Schwantes, "Warren Buffet Says Integrity Is the #1 Trait to Hire For. Ask These 4 Questions to Screen Out the Imposters," Inc., March 6, 2024, https://www.inc.com/marcel-schwantes/warren-buffett-interview -for-integrity-to-screen-out-impostors.html.

8. Jeffrey Ptak, "Bad Timing Cost Investors One Fifth of Their Funds' Returns," Morningstar, August 2, 2023, https://www.morningstar.com /funds/bad-timing-cost-investors-one-fifth-their-funds-returns.

9. "Quantitative Analysis of Investor Behavior," Dalbar.com, accessed August 4, 2024, https://www.dalbar.com/ProductsAndServices/QAIB.

10. Murray Coleman, "Dalbar QAIB 2024: Investors Are Still Their Own Worst Enemy," Index Fund Advisors, updated April 8, 2024, https://www.ifa.com /articles/understanding-investor-behavior-portfolio-performance.

11. James Picerno, "Investor Returns vs. Market Returns: The Failures Endure," *Capital Spectator*, September 21, 2017, https://www.capitalspectator.com /investor-returns-vs-market-returns-the-failure-endures.

12. Gary P. Brinson, Brian D. Singer, and Gilbert L. Beebower, "Determinants of Portfolio Performance II: An Update," *Financial Analysts Journal* 47, no. 3 (May/June 1991), https://www.jstor.org/stable/4479432.

13. Brinson, Singer, and Beebower, "Determinants of Portfolio Performance."

14. Adam Hayes, "Behavioral Finance: Biases, Emotions and Financial Behavior," Investopedia, updated August 20, 2024, https://www .investopedia.com/terms/b/behavioralfinance.asp.

15. Cory Mitchell, "Historical Average Stock Market Returns for S&P 500 (5-Year to 150-Year Averages)," TradeThatSwing, June 28, 2024, https:// tradethatswing.com/average-historical-stock-market-returns-for-sp-500-5 -year-up-to-150-year-averages.

16. Mitchell, "Historical Average."

17. *2024 Long-Term Capital Market Assumptions* (Invesco Solutions, 2024), https:// www.invesco.com/content/dam/invesco/apac/en/pdf/insights/2023 /december/LTCMA-USD-Dec-2023.pdf.

18. "S&P 500 (TR) (SP500TR)," Yahoo Finance, January 2007–December 2008, accessed August 6, 2024, https://finance.yahoo.com/quote/%5ESP500TR /history.

19. "Historical Performance of the ICE US Treasury 7–10 Year Bond Index," Blacktest by Curvo, accessed August 1, 2024, https://curvo.eu/backtest/en /market-index/ice-us-treasury-7-10-year-bond?currency=eur.

20. Marco Jacopo Lombardi and Vladyslav Sushko, "The Correlation of Equity and Bond Returns," *BIS Quarterly Review* (December 4, 2023), https://www .bis.org/publ/qtrpdf/r_qt2312v.htm.

21. Andy Polacek, "Catastrophe Bonds: A Primer and Retrospective," Federal Reserve Bank of Chicago, 2018, https://www.chicagofed.org/publications /chicago-fed-letter/2018/405.

22. Solita Marcelli, "Investing with UBS: CIO at Your Side," UBS, accessed August 25, 2024, https://www.ubs.com/us/en/wealth-management /financial-advisor-experience/articles/ubs-chief-investment-office.html.

23. Matthew Allen, "Swiss Banks Accused of Hiding Data Behind Secrecy Law," Swissinfo.ch, February 20, 2023, https://www.swissinfo.ch/eng/business /swiss-banks-accused-of-hiding-data-behind-secrecy-laws/48292728.

24. Kristi Heim, "Gates Foundation CFO Announces Resignation," *Seattle Times*, October 12, 2009, https://www.seattletimes.com/business/gates -foundation-cfo-announces-resignation.

25. Maria Di Mento, "Warren Buffett Has Given $50.7 Billion Toward Historic Pledges to the Gates Foundation and Others," Associated Press, June 23, 2023, https://apnews.com/article/warren-buffett-donations-gates -foundation-c2f6981e46c6211b16ada2704433d3c0.

26. "Mona Sutphen," Omidyar Network, accessed August 1, 2024, https:// omidyar.com/omidyar_team/mona-sutphen.

27. "Carl Gustav Jacob Jacobi," MacTutor Index, updated January 2000, https:// mathshistory.st-andrews.ac.uk/Biographies/Jacobi.

28. "Inversion and the Power of Avoiding Stupidity," *Mental Models* (blog), Farnam Street, accessed August 6, 2024, https://fs.blog/inversion.

29. *Annual Review 2010: We Will Not Rest* (UBS, 2011), 16, https://www.ubs.com /global/en/investor-relations/financial-information/annual-reporting/ar -archive.html.

30. "Junk Bond Spreads," Current Market Valuation, updated June 30, 2024, https://www.currentmarketvaluation.com/models/junk-bond-spreads.php.

RULE 5: KNOW YOURSELF AND YOUR DEEPEST MONEY ISSUES

1. "193 Quotes by Benjamin Graham," Elevate Society, accessed August 7, 2024, https://elevatesociety.com/quotes-by-benjamin-graham.

2. Alice Schroeder, *The Snowball: Warren Buffett and the Business of Life*, updated and condensed edition (New York: Bantam, 2009); Barbara Kiviat, "Warren Buffett Tells All: The Women in His Life," *Time*, September 23, 2008, https://time.com/archive/6904590/warren-buffett-tells-all-the-women-in -his-life.

3. "John Griffin," Michael J. Fox Foundation, accessed August 5, 2024, https:// www.michaeljfox.org/bio/john-griffin.

4. "Julian Robertson, Jr.," *Forbes*, April 5, 2022, https://www.forbes.com /profile/julian-robertson-jr.

5. "Daniel Kahneman: Facts," Nobel Prize, August 22, 2024, https://www .nobelprize.org/prizes/economic-sciences/2002/kahneman/facts.

6. Daniel Kahneman, *Thinking, Fast and Slow* (New York: Farrar, Straus and Giroux, 2013).

7. "Paul Tudor Jones, II," *Forbes*, accessed August 6, 2024, https://www.forbes .com/profile/paul-tudor-jones-ii.

8. Landon Thomas Jr., "The Man Who Won as Others Lost," *New York Times*,

October 13, 2007, https://www.nytimes.com/2007/10/13/business/13
speculate.html.

9. Richard Feloni, "Billionaire Investor Paul Tudor Jones Pays Tony Robbins
over $1 Million a Year and Emails Him Every Day—Here's What They Talk
About," Business Insider, October 7, 2017, https://www.businessinsider.com
/tony-robbins-coach-paul-tudor-jones-2017-10.

10. Sarah Jackson, "Warren Buffett, Who Famously Loves McDonald's, Is
Willing to Give Up a Year of His Life to Eat Whatever He Wants," Yahoo
Finance, April 12, 2023, https://finance.yahoo.com/news/warren-buffett
-famously-loves-mcdonalds-163104691.html.

11. Jackson, "Warren Buffett."

12. "Oil Crisis of the 1970s," Energy Education, accessed August 5, 2024,
https://energyeducation.ca/encyclopedia/Oil_crisis_of_the_1970s.

13. Nicolas Vega, "A Gallon of Gas Was 65 Cents in 1978—Here's How Much
It Cost Every Year Since," CNBC, April 13, 2022, https://www.cnbc.com
/2022/04/13/how-much-gas-cost-every-year-since-1978.html; "Gasoline
Prices Now 5 Times Higher Than in 1978," US Bureau of Labor Statistics,
December 5, 2013, https://www.bls.gov/opub/ted/2013/ted_20131205.htm.

14. Marcel Grzanna, "Schaffe, spare, Häusle baue," *Süddeutsche Zeitung*,
January 3, 2020, https://www.sueddeutsche.de/wirtschaft/bausparen
-schaffe-spare-haeusle-baue-1.4726122.

15. Pablo Uchoa, "How Do You Solve Catastrophic Hyperinflation?," BBC,
September 21, 2018, https://www.bbc.com/news/business-45523636.

16. "$8 in 1978 Is Worth $38.59 Today," CPI Inflation Calculator, accessed
August 5, 2024, https://www.in2013dollars.com/us/inflation/1978?
amount=8.

17. "193 quotes by Benjamin Graham."

RULE 6: CREATE LIQUIDITY, LONGEVITY, AND LEGACY BUCKETS

1. Tim Sablik, "Recession of 1981–1982," Federal Reserve History, accessed
August 4, 2024, https://www.federalreservehistory.org/essays/recession
-of-1981-82.

2. "Historical CD Interest Rates: 1984–2024," Bankrate, accessed August 6,
2024, https://www.bankrate.com/banking/cds/historical-cd-interest-rates
/#80s.

3. "Principles of Microeconomics (2021.A.01)," Saylor.org Academy, accessed
August 4, 2024, https://learn.saylor.org/mod/book/view.php?id=31181&
chapterid=7477.

4. Troy Segal, "Mental Accounting: Definition, Avoiding Bias, and Example," Investopedia, updated May 22, 2024, https://www.investopedia.com/terms/m/mentalaccounting.asp.

5. Paul D. Kaplan, "What Prior Market Crashes Taught Us in 2020," Morningstar, updated July 23, 2020, https://www.morningstar.com/features/what-prior-market-crashes-can-teach-us-in-2020.

6. "How Long Do Bear Markets Last?," Stash, January 10, 2024, https://www.stash.com/learn/how-long-do-bear-markets-last.

7. Marianna Mamou and Justin Waring, "Personalized Investment Advice in the Context of a Wealth Plan: UBS Wealth Way," UBS, July 19, 2023.

8. Laura Rodini, "What Was the COVID-19 Stock Market Crash of 2020? Causes and Effects," TheStreet, updated November 10, 2022, https://www.thestreet.com/dictionary/covid-19-stock-market-crash-of-2020.

9. "Bernardine's Story: The Renaissance of Bernardine Rosenthal," UBS, accessed August 5, 2024, https://www.ubs.com/global/en/wealth management/about-us/client-stories/2023/bernardines-story.html.

10. Bernardine Williams Rosenthal, *Under the Noodle String* (Xlibris US, 2020).

11. Vartika Gupta et al., "Prime Numbers: Markets Will Be Markets: An Analysis of Long-Term Returns from the S&P 500," McKinsey, August 4, 2022, whttps://ww.mckinsey.com/capabilities/strategy-and-corporate-finance/our-insights/the-strategy-and-corporate-finance-blog/markets-will-be-markets-an-analysis-of-long-term-returns-from-the-s-and-p-500.

12. Bill Sowles, interview by Richard C. Morais, December 12, 2023; fact-checked story details on recorded follow-up call, January 31, 2024.

13. Mark Andersen et al., "Endowment-Style Portfolio (ESP)," UBS Chief Investment Office GWM, January 2024.

RULE 7: ONCE FINANCIALLY SECURE, MASH UP THE RULES TO BECOME AN IMPACT INVESTOR

1. "The Artist's Father," Museu Picasso, accessed August 1, 2024, https://museupicassobcn.cat/en/collection/artwork/artists-father-25.

2. "Pablo Picasso Blue Period," Masterworks Fine Art Gallery, accessed August 1, 2024, https://www.masterworksfineart.com/artists/pablo-picasso/blue-period.

3. Sabine Rewald, "Cubism," Metropolitan Museum of Art, October 2004, https://www.metmuseum.org/toah/hd/cube/hd_cube.htm.

4. Pagan Kennedy, "William Gibson's Future Is Now," *New York Times*, January 13, 2012, https://www.nytimes.com/2012/01/15/books/review/distrust-that-particular-flavor-by-william-gibson-book-review.html.

5. "What You Need to Know About Impact Investing," Global Impact Investing Network, January 1, 2023, https://thegiin.org/impact-investing /need-to-know/#what-is-impact-investing.

6. "What Is Sustainable Investing?," CFA Institute, accessed August 5, 2024, https://www.cfainstitute.org/en/rpc-overview/esg-investing/sustainable -investing.

7. "Dr. Rozett Phillips Joins GIBS Executive Team," Gordon Institute of Business Science, University of Pretoria, March 8, 2021, https://www.gibs .co.za/news/dr-rozett-phillips-joins-gibs-executive-team.

8. Richard C. Morais, recorded interview with Rozett Phillips on October 10, 2022; fact-checking interview recorded on November 11, 2022.

9. Joyce Chimbi, "Africa's Vast Arable Land Underutilized for Both Cash and Food Crops," Global Issues/Inter Press Service, Jan. 16, 2023, https:// www.globalissues.org/news/2023/01/16/32820#:~:text=Outside%20of%20 countries%20such%20as,the%20world's%20uncultivated%20arable%20land.

10. Landry Signé, "Africa Youth Leadership: Building Local Leaders to Solve Global Challenges," Brookings Institute, March 27, 2019, https://www .brookings.edu/articles/africa-youth-leadership-building-local-leaders-to -solve-global-challenges/.

11. "The Sustainable Development Agenda," United Nations, accessed September 20, 2024, https://www.un.org/sustainabledevelopment /development-agenda-retired/#:~:text=On%201%20January%202016%2C %20the,Summit%20%E2%80%94%20officially%20came%20into%20force.

12. Dana Vorisek and Shu Yu, "Understanding the Cost of Achieving the Sustainable Development Goals" (Policy Research Working Paper 9146, World Bank Group, February 2020), https://documents1.worldbank.org /curated/en/744701582827333101/pdf/Understanding-the-Cost-of-Achieving -the-Sustainable-Development-Goals.pdf.

13. "Summary," IMF Working Papers, Decomposing Climate Risks in Stock Markets, accessed August 26, 2024, https://www.imf.org/en/Publications /WP/Issues/2023/06/30/Decomposing-Climate-Risks-in-Stock-Markets -534307.

14. Simon Smiles et al., *Awareness, Simplification, and Contribution* (white paper, UBS, January 2019), 9, https://catalogue.unccd.int/1124_wef-wp-final.pdf.

15. Marina Gerner, "Impact Investing Could Change Capitalism Forever," Raconteur, August 9, 2020, https://www.raconteur.net/finance/sir-ronald -cohen.

16. Lisa Cox, "From Refugee to Venture Capitalist to Social Impact Pioneer," *Forbes*, updated August 20, 2018, https://www.forbes.com/sites/sorenson

impact/2018/07/30/from-refugee-to-venture-capitalist-to-social-impact
-pioneer/?sh=6801cd146886.

17. Gerner, "Impact Investing."

18. "Sir Ronald Cohen," Social Finance, accessed August 1, 2024, https://
socialfinance.org/person/sir-ronald-cohen.

19. Rockefeller Foundation, "The Success of the Peterborough Social Impact
Bond," press release, August 8, 2014, https://www.rockefellerfoundation
.org/insights/perspective/success-peterborough-social-impact; David
Ainsworth, "Peterborough Social Impact Bond Investors Repaid in Full,"
Civil Society, July 27, 2017, https://www.civilsociety.co.uk/news/peter
borough-social-impact-bond-investors-repaid-in-full.html.

20. Social Finance, "Peterborough Social Impact Bond Reduces Reoffending
by 8.4%; Investors on Course for Payment in 2016," press release, August 7,
2014, https://www.slideshare.net/RockefellerFound/peterborough-social
-impact-bond-reduces-reoffending-by-84-percent.

21. Jet Powell, "Reducing Reoffending in Peterborough," Social Finance,
accessed August 4, 2024, https://www.socialfinance.org.uk/work/reducing
-reoffending-in-peterborough.

22. "Historical Highlights of the IRS," IRS, updated October 23, 2023, https://
www.irs.gov/newsroom/historical-highlights-of-the-irs.

23. "What Is a Private Foundation?," Fidelity Charity, accessed August 6,
2024, https://www.fidelitycharitable.org/guidance/philanthropy/private
-foundations.html.

24. Robert H. Hull, "Good Governance: Basic Rules for Governing a Family
Foundation," National Center for Family Philanthropy, October 24, 2019,
https://www.ncfp.org/knowledge/basic-rules-for-governing-a-family
-foundation.

25. "Cruise Ships," Friends of the Earth, accessed August 25, 2024, https://foe
.org/projects/cruise-ships.

26. George Lawton, "A Timeline and History of ESG Investing, Rules, and
Practices," TechTarget, August 16, 2024, https://www.techtarget.com
/sustainability/feature/A-timeline-and-history-of-ESG-investing-rules-and
-practices.

27. "Technology: Bacteria Make a Meal of Oil Slicks," NewScientist,
September 22, 1990, https://www.newscientist.com/article/mg12717353
-100-technology-bacteria-make-a-meal-of-oil-slicks.

28. "Sustainable Development Goals: Background on the Goals," United
Nations Development Program, accessed August 25, 2024, https://www
.undp.org/sdg-accelerator/background-goals.

29. "Simon Smiles," World Economic Forum, accessed August 7, 2024, https://www.weforum.org/people/simon-smiles.

30. Emily Gustafsson-Wright, *What Is the Size and Scope of the Impact Bonds Market?* (Global Economy and Development at Brookings, 2020), 8, https://www.brookings.edu/wp-content/uploads/2020/09/Impact_Bonds-Brief_1-FINAL-1.pdf.

31. Gustafsson-Wright, *Impact Bonds Market*, 8.

32. *UBS Annual Report 2016* (UBS Group AG, 2017), 74, https://www.ubs.com/global/en/investor-relations/financial-information/annual-reporting/ar-archive.html.

33. "Bard Geesaman," LinkedIn, accessed August 25, 2024, https://www.linkedin.com/in/bgeesaman.

34. "Building Companies to Transform Patient Outcomes," MPM BioImpact, accessed August 25, 2024, https://www.mpmcapital.com/#about.

35. "Bard Geesaman Ph.D," PitchBook, accessed August 25, 2024, https://pitchbook.com/profiles/person/13620-16P.

36. "The Top 10 Venture Capital Firms for Biotechnology," Leland, May 19, 2023, https://www.joinleland.com/library/a/the-top-10-venture-capital-firms-for-biotechnology.

37. "Ansbert Gadicke," MPM BioImpact, accessed August 25, 2024, https://mpmbioimpact.com/team.

38. John S. Rosenberg, "George Daily Appointed Harvard Medical Dean," *Harvard Magazine*, August 9, 2016, https://www.harvardmagazine.com/2016/08/harvard-medical-school-names-george-daley-dean.

39. "Human Genome Project Timeline," National Human Genome Research Institute, July 5, 2022, https://www.genome.gov/human-genome-project/timeline.

40. "H. Robert Horvitz," MPM BioImpact, October 24, 2022, https://mpmbioimpact.com/team/h-robert-horvitz-ph-d.

41. UBS, "UBS Clients Help Transform the Biotech Industry Through the UBS Oncology Impact Fund," press release, August 17, 2022, https://www.ubs.com/global/en/media/display-page-ndp/en-20220817-ubs-clients-help-transform.html.

42. "Crossing the Valley," UBS, September 19, 2018, https://www.ubs.com/global/en/ubs-society/our-stories/2018/crossing-the-valley.html.

43. UBS, "UBS Raises Record $471m for Oncology Impact Investing Fund," press release, April 27, 2016, https://www.ubs.com/global/en/media/display-page-ndp/en-20160427-oncology-fund.html.

44. *UBS Annual Report 2016* (UBS Group AG, 2017), 4, https://www.ubs.com

/global/en/investor-relations/financial-information/annual-reporting/ar
-archive.html.

45. Gustafsson-Wright, *Impact Bonds Market*, 8.

46. "STRIPE 71 L.P. Investing in Oncology Impact Fund 2," UBS marketing
presentation non-UK, July 2020.

47. UBS, "UBS Clients Show the Power of Investing with USD 650 Million
Investment to Fight Cancer and Other Diseases," press release, October 6,
2021, https://www.ubs.com/global/en/media/display-page-ndp/en-2021
1006-oif-2.html.

48. "Former UBS Banker Juerg Zeltner Dies at 52: Quintet," Reuters, March 23,
2020, https://www.reuters.com/article/world/former-ubs-banker-juerg
-zeltner-dies-at-52-quintet-idUSKBN21A167.

49. Sophie Robinson-Tillett, "Investment World Pays Tribute to Impact
Pioneer Simon Smiles," Responsible Investor, March 21, 2022, https://
www.responsible-investor.com/investment-world-pays-tribute-to-impact
-pioneer-simon-smiles.

50. "World Bank Boosts Support for Vietnam's Growth and Sustainability,"
Investing.com, November 15, 2023, https://www.investing.com/news
/economy/world-bank-boosts-support-for-vietnams-growth-and
-sustainability-93CH-3234869.

51. World Bank, "World Bank Continues to Support Upgrading Georgia's
Major Transport Route," press release, November 8, 2017, https://www
.worldbank.org/en/news/press-release/2017/11/08/world-bank-continues
-to-support-upgrading-georgias-major-transport-route.

52. "Debt Products FAQs," World Bank Group, August 1, 2024, https://
treasury.worldbank.org/en/about/unit/treasury/ibrd/debt-products-faqs.

53. Gethana Shashitharen and Kim Crawford, "Multilateral Development
Bank Bonds: A Sweet Spot in Fixed Income Sustainable Investing," LSEG,
December 11, 2023, https://www.lseg.com/en/insights/ftse-russell
/multilateral-development-bank-bonds-a-sweet-spot-in-fixed-income
-sustainable-investing.

54. "Solactive UBS Global Multilateral Development Bank Bond USD 25%
Issuer Capped Index," Trackinsight, accessed August 25, 2024, https://www
.trackinsight.com/en/index/solactive-ubs-global-multilateral-development
-bank-bond-usd-25-issuer-capped-index.

55. "Green, Social, Sustainability, and Sustainability-Linked (GSSS) Bonds,"
World Bank, October 2023, https://thedocs.worldbank.org/en/doc/3d31
3e4819de8d6bcb4238f253874b0f-0340012023/original/GSSS-Quarterly
-Newsletter-Issue-No-5.pdf.

56. Mara Dobrescu, "As Demand for Green Bonds Grows, Assets in Sustainable Funds Surge," Morningstar, May 9, 2023, https://www.morningstar.com/sustainable-investing/demand-green-bonds-grows-assets-sustainable-bond-funds-surge.

RULE 8: ALIGN YOURSELF WITH THE FUTURE OF WEALTH MANAGEMENT

1. "Po-Lin's Story: Destiny and the Buddhist Gods," UBS, accessed August 25, 2024, https://www.ubs.com/global/en/wealth-management/meet-our-clients/2023/destiny-and-the-buddhist-gods.html.
2. "Pavle's Story: Net-Zero Emissions; Energy's Holy Grail," UBS, accessed August 25, 2024, https://www.ubs.com/global/en/wealth-management/meet-our-clients/2023/net-zero-emissions.html.
3. Chantal Beck et al., *The Future Is Now: How Oil and Gas Companies Can Decarbonize* (McKinsey, January 2020), 3, https://www.mckinsey.com/industries/oil-and-gas/our-insights/the-future-is-now-how-oil-and-gas-companies-can-decarbonize.
4. "Pavle's Story."
5. "Pavle's Story."
6. "Pavle's Story."
7. Michel Martin and Julia Simon, "New Satellite Is Designed to Track Methane Emitted from the Oil and Gas Industry," NPR, March 5, 2023, https://www.npr.org/2024/03/05/1235911143/new-satellite-is-designed-to-track-methane-emitted-from-the-oil-and-gas-industry.
8. "Renewable Energy Targets," European Commission, accessed August 25, 2024, https://energy.ec.europa.eu/topics/renewable-energy/renewable-energy-directive-targets-and-rules/renewable-energy-targets_en.
9. "Pavle's Story."
10. "Pavle's Story."
11. "Faizal's Story: If You Give, You Get," UBS, accessed August 25, 2024, https://www.ubs.com/global/en/wealth-management/meet-our-clients/2023/if-you-give-you-get.html.
12. "Pablo's Story: Building Better," UBS, accessed August 25, 2024, https://www.ubs.com/global/en/wealth-management/meet-our-clients/2022/building-better.html.
13. "Model T," Encyclopedia of Detroit, Detroit Historical Society, accessed August 25, 2024, https://detroithistorical.org/learn/encyclopedia-of-detroit/model-t.
14. Lidia Dinkova, "Unmasking the Developers of South Florida's Biggest

Live Local Act Project," Real Deal, July 11, 2024, https://therealdeal.com /miami/2024/07/11/who-are-live-local-act-developers-pablo-castro-laura -tauber.

15. "Suchitra's Story: Chemical's Circular Economy," UBS, accessed August 25, 2024, https://www.ubs.com/global/en/wealth-management/meet-our -clients/2023/chemicals-circular-economy.html.

16. "Indorama Ventures Revenue in 2023," Indorama Ventures, accessed September 13, 2024, https://sustainability.indoramaventures.com/storage /content/document/misc/2023/revenue-in-2023.pdf.

17. "We Are America's Beverage Companies," American Beverage, accessed September 13, 2024, https://www.americanbeverage.org.

18. "Suchitra's Story."

19. "FIJI Water Transitions Iconic Bottle to 100% Recycled Plastic in the US," FIJI Water, August 15, 2022, https://www.prnewswire.com/news -releases/fiji-water-transitions-iconic-bottle-to-100-recycled-plastic-in-the-us -301605349.html.

20. Afdhel Aziz, "The Power of Purpose: The Business Case for Purpose (All the Data You Were Looking for Pt 1)," Forbes, May 2, 2020, https://www .forbes.com/sites/afdhelaziz/2020/03/07/the-power-of-purpose-the-business -case-for-purpose-all-the-data-you-were-looking-for-pt-1.

21. The Business Case for Purpose (Harvard Business Review Analytic Services, 2015), https://assets.ey.com/content/dam/ey-sites/ey-com/en_gl/topics /digital/ey-the-business-case-for-purpose.pdf.

22. Melody Brue, "Green Hushing in the Corporate World: Why ESG Is No Longer a Topic of Discussion," Forbes, June 21, 2023, https://www.forbes .com/sites/moorinsights/2023/06/21/green-hushing-in-the-corporate-world -why-esg-is-no-longer-a-topic-of-discussion/.

23. Abby Schultz, "Only 5% of U.S. Foundations Invest for Impact, Study Finds," Barron's Penta, February 29, 2024, https://www.barrons.com/articles /only-5-of-u-s-foundations-invest-for-impact-study-finds-c4fb34d4.

24. R. J. Reinhart, "Global Warming Age Gap: Younger Americans Most Worried," Gallup, May 11, 2018, https://news.gallup.com/poll/234314 /global-warming-age-gap-younger-americans-worried.aspx.

25. "Private Equity and Venture Capital," Preqin, accessed August 25, 2024, https://www.preqin.com/academy/lesson-4-asset-class-101s/private-equity -venture-capital.

26. Chris Davis, "Private Equity: What It Is and How to Invest," NerdWallet, July 2, 2024, https://www.nerdwallet.com/article/investing/private-equity -investments.

27. "Cerulli Anticipates $84 Trillion in Wealth Transfers Through 2045," Cerulli Associates, January 20, 2022, https://www.cerulli.com/press -releases/cerulli-anticipates-84-trillion-in-wealth-transfers-through-2045.

28. "Cerulli Anticipates."

BONUS RULE: UNDERSTAND THAT INVESTING IS AN EXERCISE IN HUMILITY

1. "Chuck Norris Trading Facts," HedgeNordic, August 18, 2011, https:// hedgenordic.com/2011/08/chuck-norris-trading-facts.

2. "Average Annual Resident (In-State) Full-Time Undergraduate Tuition Charges at N.J. Independent Colleges and Universities: Academic Years 1990–91 Through 2007–08," NJ.gov, accessed August 1, 2024, https://www .nj.gov/highereducation/statistics/TUITweb08.htm.

3. Shahar Madjar, "Gradually and Then Suddenly," *Daily Mining Gazette*, October 23, 2023, https://www.mininggazette.com/news/2023/10 /gradually-and-then-suddenly.

4. "The Gulf War, 1991," Office of the Historian, United States Department of State, accessed August 1, 2024, https://history.state.gov/milestones/1989 -1992/gulf-war.

5. "Remarks by President Bush ('This Will Not Stand, This Aggression Against Kuwait')," Margaret Thatcher Foundation, August 5, 1990, https:// www.margaretthatcher.org/document/110704.

6. The 70–80 percent paratrooper fatality rate the commander cited appears to be based on the fatality estimates provided to General Eisenhower just prior to D-Day. "Supreme Allied Commander: Eisenhower and the Planning for D-Day," National Parks Service, updated May 24, 2024, https://www.nps.gov /articles/000/eisenhower-plans-for-d-day.htm; Val Lauder, "Eisenhower's 'Soul-Racking' D-Day Decision," CNN, updated June 6, 2014, https://www .cnn.com/2014/06/05/opinion/lauder-eisenhower-d-day-anguish/index .html. Several reports state that, of the 13,400 paratroopers who boarded planes, 2,499 American paratroopers became casualties (dead, missing, or wounded) on D-Day. Peter Crean, "The Airborne Invasion of Normandy," National WWII Museum, June 6, 2024, https://www.nationalww2museum .org/war/articles/airborne-invasion-normandy. Due to the chaos of war, historians are still not sure what the actual fatality rate was. Dave Roos, "How Many Were Killed on D-Day?," History, June 3, 2019, https://www .history.com/news/d-day-casualties-deaths-allies.

7. "Denali," *National Geographic*, accessed August 3, 2024, https://education .nationalgeographic.org/resource/denali/.

8. James Morton Turner, "Challenge and Teamwork Drive a Diverse Group to Climb," *Princeton Alumni Weekly*, November 8, 2000, https://swh.princeton .edu/~paw/archive_new/PAW00–01/04–1108/features1.html.

9. "Outdoor Action Student & Alumni Expeditions," Outdoor Action, Princeton University, accessed August 5, 2024, https://www.princeton.edu /~oa/reports/oaex.shtml.

10. Iver Peterson, "Campus Journal; Twin Goals: $250,000 for AIDS and a Lofty Peak," *New York Times*, September 16, 1992, https://www.nytimes .com/1992/09/16/news/campus-journal-twin-goals-250000-for-aids-and-a -lofty-peak.html.

11. "An AIDS Summit," People.com, updated July 26, 1993, https://people.com /archive/an-aids-summit-vol-40-no-4/ (content no longer available).

12. "Denali."

13. "AIDS Summit."

14. Robin Marks, "Guide Scott Fischer Dies on Mount Everest," Zone Network, 1996, https://www.mountainzone.com/climbing/fischer/fischer.html.

15. K2 Climber, "'Mountains are not fair or unfair, they are just dangerous.'— Reinhold Messner," Facebook, March 10, 2023, https://www.facebook.com /photo.php?fbid=587747760051504&id=100064488566914&set=a.35033195 0459754.

16. "Rob Hess," Mountain Guides, accessed August 4, 2024, https://the mountainguides.com/guide/rob-hess.

17. "AIDS Summit."

18. "There and Back Again," Tolkien Gateway, modified January 2023, https:// tolkiengateway.net/wiki/There_and_Back_Again.

19. Clay Holton, "The Truth About Y2K: What Did and Didn't Happen in the Year 2000," Investopedia, May 31, 2024, https://www.investopedia.com /terms/y/y2k.asp.

20. "Testimony of Governor Edward W. Kelley, Jr.: The Federal Reserve's Efforts to Address the Year 2000 Computer Problem," Federal Reserve Board, April 28, 1998, https://www.federalreserve.gov/boarddocs /testimony/1998/19980428.htm.

21. "David Goel," Crunchbase, accessed August 4, 2024, https://www.crunch base.com/person/david-goel.

22. "Fed Stockpiles Cash for Y2K," *Wired*, December 10, 1999, https://www .wired.com/1999/12/fed-stockpiles-cash-for-y2k.

23. "Jim Cramer," CNBC, accessed August 1, 2024, https://www.cnbc.com /jim-cramer-bio.

24. "George Q. Daley, MD, PhD," Harvard Medical School, accessed August 5, 2024, https://hms.harvard.edu/faculty-staff/george-q-daley.

25. "Securities and Exchange Commission, Washington, D.C. 20549: Form 10-K," in *WorldPort Communications, Inc., 1998 Annual Report*, Getfilings.com, December 31, 1998, http://getfilings.com/o0000950144-99-003884.html.

26. "WorldPort Communications Inc. (Houston, TX) Signed Papers to Acquire EnerTel, an Alternative," Lightwave + BTR, June 1, 1998, https://www.lightwaveonline.com/business/mergers-acquisitions/article/16655596/worldport-communications-inc-houston-tx-signed-papers-to-acquire-enertel-an-alternative.

27. Devanesan Evanson, "Six Investing Rules," *New Straits Times*, February 1, 2023, https://www.nst.com.my/opinion/columnists/2023/02/875636/six-investing-rules.

28. Jake Lloyd-Smith, "Energis Pays Pounds 352M for Dutch Telco," *Independent*, November 12, 1999, https://www.independent.co.uk/news/business/energis-pays-pounds-352m-for-dutch-telco-1125392.html.

29. "Banks Grab Energis From Brink," CNN, July 16, 2002, https://www.cnn.com/2002/BUSINESS/07/16/energis/index.html.

30. Gershon Ben Karen, "Everybody Has a Plan Until They Get Punched in the Face," Krav Maga Yashir, August 20, 2019, https://www.bostonkravmaga.com/blog/self-defense/everybody-has-a-plan-until-they-get-punched-in-the-face.html.

ABOUT THE AUTHORS

MARK H. HAEFELE

Mark Haefele has been the chief investment officer of UBS Global Wealth Management since 2014. UBS's chief investment office (CIO) was again named "Best Private Bank for Chief Investment Office" in the *Financial Times*–owned Professional Wealth Management / The Banker Global Private Banking Awards in 2023, while UBS was recognized in 2024 by *Euromoney* as the "World's Best Bank."

Mark graduated summa cum laude from Princeton University. He holds AM and PhD degrees from Harvard University, where he was an acting dean and lecturer. He has an MA from the Australian National University, where he was a Fulbright Scholar.

Mark was the cofounder and co–fund manager at Sonic Capital and served as a managing director at Matrix Capital Management. Mark appears frequently in numerous financial media around the world.

RICHARD C. MORAIS

Richard C. Morais is an award-winning business journalist and novelist. Richard has published three novels, including *The Man with No Borders*, an Amazon "First Read" about a Spanish private banker living in Zurich, but he is best known for the *New York Times* and international bestseller *The*

Hundred-Foot Journey, a culinary novel that Steven Spielberg and Oprah Winfrey turned into a 2014 film starring Helen Mirren and Om Puri.

Richard was also the editor who built *Barron's Penta*, a glossy magazine for wealthy families, and served as *Forbes*'s European Bureau chief, the business magazine's longest-serving foreign correspondent. Richard has uniquely won three awards and six nominations at the Business Journalist of the Year Awards, and he was named the 2015 Citizen Diplomat of the Year—the highest honor granted by Global Ties US, a private-public partnership sponsored by the US State Department—"for promoting cross-cultural understanding in all of his literary work."